D0560996

A THEOLOGY OF CHURCH GROWTH

A THEOLOGY OF CHURCH GROWTH

George W. Peters

ZONDERVAN
PUBLISHING HOUSE
OF THE ZONDERVAN CORPORATION
GRAND RAPIDS, MICHIGAN 49506

A THEOLOGY OF CHURCH GROWTH
Copyright © 1981 by The Zondervan Corporation
Grand Rapids, Michigan

Library of Congress Cataloging in Publication Data

Peters, George W
    A theology of church growth.

(Contemporary evangelical perspectives)
Bibliography: p.
1. Church growth.   2. Church.   I. Title.
BV652.25.P47   266'.001   80-27050
ISBN 0-310-43101-8

Edited by Diane Zimmerman and Edward Viening
Designed by Edward Viening

Printed in the United States of America

Contents

FOREWORD

Dr. George W. Peters is without doubt one of today's leading missiologists. Being a theologian and a missiologist, he is eminently qualified to speak with authority on the theology of church growth. He has seen, studied, analyzed, and reported on church growth in all parts of the world; consequently, he writes from practical observation and experience as well as from a theoretical point of view.

The book is most timely, coming as it does when the principles of church growth are beginning to be applied here at home. Pastors as well as missionaries and administrators will benefit from a reading of this excellent book.

George Peters can always be counted on to be biblical in his approach, practical in his application, and balanced in his presentation. He has no time for passing fads and fancies. While fully aware of the mistakes of the nineteenth-century pioneers, he is too good a historian to condemn them out of hand. Their good points far outnumber their bad ones. His sane, moderate approach is clearly seen in his treatment of such controversial subjects as the role of miracles, homogeneous units, evangelism-in-depth, and the Westernization of missions.

Particularly helpful and refreshing is his constant emphasis on the great fundamentals: the sovereignty of God, the centrality of Christ, the ministry of the Holy Spirit, the importance of the church, and the priority of evangelism. When it comes to methodology, he is convinced that right ends must be achieved by right means. While not happy with all aspects of the church growth school of thought, the author is in agreement with its basic insights. He even defends the numerical emphasis of church growth; at the same time, he warns against sacrificing quality for quantity.

This is the first definitive work devoted entirely to the theology of church growth. As such, it will make a significant contribution to the growing body of literature on this important topic. I heartily recommend it.

J. Herbert Kane
Trinity Evangelical Divinity School

PREFACE

Christian missions has always been concerned about church growth; in fact, research into church growth has accompanied missions for over a century.[1] Today church growth is a popular topic, and literature on the subject is having a heyday. More than one hundred titles have been released by publishers in recent decades.

These reports and analyses stem principally from two sources. Fifteen studies presented in thirteen volumes were prepared by a task force of researchers and experts under the sponsorship of the Commission of World Mission and Evangelism of the World Council of Churches in Geneva. The series is entitled *World Studies of Churches in Mission.* The purpose of the research was to establish the vitality of the church as manifested in both numerical expansion and creative response to the environment. This series presents case studies from Africa (Uganda, Brazzaville, Togo, Rhodesia), Latin America (Chile), Solomon Islands, Indonesia (Java), Japan (Tokyo), India, Germany (Hamburg), Britain, and the United States (Michigan). Some books are well written and carefully researched, and present a vast amount of material, although some of it is merely accumulated. The studies are lacking in uniformity and unity both in objective and in answers to the fundamental research undertaken. Thus each book must be taken on its own merit. Some of the books are still available through Friendship Press, New York.[2]

The second main source of literature comes out of the School of World Mission and the Institute of Church Growth of Fuller Theological Seminary in Pasadena, California. Scores of titles on the subject have been published either by the William B. Eerdmans Publishing Company (Grand Rapids, Mich.) or by the William Carey Library (South Pasadena, Calif.). Several of these volumes make substantial contributions to the field of missiology and church growth.[3] Many present general information on specific countries or specific missions; although much of the research seems superficial, resembling unverified, merely accumulated data styled to establish a thesis rather than to discover historical facts, realities, and dynamic principles.

The Fuller School is concerned mainly with numerical expansion, with an emphasis on church multiplication. The school, however, demands our attention. It has made significant contributions to evangelical missions in specific emphases. Its work has focused on the church of Jesus Christ as manifested in local congregations and on the biblical fact that God wants His church to grow and multiply. It has emphasized the facts that (1) there are seasons in the mission world, (2) there are vast strata of society and total communities that constitute ripened harvest fields, and (3) the gospel moves most effectively along lines of social, professional, and filial relationships. The school has also successfully insisted that the behavioral sciences, rightly applied, can become a most useful aid in gospel communication, church expansion, and theological formulations.

None of these emphases is new. They have surfaced before in the history of missions. Their present value lies in their clearer definition and their integration in mission operations. The concern expressed by Shenk, however, seems justified when he writes: "For a movement that has shown capacity to grow and refine its scientific theoretical framework, there has been a corresponding lag in development in its theological foundations."[4]

Besides these two principal schools of research and literature, newer research agencies are being developed. Latin American researchers (San Jose, Costa Rica) are not interested in numerical growth primarily but more with the church's role in the restructuring of society in accordance with humane and just principles as deduced from the gospel of the kingdom of God.

The recently established U. S. Center for World Mission in Pasadena is concentrating its research principally on unreached people. It is concerned with evangelism and church growth among people who, because of social barriers (e.g., the caste system of

India), or geographical difficulties (e.g., tribal people and vast pockets in Africa), or religious prejudices and obstacles (e.g., the Muslim people), have remained relatively unaffected by the gospel.

The Nairobi (Kenya) Center is interested mostly in the independent church movement in Africa and studies its causes, characteristics, dynamics, and consequences. The Lausanne Continuation Committee seems more concerned with general effectiveness in evangelism and church growth than with specific theories, areas, and people.

In addition to the above research groups on church growth, Dr. J. Edwin Orr has published a number of volumes on the great awakenings around the world. His one-volume work *The Light of the Nations* has grown into more than a score of volumes, and a new "school of church growth" could easily evolve from this literature.[5] Certainly Dr. Orr has accumulated a vast amount of material on this subject, and his evidences cannot be brushed easily from the table. It is my conviction that he deserves more hearing than he is receiving, especially now that missions is moving into a new phase of evangelization and church expansion.

The relationship between revival and church growth cannot be denied—it is a fact of history. Studies of Christian expansion at home and in the Third World bear out that fact. Korea, India (Assam, Andhra Pradesh), Indonesia, and East Africa stand out as testimonies.[6] The two great revival/evangelism agencies, the Southern Baptists and the Assemblies of God, are the fastest-expanding movements around the world.[7] They are contemporary witnesses of a revival church-growth theory, even as the Book of Acts is our biblical and first-century witness. Revival is released and relayed, and a tremendous expansion of the Christian church results from it. While the Southern Baptists operate more in revival/evangelism pulsations, the Assemblies of God have been successful in many areas of the world in maintaining a revived state and continuous growth.

It is not out of order to associate the late historian and missiologist Kenneth Scott Latourette with this theory. His *wave theory* is principally a revival church-growth theory.[8]

In addition to the above schools and sources, individual research-ers have conducted independent studies and published them in book form. Such is the book *Followers of the New Faith* by Emilio Willems, a study of Brazil and Chile that is by far the most penetrat-ing and most stimulating research that has been made on Latin America.[9] F. Peter Cotterell has provided us with a study of the Evangelical Church in Ethiopia under the title *Born at Midnight.* It is a fine, scholarly, and scientific piece of work.[10] Harold R. Cook has published a very readable book, *Historic Patterns of Church Growth,* that examines five different churches.[11] Recently Donald Palmer has released a report of the Pentecostal explosion in Colom-bia under the title of *Explosion of People Evangelism.*[12] A rather penetrating and stimulating study of the decline of some and the growth of other American churches has been made by Dean M. Kelley in his book *Why Conservative Churches Are Growing.*[13]

Agencies have also arisen in Canada and the United States with considerable and efficient staffs to counsel and assist churches in growth and multiplication.

We can only thank the Lord for all the honest efforts that are being put forth not only in evangelizing but also in bringing people into established fellowships for nurturing, maturing, and equipping in the service of the Lord. New insights have been disseminated, principles defined, concepts illuminated, and theories formulated and some vigorously propagated. It must be admitted, however, that the theories of church growth are more or less at the stage of hypothe-ses and need the continued sobering and modifying judgments of science and theology. It is evident that research depends on the tools employed, the nature of growth to be discovered, the purpose that the research is to serve, and, not least, the presuppositions and preparation of the researcher. Little agreement exists among the schools and researchers of church growth and expansion. The vast amount of material needs to be sorted out and synthesized. The priorities and emphases found in the Scriptures must be established.

A Theology of Church Growth is the result of years of classroom lectures on missionary methods, principles of church growth, and cross-cultural evangelism. In outline form the material has also been discussed with missionaries and national pastors at numerous work conferences in various parts of the world. It is presented here in printed form in response to the many requests that have come from students and conference participants.

The book is not a polemic that seeks to interact with the various publications on the subject or the several schools that are advocating their specific theories. Quotations and references, therefore, are held to a minimum. Neither is this an apologetic to defend church growth and multiplication. I take this for granted. The Book of Acts is clear on this point.

My approach is to be principally scriptural. I aim to set forth what I believe to be a biblical framework for defining strategies and operating principles for church growth. While at first I draw from the whole Bible, I focus later on the Book of Acts. It is my firm position that Acts is an authentic record of apostolic times and mission and that it was written by Luke, a companion of Paul, who assures us of having done careful research and giving us a true record.

There are many fine expository books on Acts that deal with many issues and doctrines of the book as well as provide excellent material for devotion and general inspiration. In recent years some publications have emphasized the church of Acts and its progressive expansion. Therefore, much material is available.[14]

Given to us under the guidance of the Holy Spirit, the Scriptures are our safest directive but also our sharpest critic in the whole matter of church growth. While I fully realize that built into Acts are a cultural flexibility and adaptabilily in methods of operation and communication, there are many absolutes that refuse domestication and acculturation. They will not bend to any accommodation. They are divinely fixed principles for all times and cultures. To find the line of demarcation between what is absolute and what is relative is not always easy. It will require mutual respect when we differ, tolerance when we disagree, and much dialogue to bring us closer together for mutual enrichment—all of this for the cause of the *one* Master whom we are serving.

I was first introduced to the concept of church growth in studies in the Kennedy School of Missions in Hartford in 1945–1947. Here I became acquainted with men such as J. Waskom Pickett, Dean M. Pitt, J. Merle Davis, Daniel J. Fleming, and others. Many of the present-day defined principles of church growth were discussed and evaluated from the historical, cultural, sociological, and theological perspectives. I brought back with me much valuable material that has enriched my classroom lectures. Of course, much has been added since those days. Of special inspiration have been the writings of J. Waskom Pickett, John V. Taylor, Donald McGavran, Emilio Willems, Robert Lee, and Christian Lalive d'Epinay. Other sources have become so much a part of my thinking that it becomes impossible to separate these elements from one another.

I also gratefully acknowledge the comments and suggestions made by the following colleagues after they read an early draft of the manuscript: Arthur Glasser, Peter Wagner, Arthur Johnston, John Gration, Hans Kasdorf, and Henry Schmidt.

Research in social anthropology and social psychology has greatly enriched the whole field of mission operations. Church growth is a lively subject today and deserves our attention. I hope that my presentation can make some contribution to the growth of the church of Jesus Christ around the globe for the glory of our blessed Lord.

1

Church Growth—
Source, Leitmotif, Meaning

The Book of Acts constitutes the primary and also the most safe and the most conclusive source on church growth and church multiplication. It is my impression that Luke, the author of Acts, according to his own introductory words is not so much interested in presenting to us a dogmatic view of the church as such or even great doctrines about it. Rather he purports to present to his readers a living and reliable report on Christianity as a dynamic movement. Therefore he brings before us the church in its beginning and in its expansion from Jerusalem to Rome.

Acts is a showcase of a "new religion." This new religion began in Jerusalem, and its central message was about One who was crucified and raised again, who ascended into heaven, and who sent the Holy Spirit from heaven. It was carried forward by a group of "unlearned men" of Galilee. A former zealous Pharisee named Saul, who was converted on the way to Damascus by a unique appearance of the Lord, became its great exponent and proponent and apostle to the non-Jewish world. The new religion overcame all barriers and leaped all boundaries to become a supranational, suprracial movement and institution—the international church of Jesus Christ. Here is church growth as a divine-human movement.

From Luke's report we can deduce principles, practices, and patterns and can observe powers that advanced the church of the apostles and early disciples to the ingathering of countless converts. We can see how it expanded geographically, much to the consternation of Jews and Romans alike. Here was a movement on the march.

In order to observe the dynamic of this movement, we need to see that Acts unfolds the progressive development of the church. There is no full-orbed church on any of the first pages; only gradually and progressively does it appear. There are at least four stages in this gradual unfolding, and only after chapter 13 has the church become what the church ought to be. We note the following progression: Acts 2–5, the church is presented as a qualitative community; Acts 6, the church is seen as evolving as a serviceable structure; Acts 8–12, the church is evangelizing in related communities; and Acts 13, the church is moving out in aggressive world evangelism. These stages will be further explored and expounded in Part 3.

As a guide to the book we turn first to the leitmotif passage of Acts to find several general directives on basic principles.

CHURCH GROWTH AND THE LEITMOTIF OF ACTS

The Book of Acts is the primary textbook in world evangelism and church growth. We are not misreading the author if we accept the introductory verse as a statement of the purpose of the book and Acts 1:8 as the leitmotif in the interpretation of the presentation. It is significant that the leitmotif was spoken by our Master who on a previous occasion had assured His disciples that He would build His church (Matt. 16:13–21). In Acts 1:8 are His principal directives for this *great building program;* these directives are gradually unfolded. "But you shall receive power when the Holy Spirit has come upon you; and you shall be My witnesses both in Jerusalem, and in all Judea and Samaria, and even to the remotest part of the earth." Five basic truths are uncovered from the leitmotif text that dominate the Book of Acts.

1. *The Holy Spirit is the divine agent* to initiate, supervise, energize, and accomplish the purpose of God in the church-building program. He is the Paraclete, the administrator, executor, and realizer of the program. In Him God is immanent in this world in power and executive authority. On the day of Pentecost the Holy Spirit created for Himself a body, the church of Jesus Christ. He resides in the church and He operates through the chruch in a redemptive manner in the world. He relates Himself to the true church of believers in a similar manner as He does to the Word of God written. Accordingly the church becomes the primary agent of the Paraclete to execute and accomplish the purpose of God. The church thus is purposive in its origin, existence, and operation. It is never an end in itself. This is the deep significance of Pentecost, for Pentecost was not merely a great event. It was an event with a glorious purpose divinely designed and divinely executed. (The relationship of the Holy Spirit to the church is discussed in chapter 3.)

On the day of Pentecost a power and a revival were released from heaven in the Person of the Holy Spirit who now operates principally through the word of God written as *His means* and the living church of Jesus Christ as *His agency*. (See chapters 5–7.) Thus the power and revival focused in the Holy Spirit are to be relayed through this means and this agency. Such is the high and holy calling of the church.

2. *The apostles of Jesus Christ are the representatives* of the church of Jesus Christ and the initial agents of the Holy Spirit through whom the divine purpose is to be initiated and directed. The apostles together with some New Testament prophets are recognized as the foundation of the church. Carefully, however, the text circumscribes the foundation and adds that Christ Jesus Himself is the cornerstone (Eph. 2:20). The unique position of the apostles in the beginning ministries of the church is recognized throughout the New Testament—only they are known as *the apostles of Jesus Christ,* while others are known simply as apostles or as apostles of the church. (The role of these servants of God is looked at in chapter 7.)

3. *Witnessing or oral communication is to be the major means* of accomplishing the divine purpose as outlined in Acts 1:8. No specific method is designated. Neither is there any reference to miracles, wonders, and signs or other accompanying startling phenomena, though these are not necessarily excluded from the program as Acts testifies. While oral communication is the major means, it is not necessarily the exclusive means. The means may well include service and suffering. Certainly suffering is included, for the word *witness* is a translation of the Greek word from which we get our word *martyr*. It is evident from Acts that the apostles repeatedly speak of themselves as witnesses.

4. *Jesus Christ Himself is the content* of the Christian message. "You shall be witnesses unto me" (kjv). The chief purpose of the Holy Spirit is to bear witness of the Son (John 15:26; 16:14) and draw all men to the Son (John 12:32). Somewhat later the apostles clearly defined the One they were preaching by assigning to Him many descriptive titles and pointing to the centrality of the Cross, the Resurrection, and the Ascension.

The Christian church is not sent forth to propagate its philosophy, great ideals, theological systems, ecclesiastical dogmas, structures, religious ideologies, doctrinal creeds, and church confessions. It is bound to a *person* and must witness to a *person*. However, it must be the *person* as authentically revealed in the Scriptures—he who believes in me *as the Scripture said* (John 7:38). The Christian knows no other Jesus, no other Christ, no other Savior, no other Lord, except as He is disclosed in the Bible. The search for the "real Jesus" ended when Luke wrote his Gospel on the "Historical Jesus," John his Gospel on the "Dogmatic Jesus," and Paul his epistles on the "Kerygmatic Jesus Christ the Lord." The Bible-believing Christian rests on these documents as authentic and conclusive. He joins the apostles in witnessing to this Jesus as the Son of God and Savior of humankind. (A further discussion on the message is found in chapter 6.)

5. *The total inhabited world is to become the sphere* of God's gracious operations and gospel proclamation. There is to be a directional change from the centripetal universality of the Old Testa-

ment to a centrifugal universality of the New Testament. This is a radical departure from the methodology of the Old Testament, from the practice of Jesus Himself, and from His initial instructions to His disciples (Matt. 10:5; 15:24). According to the Old Testament the Gentiles were to *come* to Jerusalem to hear the message and be instructed in the Word of God. All could hear it, all could experience and possess it, but the Law (the message) was to go out from Jerusalem. This is centripetal universality. After Pentecost a centrifugal principle is to operate.[1] *The command—"Go you"—is emphatic.* A new era needs a new methodology. The new method must become the operative principle of a living church in and by the Holy Spirit. Only thus will the purpose of God be accomplished in our age as He gathers out a people for His name from among the nations of the world (Acts 15:14).

It is noteworthy that the repeated conjunction *and* in Acts 1:8 binds the regions together. It coordinates them and directs that such proclamation is to be simultaneous and no area is to have special preference. Had the church observed this principle, the whole world would long ago have heard the gospel of our blessed Lord Jesus Christ. (This point will be discussed further in chapter 12.)

The above points are the major concepts of Acts 1:8 and constitute the major emphases of the book before us. The time of promise is giving way to the time of realization. The *eschaton* is moving in on the inhabitants of the world. Reality has broken in on the world in an unprecedented manner. The Holy Spirit indwells His agents to make known to all the world what God has provided. The world must be called to repentance from sin and to faith in Christ Jesus in order to participate in the reality that God is offering to all mankind.

It may seem strange that the leitmotif passage does not mention the church. The passage speaks of the Holy Spirit, power, the personnel, witnessing, the message, and expansion—but not of the church. In this omission Acts 1:8 is not alone. The church is not mentioned in any of the editions of the Great Commission in the Gospels (Matt. 28:18–20; Mark 16:15–16; Luke 24:45–48; John 20:19–23). Neither is it mentioned in the commissioning of Paul as recorded by Luke in Acts (9:15–16; 22:14–15; 26:16–18). However, the church is mentioned more than twenty times in Acts and is written indelibly into the record. The apostles seemingly did not go out to "plant" churches. They were not commissioned to launch out toward that goal. They were sent forth to preach the gospel. Yet, wherever Acts 1:8 was faithfully discharged, a church was born. The Holy Spirit brought it about and formed it. Thus a functional tie between gospel preaching and church planting, nurture and growth, is clearly established. We may therefore confidently state that the church is germinal in the gospel as evangelism is germinal in a New Testament church.

THE MEANING OF CHURCH GROWTH

While it is a fact of revelation that we are living uniquely in the age of the church of Jesus Christ, this does not mean that the church is an end in itself. The church must be forever a servant church. It is to serve as the instrument and agent of the Holy Spirit, who indwells the church, to accomplish the divinely ordained program and purpose, which reaches out toward all humankind and anticipates the global expansion of the church.

1. *The growth concept.* Growth is not inconsistent with divine reality. We read of Jesus, the Son of the living God, that He *grew* (Luke 2:40, 52). The kingdom is likened unto a mustard seed that *grew* into a great tree (Matt. 13:31–32). The church is also to *grow* (Eph. 4:16) until it enfolds members "out of every kindred, and tongue, and people, and nation" (Rev. 5:9, KJV). Growth is not contrary to divineness or to perfection.

While we ascribe all ultimate causes of growth to the Holy Spirit, church growth takes place in history and within human society. On the human level, therefore, it develops according to principles, procedures, patterns, and methods that conform to human cultural and societal movements. Because of this we may well ask, What kind of church is it that adds members and multiplies, that prospers and grows? The Book of Acts furnishes us with the basic material from which we can deduce and define specific principles of growth whose validity was demonstrated in apostolic times and in succeeding history.

Seven Dimensions of Church Growth

1. Divine worship
2. Fellowship ministrations
3. Biblical conceptualization
4. Community evangelization
5. Environmental accommodation
6. Societal Christianization
7. Global proclamation

Kinds of Growth

1. Quantitative growth
2. Qualitative growth

Manner of Growth

1. Biological growth
2. Spontaneous growth
3. Planned growth
4. Growth through special crises

Diagram 1

Before we enter on a study of details, let us first agree on the meaning of church growth. Diagram 1 shows seven dimensions of church growth, and it would be difficult to pinpoint the most important quality. At one time or another each one must receive its share of emphasis. In our studies, however, we focus mainly on one particular aspect—global proclamation, with the expectation of global church expansion. While this inevitably involves all other qualities, we are looking at numerical growth and geographical expansion.

2. *The fact of growth in Acts.* For many people church growth has become almost synonymous with numerical increase and geographical expansion. While quantitative growth is only one aspect, it is most certainly present throughout the Book of Acts, and the geographical expansion is laid out in our leitmotif passage. This passage

not only implies but also necessitates numerical growth. We read in Acts of 120 believers (1:15) to whom 3,000 are added (2:41). Because this event took place in the temple and because of the manner of address used by the apostles (2:37), it is quite safe to surmise that these 3,000 souls were men, heads of that many families. This body soon became 5,000 men (4:4) to whom *multitudes* were added, both men and women (5:14). Hereafter the number of the disciples increased in Jerusalem greatly (6:7) and a large company of priests were obedient to the faith (6:7). A great revival in Samaria took place (8:5–25). After this we read that churches in Judea, Galilee, and Samaria multiplied (9:31), and that all who dwelt at Lydda and Sharon and many at Joppa believed (9:35, 42). A strong movement in Antioch is recorded and great numbers believed and turned to the Lord (11:21, 24, 26). The first part of Acts concludes with the statement: "But the word of the Lord continued to grow and to be multiplied" (12:24). In Acts 21:20 James, summarizing the results of the growth of the church, informs us that there were tens of thousands (Greek: *myriads*) of Jewish believers in Jerusalem and the community. Thus Acts provides a clear record of the numerical expansion of the church among the Jews.

There are similar accounts of the quantitative growth of the church outside of Palestine (13:48–49).

Major passages in Acts indicating church expansion include the following:

Antioch in Pisidia	13:43–44, 48–49
Derbe	14:20–21 (many)
Galatia	16:5 (the churches increased in numbers)
Thessalonica	17:4 (a great multitude)
Berea	17:12 (many believed)
Corinth	18:8–11 (I have many people in this city)
Rome	28:24, 30–31

We find such expressions as: "The word of the Lord was being spread through the whole region" (Antioch and Pisidia, 13:49); "The churches were being strengthened ... and were increasing in number daily" (16:5); "All who lived in Asia heard the word of the

Lord, both Jews and Greeks" (Ephesus, 19:10); "Preaching the kingdom of God . . . with all openness, unhindered" (Rome, 28:31); ". . . so that from Jerusalem and round about as far as Illyricum, I have fully preached the gospel of Christ" (Rom. 15:19); "But now, with no further place for me in these regions" (Rom. 15:23) I will proceed to Spain.

Quantitative growth and geographical expansion are important in the light of facts presented in the New Testatment.

3. *Possible illusion of growth.* Quantitative growth, however, can be deceptive. It may be no more than the mushrooming of a mechanically induced, psychological or social movement, a numerical count, an agglomeration of individuals or groups, an increase of a body without the development of muscle and vital organs. It may be Christendom in the making but not Christianity breaking through. Many mass movements of the past and community and tribal movement have been just that. An example is found in the mass accessions in Europe, particularly in France and Russia, when many were driven to baptism and drawn into the church, resulting in a mass of people professing Christendom but not in a dynamic, vibrant, growing, and responsible church of Jesus Christ. As soon as the pool of resources and relationships had been exhausted, accessions ceased and the body began to wilt and decay. The movement soon ran dry, leaving a different type of spiritual desert. A change of religious affiliation had taken place but hearts had not been changed. Lives had not been touched by God and consequently had not been transformed. As a result, astrology, occultism, and spiritism still have a tremendous hold on multitudes of people. All this indicates that it was principally an induced political, sociological, and psychological movement. It was not a Spirit-born, living organism as it was in the Book of Acts. Of course, there were living cells in the masses, but they were a small remnant who had to struggle bravely to survive in a sea of Christo-paganism and syncretism. In much of Europe Christianity became an ecclesiastical establishment rather than the church of the living God. The Reformation made a significant doctrinal and ecclesiastical change, and sporadic revivals and pietism aided the believers and spread consid-

erable light.[2] However, never did the light of the gospel really break through on the mass of people.

It has been argued that most people have come into the church in large group movements and that this is the most natural way for them to come. Most of Europe, Russia included, has come via that route. In modern missions the mass movements of India, the community movements of Indonesia, and the tribal movements of the islands and in Africa support this argument. It is a record of history that Christendom as a religious phenomenon and establishment has been an expanding entity. The mustard seed has become a large tree stretching its branches over the whole globe. In this century it can be spoken of as an ecumenical church in the sense of being present in the whole inhabited earth. It must be admitted, however, that to a great extent this expansion of the form, profession, and name of Christendom has little resemblance to the Christianity defined in the New Testament and the church portrayed in the Book of Acts.

In many ways the expansion of Christendom has come at the expense of the purity of the gospel and true Christian order and life. The church has become infested with pagan beliefs and practices, and is syncretistic in theology as evidenced in the larger and ancient branches of Christendom. Large segments have become Christo-pagan.

Such corruption, however, must not be attributed solely to the mass accessions by profession of faith but rather to doctrinal ignorance and indifference, to negligence of Christian standards, and to stereotyped ways of dealing with mass accessions. Had the church faithfully practiced the formula of Acts 2:42, much could have been saved for the cause of the Lord. The lack of creativity, the inflexibility, the structural and cultural conservatism, the exchange of the gospel for semi-Christian philosophies, sacramentalism, ecclesiastical establishment and liturgical performances, and the stereotyped ways of dealing with life situations and movements are some of the most serious "crimes" the church has committed against the gospel and humanity. Such attitudes have choked the life of the church, repelled the masses, and paralyzed the movement of the church. The miracle of it all is that the gospel and a remnant church have survived throughout the centuries.

Today the church again finds itself experiencing large mass accessions. How can we avoid duplicating in the Third World what has happened in large parts of Europe and what is happening more and more in America and parts of the British Commonwealth—Canada, New Zealand, Australia, and South Africa?

That such miscarriage need not take place is evidenced by the Book of Acts, by present-day experiences in Korea, and by some movements in Indonesia, Burma, Assam, and sections of Africa.[3] Therefore we are faced with the weighty question: How can we strengthen the impending great movements and truly lead people to real life in Christ and not merely to a change of religion? The historical patterns need not cause us to avoid large movements to Christ. Rather, our concern is how we can monopolize people movements for the kingdom of God in such a manner that large and healthy churches result.

A simple answer is that evangelism, church planting, and church growth must find their orientation in the Bible. A return to the principles and practices unfolded in the Book of Acts is the only reliable answer.

However, the Book of Acts and the church in Acts cannot be studied in isolation. Revelation is orderly and progressive. It is a simple fact that the New Testament follows the Old Testament. It is built on it. It in not the total pyramid of revelation, but without it the Old Testament would have no summit. The Testaments belong together as the base and the crown belong together. Each has its value and its grandeur. Likewise, Acts is preceded by the Gospels and followed by the Epistles with their doctrinal and ethical unfoldings. Therefore, Acts and the church must be seen in a total revelational perspective.

We turn in Part 1, therefore, to the theological foundations in order to find the proper place of the church in the total realm of revelation. Having found the place of the church in its theological framework, we explore in Part 2 some biblical principles of church growth. Finally, in Part 3, we turn to a closer study of the kind of church Luke presents as having flourished and prospered to the joy and salvation of many.

Part One

Theological Foundations of the Church

2

The Church in
Theological Perspective

The priority truths set forth in the Bible may be likened to a series of concentric circles. It is important to observe and preserve such priority in biblical interpretation and set the great doctrines into this divine frame of reference. When I speak of the innermost circle as representing God, the next circle Christ, and the third circle the Holy Spirit, I do not mean this in the gnostic manner in which God the Father is more deity than the other persons of the Trinity and the Holy Spirit is less than the other persons. I hold firmly to traditional Trinitarianism, which believes in the coequality and coeternity of all three persons of the Trinity. With this premise and from this position we begin our studies, emphasizing in sucession: Biblical Theocentricity—the God of the Bible; New Testament Christocentricity—the Christ of the Bible; New Testament Pneumatology—the Spirit of God; New Testament Theocracy—the Kingdom of God; New Testament Ecclesiology—the Church of God; New Testament Cosmology—the World of God.

BIBLICAL THEOCENTRICITY

At the very heart of a series of circles in biblical revelation is the doctrine of God. The Scriptures are emphatically theocentric in considering the universe; the history of humankind; and the nature, life, and purpose of man. Clearly the Word states that all things are from Him, and through Him, and to Him and that in the end God will be all in all (Rom. 11:36; 1 Cor. 15:28). Only a theocentric perspective of the Bible gives us the right direction and can save us from humanism in any form—individual, societal, ecclesiological, or cosmological. The peril of humanism in these various forms may not be equally great, but the consequences are disastrous in every case. God is and remains the final cause and source, the supreme initiator and actor, and the ultimate perspective and goal of all existence, being, events, and processes. That majestic first statement in the Bible—"In the beginning God"—reminds us that God is and remains the fundamental and ultimate basis of all that is and comes to pass. He is the *"I am who I am,"* the self-existent One, the self-sufficient One, the self-impelling and compelling One (as revealed to Moses), the God over all (Paul). He is the "God in heaven above, and on the earth below," "the Lord of all the earth" (Joshua); "the true God; He is the living God and the everlasting king" (Jeremiah); "the everlasting God, the Lord, the Creator of the ends of the earth" (Isaiah). God is God and not man (Hosea).

In the beginning of beginnings (*Uranfang*) God created the heavens and the earth and all the hosts of them. He is the God of creation, history, and providence. He is the God of salvation and consummation. In Him the ends of the eternal counsel and eternal purpose meet to form a perfect circle (not cycle). Any study of Christianity (and church growth) that does not find its source, power, perspective, and focus in God will inevitably result in warped views, emphases, and conclusions. The Bible is "fanatic" in its position on theocentricity. The Scriptures will never yield to any man-centeredness human self-interest, or even church-centeredness. In our days evangelical missiology has become as dangerously ecclesiocentric and anthropocentric as it was formerly soteriocentric. Such emphases are off center and unwholesome. All nontheocentricity is doctrinal dissent that eventually and inevitably leads to humanism, idolatry, or atheism (the ultimate form of idolatry).

1. *Theocentricity and humanity.* Our emphasis on theocentricity is not mere theological exercise. It is true to the Bible and it is fundamental to the individual's wholeness.

Human beings are a creation of God, created in the image of God and for the purpose of God, and with eternity and eternal issues engraved in their being. Two qualities refuse to be eradicated from their existence. They are possessed by a sense of creatureliness on the one hand and an awareness of God-relatedness on the other hand. Such existence expresses itself in a feeling of dependence and a consciousness of responsibility.

Individuals are aware that they do not have the originating and sustaining resources of life within themselves. They cannot maintain themselves at will and forever. Humans know themselves to be creatures limited by time and dependence. No matter how they may strive, they cannot save themselves from peril, illness, and death, the dreaded enemy of all existence.

Humankind has interpreted the content of awareness of creatureliness in various ways. Yet they cannot eradicate the existential experience as such. It haunts them in all that they are and do. The sense of creatureliness became Satan's point of contact with humans in the Garden of Eden, and they sought to overcome it by an act of disobedience. This pursuit has continued, and today science has become the tool and hope in humanity's search to conquer the sense of creatureliness. Individuals want to be their own creator and lord. They want to be autonomous, self-existent beings in order to be relieved of feelings of dependence and sense of accountability.

Humankind's awareness of God-relatedness has expressed itself in religious quest and in building religious systems and institutions, temples and shrines. The strength of God-awareness can be measured by the cost, sacrifices, and devotion in religion that have devoured the substance and life of multitudes of people. Not having been able to find satisfaction and quietude of heart in religion, people have resorted to rationalization. Modern psychology of religion and history of religion or outright and bold atheism are their attempts to shake off the sense of God-relatedness. However, neither view has been able to win the allegiance of the masses of people. Even in atheist France and communist Russia the multitudes are religious, and the present sweep of oriental mysticism and occultism in the West is a hidden cry of the human being's God-awareness. Humankind persists in a vague and undefined but dynamic awareness of God-relatedness. They are possessed by a feeling that they can live properly and function dynamically only in a sound God-relatedness whatever this may be religiously, theologically, or philosophically.

A vivid reminder of this truth was seen in a *Time* magazine report (31 January 1977) of a 1977 celebration in India described as "The Holiest Day in History." It was the celebration of the "Jar Festival" (Kumbh Mela) when some 50 million Maha Nirvana Hindu pilgrims from all parts of India made their way to the river bank near Allahabad where the Yamuna River meets the Ganges River. It is here, according to Indian mythology, that every twelve years the waters receive sanctifying power to wash away all sins and stains and assure eternal salvation for all who plunge into the holy waters.

Human beings know that they are out of relationship with God and seek to restore their God-relatedness. Thus the continued yearning for salvation and the persistence of religious rites and sacrifices. Humanity is built by nature, design, and purpose for theocentricity. Only as people find the true and living God can they find rest and fullness of life.

2. *The significance of the God concept.* It is not too difficult to establish from history that the God concept is the regulative concept of all that the individual is, thinks, and does. It is also the all-determining concept of the religion and philosophy by which each person lives. As the concept of God is, so the person himself becomes in thought, life, and religion. Therefore in all studies of comparative religion the primary factor is the concept of God or deity. Humankind's perception of ultimate reality is the core around which total being and existence revolve. This is why theocentricity is so heavily underscored in the Old Testament and why the writers raised questions like these: "Who is a God like Thee?" "To whom then will you liken God?" (Mic. 7:18–19; Isa. 40:18, 25).

The existence, supremacy, uniqueness, and living presence of God in the universe and in human history is a biblically revealed reality that brings peace and security, and also fear and dread to humankind. God is God and not man! He is before all, above all, and in all, and is the same from eternity to eternity. "Before the mountains were born, / Or Thou didst give birth to the earth and the world, / Even from everlasting to everlasting, Thou art God" (Ps. 90:2).

3. *Theocentricity and idolatry.* Because of the emphasis on theocentricity, the Bible is vehement against idolatry. It forbids it in unmistakable terms (Exod. 20:2–5). It ridicules it as it does no other sin and evil (Isa. 41:26–29; 44:9–20; 46:1–9). Idolatry will be punished mercilessly (Deut. 17:2–7; 13:12–18). It is the climaxing sin of the people of Israel. An idol is an abomination to the Lord. The New Testament does not moderate the tone but continues in the same vein (Acts 19:19, 26; 1 Cor. 8:4; 2 Cor. 6:14–18; 1 Peter 4:3; Rev. 21:8).

The entire Bible knows neither compromise nor tolerance in relation to idolatry. Positive aspects are never ascribed to idolatry, nor are positive characteristics and actions attributed to idols. Biblically, there are no psychological, social, moral, or religious values in images. Paul's classic presentation of the origin and evil results of idolatry in Romans 1:18–32 is not the tirade of a narrow-minded theologian or fanatic missionary. These words are a just summary of all that the Old and New Testaments express and history verifies. In this area the Bible legislates total and uncompromising intolerance. The major reason for the Bible's attitude seems to be that idolatry distorts the concept of one God and casts God into the image of the creature and according to the creature's evil imagination. God is re-created in the image of sinful humanity. The creature becomes the creator of the god. This is biblically intolerable. God is God, and only as He discloses Himself can He be known. He alone is to be loved, worshiped, and served (Deut. 6:5; 10:12–14; 11:1, 13, 22; 30:6; Matt. 22:37; Mark 12:30, 33; Luke 10:27). The Bible is from beginning to end theocentric; the human being is created for such a God and can find rest only in such a position. Thus theocentricity is biblical and God-honoring. A church, therefore, that expects to thrive, to meet the biblical standards, and to meet humankind's deepest needs and demands must be theocentric in its message, emphasis, perspective, and goal.

NEW TESTAMENT CHRISTOCENTRICITY

The second innermost circle definitely represents Jesus Christ and relates to the christocentricity particularly of the New Testament in that "God was in Christ." This is the great mystery of the New Testament. That God is "manifested in the flesh," and is "reconciling the world to Himself" (1 Tim. 3:16; 2 Cor. 5:18–21) is the good news to all humankind. The New Testament is a grand portrait of Christ Jesus the Lord. The Gospels present Him principally in His incarnation ministries. The Book of Acts portrays Him as the glorified Lord in His church-expanding ministries. The Epistles show Him in His glorification ministries. The Book of Revelation reveals Him in His historic-cosmic consummation ministries.

He is the Prophet, Priest, and King, the Lord of Lords in whom cosmos is created, redeemed, and consummated. Christ Jesus is the Mediator between God and humans—the representative of God to humans and of humans to God, the sole sufficient and efficient go-between (*goel*—kinsman redeemer). He is the God-man in the full and true sense of the word as no other being is, ever will be, or can be (1 Tim. 2:5–6; 1 John 2:1–2). Only in this way could He become the *Prophet* like Moses (Deut. 18:15–19; John 1:21, 45; Acts 3:22–23; 7:37). As prophet He declared God and revealed Him perfectly in His person, purpose, and message (John 1:18). No fuller disclosure of God to humanity is necessary or possible (Heb. 1:1–3). Only as the incarnate One could He become the *Priest* after the order of Melchizedek (Heb. 5:5–10; 7:1–10) who can truly enter into our experiences (Heb. 4:14–16) and reconcile us to God by becoming the sacrificer and the lamb offering (John 1:29; 1 Peter 1:18–19). As the *Lamb of God* portrayed in Isaiah 53 He fulfilled the rich typology of the Old Testament. And by the will and power of God He became the first fruits of resurrection (1 Cor. 15:20; Col. 1:18). As priest He is now the mediator and intercessor for God's people to appear for them in the presence of God (Heb. 9:24; 1 John 2:1–2).

Only as the truly human One could He become the perfect *Servant of Jehovah* to manifest and magnify God to His people in serving them in all their needs (Mark 10:45; Luke 4:18–19). Only as the incarnate One could He become the Man, the Man Christ Jesus (Rom. 5:15; 1 Cor. 15:21; 1 Tim. 2:5). As the Son of David (Matt. 1:1; 15:22), the Son of God, and Son of man He becomes *the Lord of Lords and King of Kings* and rules for God in and over humankind. In a progressive and sure manner He brings the kingdom of God to a perfect consummation (1 Cor. 15:20–28; Rev. 19:11–21). Therefore John portrays the Son of God not only as the *Lamb* that bears the sin of the world but also *the Lamb of consummation* (mentioned seven times in Revelation—21:9, 14, 22, 23, 27; 22:1, 3).

Jesus Christ the Lord is vividly portrayed as Prophet, Priest, Lamb of God, Servant of Jehovah, and King of Kings. The truths of His incarnation, perfect life and teaching, atoning death on the cross, victorious bodily resurrection from the dead, triumphant exaltation to the right hand of God as *Mediator* between God and humanity, and glorious return to consummate the plan and purposes of the ages constitute the central message of the New Testament (1 Tim. 3:16; cf. Acts 2:22–23, 30–33; 3:13–18; 4:10–12; 5:30–31; 10:36–43; 13:23, 33–39; Phil. 2:5–11; Rev. 1:1). These facts are the objective content of the gospel of God, the surety of our salvation, and the foundation of the church of God. The Bible emphatically declares that there is no salvation in any other "for there is no other name under heaven that has been given among men by which we must be saved" (Acts 4:12). This uniqueness of Christ and the exclusion of all other names is not easy to maintain in a world of religious pluralism, relativism, and accommodation. Yet, this truth is the emphatic declaration of the New Testament and is in harmony with the Old Testament, which maintains the sole Saviorhood of Jehovah (Isa. 43:11; 44:6). Christocentricity is the stamp and seal of the New Testament. Christ is the Alpha and the Omega (Rev. 1:8; 21:6).

NEW TESTAMENT PNEUMATOLOGY

The third circle bears the imprint of the Holy Spirit, who is mentioned more than 250 times in the New Testament. The descriptive titles and vivid symbols of the Holy Spirit; the portrayals of His activities in and relationships to the individual believer, the church, and the world; the great pentecost event with its resultant consequences—all these speak of the greatness and fullness of the Holy Spirit. Too little have the people of God recognized that we are living in the "age of the Holy Spirit" and that He is the Paraclete of God in this age. In its history the church has only occasionally emphasized this fact. In general, the Holy Spirit has been neglected or treated as nonrational, mysterious, mystifying, or impersonal. He has been little honored and even less obeyed, little appropriated and experienced. As a result, the church has felt again and again a tremendous void. Occasional local revivals have not filled the vacuum and in many places the void has become a desert. What a tragedy for the church and the world! The church, instead of being an Elim with its wells of water to refresh the weary pilgrims, has often been a Marah with its bitter water that no one could drink. Yet the Holy Spirit is present in the world and He will accomplish the purpose of God. (A more detailed study of the Holy Spirit's ministry in the world is found in chapter 4.)

New Testament Theocracy

The fourth circle must be devoted to the kingdom of God.[1] This is not a human utopia but a biblically revealed, divine reality. The concept, which had its roots in the Old Testament, was central in the proclamation of our Lord as the Gospels clearly indicate. Our Lord began His ministry with the preaching of the kingdom of God. Mark tells us: "Jesus came into Galilee, preaching the gospel of God, and saying, 'The time is fulfilled, and the kingdom of God is at hand; repent and believe in the gospel'" (Mark 1:14–15). The message of the kingdom continued to be a priority during His life of ministry; and, as Luke informs us, after His resurrection He continued to speak to the apostles "of the things concerning the kingdom of God" (Acts 1:3). Thus it is a focal, and even an essential, emphasis in the teaching ministry of Christ.

The concept of the kingdom of God is not nearly so evident in the ministry of the Twelve. In the sermons recorded in the Scriptures

Peter does not employ the concept. Second Peter 1:11 is his only mention of the "eternal kingdom of our Lord and Savior Jesus Christ." Similarly James writes only once of "the kingdom which He promised to them who love Him" (James 2:5). The concept is not found in John's three epistles and is brought out in his Gospel only when he directly quotes the Master (John 3:3, 5; 18:36). Neither does Jude's epistle refer to it.

Paul became its standard-bearer. We read that Paul went about proclaiming the kingdom of God (Acts 14:22; 19:8; 28:23, 31). In his epistles he expounds the present-day spiritual nature of the kingdom as consisting not in food and drink but in "righteousness and peace and joy in the Holy Spirit" (Rom. 14:17). Its moral nature and its otherworldliness in values, nature, destiny, and realization are emphatically set forth in 1 Corinthians 6:9–10; 15:50; Galatians 5:21; Ephesians 5:5; and 2 Timothy 4:18.

That Paul should become the standard-bearer of the kingdom emphasis is more remarkable in that he is also the foremost exponent of the divine origin, composition, purpose, and position of the church of Jesus Christ. His theological lines are very precise. It is a fact of exegesis that he nowhere completely identifies the church with the kingdom. In fact, his symbolism and metaphors about the church do not allow this. It could not be said of the kingdom that it is the body of Christ, the bride of Christ, the temple of the Holy Spirit, or the priesthood of God. While the apostle does not completely identify the church with the kingdom, neither does he totally separate them as two distinct entities. While there may be some polarities in their relationship, there seemingly are no conflicts or even tensions in the mind and theology of Paul.

In the history of the Christian church the kingdom of God emphasis has come to the forefront at various times and for various reasons. The debate has been on at least since Augustine wrote *The City of God*. It has continued throughout the centuries and is a most lively issue in our day. The issue is not merely between dispensational hermeneutics and traditional theology or between proponents of amillennialism, premillennialism, and postmillennialism. The issue is not only one of hermeneutics but also of a philosophy and purpose of history and God's plan for the realization of the redemption of mankind and the cosmos (Rev. 21:22). The basic question deals with the nature of the kingdom of God and a definition of its relationship to the church, to Israel, to the nations, and to the world mission and missions of the church. Eschatology enters heavily into the discussion.*

Certain specifics seem evident from Scripture: (1) the sure but progressive realization of the kingdom; (2) the complicated nature of the kingdom and the difficulty in defining it; (3) the presence of some universal qualitative characteristics of the kingdom throughout all ages—a fact that makes sharp distinctions most difficult.

1. *The progressive realization of the kingdom.* It is evident that the Scriptures uphold an age of promise and an age of realization. But the New Testament hardly warrants and even less demands the full realization of all promises *in our age.* There is a gradualism or progressivism evident in the Book of Revelation.

There is a present age (Rev. 1–19), a millennium to come with concluding judgments (Rev. 20:1–15), and an age with a new heaven and a new earth (Rev. 21:1–22:5). A similar gradualism is

---

*Theories of the "hiddenness of the kingdom" (continental Lutheran), the expanding kingdom through the ministry of the church of Jesus Christ and its Christianizing and moderating influence (Reformed), the identification of the church with the kingdom and its growth and expansion (Anglican), the "already" and the "not yet" aspects of the kingdom, have made themselves heard in history and at great councils. For example, see the Willingen documents of the International Missionary Council of 1952. At this council the continental Lutheran, the Reformed (mostly Dutch), the Anglican, and the American delegates locked horns and debated heartily and heatedly, each one tenaciously holding and defending his position. While shedding some light on the subject, the council was not able to agree and come to definite conclusions. In the ensuing decades the matter has been seriously complicated by the new theory of "realized eschatology" (C. H. Dodd of London). The Christian church must be prepared to continue the debate in a sharpened manner. With the coming of the "Theology of Liberation," "African Theology," "Creation Theology," and the "Missio Dei" in the world, the struggle is bound to intensify and enlarge.[2] For this the church of Jesus Christ must be prepared without permitting itself to become bitter and antagonistic. This calls for serious dialogue.

stated in 1 Corinthians 15:20–28. Speaking of the Resurrection, Paul informs us that Christ is the first fruits, afterwards those who are Christ's at His coming, then comes the end. Paul also speaks of the present age and the age to come (Eph. 1:21). Because "age" is a time-word in its first usage, it may well be that the second usage also is a time-word and does not refer to the eternal state.

All reality resides in Christ (Col. 1:19; 2:9). In Him all the promises of God find their yea and amen (2 Cor. 1:20, KJV). From His fullness we have all received, and grace for grace (John 1:16). Such fullness, however, is portioned out according to His sovereign will and pleasure and according to His ever-blessed wisdom (1 Cor. 12:11; Eph. 1:5, 9) and seems to become the experience of mankind in three stages in a specific order and through God's gracious intervention in history and the cosmos.

It is evident that we live in the experience of *spiritual realization* of such blessings (Eph. 1:3–14). It is also evident that we are living in the experience of the "*earnest* of our inheritance until the redemption of the purchased possession" (Eph. 1:14, KJV). The *until* is significant. A greater measure of realization is awaiting the saints of the *Millennium* when to the spiritual blessings (Eph. 1:3, in the heavenlies), will be added physical, material, social, moral, political, economic, and religious blessings. Freedom from want, freedom from fear, and freedom of propagation and conversion without restrictions from government and society will be enjoyed by humankind because of the presence and rulership of Jesus Christ. The national, spiritual restoration of Israel is clearly stated in hundreds of passages in the Old Testament. It is also implied in such New Testament passages as Matthew 19:27–29; Acts 3:19–26; 15:13–18; Romans 11:12, 15–29 (perhaps also in 2 Cor. 3:14–16). Israel will thus fully share in the millennial blessings and will be a blessing bearer in this world.

Even in the millennium, however, sin will still mar much of life and hinder the free flow of the blessings of God (Rev. 20:7–9). As the presence and gracious ministry of the Holy Spirit today does not lead all people to repentance and faith in Christ and subsequently into the blessings of the Lord, so even the glorious presence and gracious reign of the Lord in the millennium will not convert all people to the truth and realization of His blessings. It will be necessary to rule nations and individuals with a "rod of iron" (Ps. 2:9).

The fullness of the blessings of God will come in the *consummation* as John sees it experienced in Revelation 21:1–22:5. Here are blessings without measure. Here righteousness will not only reign but will also *dwell* and be at home. Here is *realized eschatology* in the fullest sense of the term. To read all of this into our age or even into the millennium seems unwarranted. The kingdom of God is, indeed, realized and in the process of realization, but at least three interventions of God will usher in its full realization (Rev. 19:11–21; 20; 21).

2. *The nature of the kingdom of God.* The kingdom of God is a reality of history and beyond history. History can neither produce it nor exhaust it. It is in history but not of history. The nature and complexity of the kingdom is seen in part from such scriptural statements as these: the kingdom must be preached (Mark 1:15; Luke 4:43; 9:2, 60; Acts 8:12; 20:25; 28:31); it must be sought (Matt. 6:33); it must be received (Mark 10:15; Luke 18:17); it must be entered (Mark 9:47; John 3:5; Acts 14:22); it can be seen (Mark 9:1; Luke 9:27; John 3:3); it can be possessed, expressed, and manifested (Rom. 14:17; 1 Cor. 4:20); it can be taken from a people (Matt. 21:43); it can be forfeited (1 Cor. 6:9–10; Gal. 5:19–21; Eph. 5:5–6).

The kingdom is the *spiritually qualitative existence* in which God's rule is acknowledged, loved, and obeyed by rational creatures and His presence is supreme and worshiped (1 Cor. 15:28). It is the *realm* from which all sin and works of darkness are excluded (Rev. 21:8, 27). It is the *sphere* that can be entered by sinful man only by means of personal regeneration by the Spirit through a faith relationship with Jesus Christ (John 3:5; Titus 3:5). It is the *divine gift* that must be received and that assures the individual of heavenly citizenship and of being an eternal heir (Eph. 2:8, 19–22). It is the *quality of eternity* that brings to a person the full blessings of God without measure (John 10:10; Eph. 3:8, 7–22). It is the *divine operation* that unites all generations of humankind into the household of God (Eph. 2:19). It is the *state of being* that perfectly unfolds the total potential of the human personality expressed in the words "we shall be like Him" (1 John 3:2; cf. 1 Cor. 13:12).

Finally, the kingdom of God may also be thought of as *that divine impact* through the church and the cosmic operations of the Holy Spirit that impinges on the kingdom of humans and that confronts the prince of the power of the air and the principalities and powers and rulers of the darkness of this world and spiritual wickedness in high places as they seek to entrench and manifest themselves in the various power structures of human society (Eph. 2:2; 6:11–12; Col. 1:13; 2:14–15).

In the kingdom are the angels that preserved their created estate and serve and worship God. In it also are the saints of the antediluvian and postdiluvian times, the saints of Israel and those who shared in the faith of the living God and the redemption hope of Genesis 3:15 (e.g., Job, Melchizedek, Naaman, the wise men from the east), the saints of our economy, the believers out of the Great Tribulation, and eventually the saved nations of the Millennium (Rev. 21:1–27; Matt. 5:34).

From the above scriptural summary it is evident that to define the kingdom of God in a simple sentence is to omit some essential aspects of it. It is one of those broad biblical concepts that defies a simple definition simply because it surpasses knowledge and belongs to those "unfathomable riches." It is progressive, dynamic, existential, and intensely practical and moral rather than static and philosophical. To paraphrase the great theologian Bengel, "It bursts every system and definition of man."

Here the wise words of O. Michel are most appropriate:

> All genuine theology is in battle against theologizing, abstracting, theorizing, and against the attempt to replace the genuine Biblical and historical motive by a philosophical transformation. Genuine theology is acquainted with insoluble tensions and self-defining thought-forms of the holy Scriptures, which cannot become a part of any human scheme nor of any theological system. At present we are in love with simplifications, while the Bible glorifies humble simplicity; at present we wish easy solutions, while the Bible strengthens us with solu-

tions for travelling; at present we wish again and again to hear ourselves while the Bible would invite us to the hearing of the naked word.[3]

The kingdom of God, then, can be described as the fullness and glory of the Godhead revealed in Christ Jesus to His intelligent creation that honors and worships Him as God and Father. It is life and gift, position and possession, rule and worship, relationship and fellowship. Because of this fullness, the kingdom cannot completely express itself nor can it be experienced fully by any age or by any one people until the glorification of humankind and the consummation of the ages. Then will we be enabled to experience its full splendor and riches and express it as it really is. This, indeed, will be realized eschatology.

3. *The universal qualitative characteristics of the kingdom.* The qualitative characteristics of the people of God of all ages and of the citizenry in the kingdom of God are the same. The ultimate destiny seems to be the same (the new heaven and the new earth, Rev. 21:1–22:5). It is the kingdom *of God*—it comes from Him, it belongs to Him, and He remains its center. It is a kingdom of righteousness, of peace, of joy (Rom. 14:17), of fullness of life (John 10:10), and of spiritual qualities that only the Holy Spirit can produce in the life of the redeemed person (Gal. 5:22–23). It can be entered only by way of regeneration by repentance from sin and faith in Christ Jesus (John 3:3, 5). Without holiness (sanctification) no person shall see the Lord (Heb. 12:14). It is because of this that Jesus Christ was made for us "wisdom from God, and righteousness and sanctification, and redemption" (1 Cor. 1:30). In the Beatitudes our Lord describes the basic disposition and attitudes of the citizens of the kingdom of God (Matt. 5:2–12). There are specific classes of people who always have been and always will be excluded from the kingdom of God (1 Cor. 6:9–10; Gal. 5:19–21; Eph. 5:5; Rev. 21:8). The kingdom of God, then, has some very specific qualitative distinctives that always have characterized and always will characterize the participants in the kingdom.

It is not in the qualitative distinctions that we find difference. Such difference, if there is any, seems to show through in the *calling* of the people of God in the different ages or dispensations and in their *experiences* according to the covenants and promises of God. God has regulated all things according to the pleasure of His eternal counsel and in keeping with His all-wise *plan* and *purpose* of the ages (Rom. 11:33–36; Eph. 1:3–14; 3:1–12). Much in Scripture is given for worship and obedience rather than for full understanding and exposition. Certainly Israel did not understand all the detailed meanings of its sacrificial system, but the people could experience blessings beyond their understanding if they believed the divine ordinances and obeyed them implicitly. So it is today. However, the differences in the promises, experiences, calling, and purposes for the people of God in the different ages of the economy of God condition the nature and degree of the unfolding and realization of the kingdom of God (Eph. 3:2, 10, 20–21). Thus within the basic unity there seems to be diversity.

The church, then, is an essential part of the kingdom of God; however, it is only a part of it. In the words of Johannes Blauw:

> Nowhere in the New Testament is the church made the equivalent of the kingdom of God but neither is the one set anywhere in opposition to the other. The church is the community gathered around Christ and gathered by Christ (and by the apostles who are proxy for Him). She is not herself the kingdom but she is its manifestation and its form. The church herself is the sign of the new future which has broken in for the world.[4]

It must be emphasized, however, that the church does not constitute, embrace, or express the whole reality of the kingdom of God. This holds true qualitatively as well as quantitatively. The blessings of the church are principally spiritual in nature as its calling is principally spiritual in nature. Its destiny is heavenly and not earthly. It is more futuristic than it is present. It has something to strive for in the coming age as well as to gain and possess in the present. Thus while the church is realized eschatology and realized kingdom of God, it is so *in part only* and its limitations must be recognized and appreciated (Acts 14:22; Rom. 14:17; 1 Cor. 6:9–11; Eph. 1:3–14; Col. 1:13; Heb. 12:28; 2 Peter 1:11).

New Testament Ecclesiology

The fifth circle represents the church of Jesus Christ. Ecclesiology is prominent in the New Testament. From a certain perspective it constitutes a central concern of the apostolic epistles because of its glorious relationship, position, and high and holy calling. Jesus Christ loved and purchased the church with His own blood (Eph. 5:25–27). He walks in the midst of the golden lampstands that represent the church (Rev. 1:10–18), and as the chief shepherd He graciously cares for His own (John 10:11, 14; Heb. 13:20–21; 1 Peter 5:1–4).

No student of the New Testament can question the prominence of the doctrine of the church in the pages of New Testament writings. It is the unique, divine institution of the New Testament. The church is the fourth institution directly originating in God and by the act of God. First is the family, second the government, third comes the appointment of Israel as the people of God, and last comes the church. While the church has many features in common with the other institutions, it is unique in its origin, design, mission, and purpose.

The church is built on the foundation of the apostles and prophets, Jesus Christ Himself being the chief cornerstone. It is the mystery hidden in ages past but now revealed to His apostles and prophets by the Spirit to make known the "manifold wisdom of God" "in accordance with the eternal purpose which He carried out in Christ Jesus our Lord" "to the praise of the glory of His grace" (Eph. 3:5, 10, 11; 1:6).

From a specific perspective the New Testament presents a theology of the church. Such a statement, however, must be carefully defined. The Bible is not a book about the church (or church growth), although this idea is not excluded from it. The apostles are not recorded as having preached about the church, nor were they commanded to do so. They were sent forth to preach the gospel. The major emphasis of the New Testament is on the salvation of God and the glorious consummation of the purpose of God in and beyond history. Ecclesiocentricity is foreign to the Bible. The verdict of J. C. Hoekendijk seems biblically justified when he says:

> In history a keen ecclesiological interest has almost without exception been a sign of spiritual decadence; ecclesiology has been a subject of major concern only in the "second generation"; in the "first generation," in periods of revival, reformation or missionary advance, our interest was absorbed by christology, thought-patterns were determined by eschatology, life became a doxology and the Church was spoken of in an unaccented and to some extent rather naive way, as being something that "thank God a child of seven knows what it is " (Luther). This child of seven should constantly cross our path whenever we set out to "engage in ecclesiology."[5]

As humanism is a general tendency of natural human beings, so ecclesiocentricity is a natural tendency of the church. Even missionary motivation, enthusiasm, and endeavor may be made subservient to this end and serve for the aggrandizement of the church. Much of church growth throughout the centuries has been just that. That such has been a strong undercurrent in the history of modern missions is well established by Hoekendijk in an article on "The Church in Missionary Thinking."[6] His distinction between an Independent Church, World Church, Autochthonous Church, and National Church is convincing evidence of the ecclesiocentricity of modern missions. Evangelical missions are no exception. This is an age when church planting, church growth, church expansion, and church multiplication have become evangelical obsessions, when sociology and anthropology have become more dominant in missiology than the Bible and theology, when technology and methodology are better known than the divine moving of the Holy Spirit.

To keep the church within the perspective of the New Testament, the four descriptions of the church by Hoekendijk need to be supplemented by others. The church should be a Reflecting Church—it should reflect the divine qualities of the One who has called it out of darkness into His glorious light (1 Peter 2:9–10). Like its Lord, the church should be a Serving Church (Matt. 11:3–6; Mark 10:45; Luke 4:16–19; Phil. 2:5–11). Finally, a church with a compelling motivation to preach the gospel of Jesus Christ is an Evangelizing Church (Acts 8:4, 5, 25, 40; 9:31; 11:19–21; 12:24; Rom. 1:8; 15:19, 30; Phil. 1:5; 1 Thess. 1:7–8).

Ecclesiology in the New Testament is therefore carefully hedged in a greater purpose of God—a purpose that includes the church but also lies beyond the church. (A more detailed study of the church follows in chapter 3).

New Testament Cosmology

The sixth circle is that of the world—the world of humankind that God loves, Christ reconciled to God, and the Holy Spirit convicts of sin and of righteousness and of judgment, and that the ambassador of Christ is commanded and constrained to reach with the gospel and persuade and beseech to be reconciled to God.

The word "world " (*kosmos*) presents a complexity of meanings. It appears in the New Testament 187 times. The apostle John majors in it: 79 occurrences in his Gospel, 23 times in 1 John, once in 2 John, and 3 times in Revelation—a total of 106 times. Paul employs it 47 times and is quite definitive in some instances.

The concept "world" bears at least a fourfold meaning. It may refer to all of humankind as it does in John 1:29; 3:16; 8:12; 17:6, and others. It may point to the cosmos or the creation in totality or the inhabited areas of the globe, which seems to be the meaning of Mark 16:15; John 17:5; Romans 1:8; Colossians 1:6; 1 Peter 1:20. It may mean humankind, or part of it, as hostile to God, to the gospel, and to the Christian and as set in opposition to all that is spiritual, godly, eternal, or Christian (John 3:19; 15:18–19; 17:14, 25; Phil. 3:18; 1 Thess. 2:14–15; 1 John 4:4). It may also mean evil systems that have been developed by humans under the influence of Satan and his hosts and that constitute chains of iniquity to hold people captive and exploit them for the benefit of sinful ends. Passages such as John 12:31; 14:30; Romans 12:2; Galatians 4:3; Ephesians 2:2; 6:12; and 1 John 2:15–17; 4:4; 5:4; 5:19 substantiate this meaning. Paul in Colossians 2:8, 20 and Galatians 4:3 seems to refer to this usage by "elementary principles of the world" and the "elemental things of the world."

The world, meaning humanity, plays a significant role in the New

Testament. It is the object of God's love but also of His wrath, of His concern, and of His judgment. It is because of the world that Jesus came (John 3:16–17) and that the church is here (Matt. 5:13–16; John 17:18). Because the concept "world" in the New Testament is not easily defined, the church's relationship to the world is very complex. John tells us that the world lies in the evil one (1 John 5:19) and that the Christian is not to love the world (1 John 2:15). To live in the world and not as the world is not an easy assignment (Rom. 12:2). To be in the world but not of it demands great wisdom and courage (John 17:14–16). To live for the world yet be against it seems like a paradox. Not to identify with the world yet not to be isolated from it, is a divine art. To be insulated from the sins of the world and not to be callous to its woes, hurts, yearnings, and aspirations requires divine sensitivity and deep spiritual discernment. These are some of the paradoxes and tensions Christians will experience, and yet they must live and minister in the world. (God's dealings with the world will be studied later.)

In conclusion of this study of priority truth we state that a theology of the church, then, is one of the great circles of doctrine revealed in the Scriptures. Ecclesiology is part of the overall theological framework that includes theocentricity, Christocentricity, pneumatology, the kingdom of God, and cosmology. The purpose of the church is to fulfill the purposes of God in the world.

From the New Testament I gather that God wants His church to grow in number, size, and impact and to expand geographically among all people of the world. It must be a church of all nations, a people that cannot be numbered. God is great as well as good. And the Holy Spirit will not permit the church of Jesus Christ to come to rest until all the world has heard the gospel of our blessed Lord and Savior. Church growth and multiplication are essential to the well-being of the church; the blessings of humankind; the accomplishing of the purpose of God; and the glory of God the Father, Son, and Holy Spirit.

3

The Church as
the Church of God

The church of Jesus Christ is a divine creation (Eph. 2:10). It finds its source in the eternal counsel of God (Eph. 1:4; 3:11). Its origin, design, composition, mission, purpose, vitality, and destiny are an expression of the love, wisdom, grace, power, and pleasure of God (Eph. 1:3–12). We, the church, are His workmanship, created in Christ Jesus (Eph. 2:10). It is the *church of God,* the household of God, the priesthood of God, the body of Christ, the bride of Christ, and the temple of God indwelt by the Holy Spirit. In many ways the church betrays strong human characteristics and is not as ideal as we would like it to be. It is portrayed in its weaknesses, sinfulness, and failures in such writings as First and Second Corinthians, Galatians, James, Jude, and Revelation. Yet it is the church of God (1 Cor. 1:2), and it knows that some day it will be presented without spot and wrinkle (Eph. 5:27). It has the promise that it will be taken from this earth before the wrath of God will visit apostate humanity and that it will enjoy the glory and presence of its Lord for all eternity

(1 Thess. 4:13–5:11; Rev. 3:10). A living, blessed hope is its portion in the midst of toil and tears, sacrifice and suffering, pressures and temptations (1 Peter 1:3–9). Indwelt by the Holy Spirit, it is led on from faith to faith and from glory to glory (Rom. 1:17; 2 Cor. 3:18).

Decisive and gracious actions of God are written into the history of humankind. These manifest themselves uniquely in the history of Israel and in the mystery and existence of the church of Jesus Christ.

THE CHURCH AND ISRAEL

From the perspective of *Heilsgeschichte* (salvation history) and the theology of the church, I conclude that the church of Jesus Christ was born on the day of Pentecost. Its relationship to the Old Testament people and mission of God is a hermeneutical debate that in the main does not concern us here. In chapter 2 we examined the relationship of the church to the kingdom of God. Here I briefly delineate the relationship of the church to Israel.

That *a functional and qualitative relationship* exists between Israel and the church is difficult to deny. Both share in the kingdom of God and constitute a part of it. Because of this they have many features in common and their spiritual heritage is very similar. To completely dissociate the church in its salvation experience (Rom. 3:21–5:21), historical significance, function, and historical purpose (1 Peter 2:9–10) from Israel is to disregard the overall and unifying purpose (singular) of the ages (plural) (Eph. 3:9) and salvation history as revealed in the Word of God. To completely identify the church with Israel and to make it the New Israel seems unwarranted and unjustifiable. They are two distinct entities in the plan and purpose of God (Rom. 9–11; 1 Cor. 10:32; Eph. 3:1–12) with separate covenants and promises.

I am quite well acquainted with the literature that seeks to bring the Old Testament in line with realized or partially realized eschatology through a process of spiritualization and transmutation of promises and covenants (a conservative view), or to demythologize, dehistoricize, and despiritualize the Old Testament (liberal) to make it a relevant example of God's presence in history.[1] But none of these approaches seems to me to be historically and theologically necessary or consistent with Old Testament meanings and values. It seems best to accept the Old Testament as actual revelation, interpret it as much as possible literally and historically, and remain consistent in hermeneutics. If the judgments of the nations and Israel have become history, and the promises about Christ's first coming have been literally fulfilled, why not believe that the promises of His second coming and the remaining promises to Israel and the nations will also be fulfilled literally? This seems most logical with a consistent hermeneutic and the unchanging character, promises, and covenants of God.

Pentecost, then, is the birthday of the church of Jesus Christ as a separate, distinct, and unique people of God, and the beginning of a new economy of God similar to the new economy of God signaled by the call of Abraham (Gen. 12).[2]

From the historical point of view we are now living in the *age of the church* with a limited unfolding of the kingdom of God. From the trinitarian perspective this seems to be uniquely the age of the Holy Spirit with the full manifestation of the spiritual blessings in Christ Jesus (Gal. 5:22–25; Eph. 1:3; 4:23–24). The challenge live, walk, and pray in the Spirit is central in the New Testament (Rom. 8:1ff.; Gal. 5:16, 25; Eph. 6:18; Jude 20). A fuller coming of the kingdom awaits the return of the Prince of Peace on this earth that will result in the national and spiritual restoration of Israel and a spiritual renovation of humankind. Justice, peace, and freedom will govern the nations of the world under the personal administration of the King of Kings and Lord of Lords. This is the time so richly portrayed in numerous promises and prophecies in the Old Testament, the time that Peter called "the period of restoration" (Acts 3:21), John spoke of as the thousand years six times (Rev. 20:2–7), and Christ described as "the regeneration" (Matt. 19:28).

The Church and Christendom

Throughout history the church has expanded greatly both numerically and geographically. Today it claims a larger professing membership than any other religion and is found on all continents and in most countries. In some areas it constitutes only a very small minority and in some it is on the decline. In some areas several prodigious religious establishments and ecclesiastical systems have evolved, constituting a kind of corpus Christianum. It is this kind of Christianity that atheism sought to dethrone in France toward the end of the eighteenth and beginning of the nineteenth centuries and that communism confronted in Russia.

In much of Christendom the wheat and the tares have become so mixed together that the true and the false, the professing and the possessing are difficult to distinguish. Culture and religion, psychology and spirituality, philosophy and theology, community and ecclesia have become fused inseparably. In the course of time symbol has replaced reality; form has been substituted for substance; ritual and performance have supplanted worship; sacraments have taken the place of faith, prayer, and communion. Monolithic hierarchical religious systems pose as the church of Jesus Christ, and the Savior of mankind is hidden in pomp, ritualism, and imagery. Salvation from sin and from eternal damnation and justification by faith in Jesus Christ alone are either unknown or in some cases denied outright.

Humanism, mysticism, socialism, ritualism, cultism, and in some instances even occultism, in their crassest forms are offered as substitutes for the gospel of God. In the final days this religious system becomes apostate (Rev. 17–18). It is out of the interreligious conglomerate that the darkest anti-Christian forces arise and not out of communism, Islam, Hinduism, or Buddhism (2 Thess. 2:1–12). That which is raised highest falls deepest and plunges into the blackness of darkness.

This dismal picture of a kind of corpus Christianum must not blind us to the fact that since Pentecost there has been and always will be the true and genuine church of Jesus Christ. Christ has assured us that He will build His church and that the gates of Hades will not prevail against it no matter what form these attacks take.

Despite the fiercest opposition, brutal oppression and murderous persecutions, numerous disruptions, tragic apostasies, fallacious accommodations and degrading syncretism, its course has demonstrated that the church is a mysterious reality. No religion has such a trail of suffering and blood, such heroism in martyrdom, such sacrificial giving to show forth as Christianity and the Christian church. No religion has aroused more bitter opposition from the outside and experienced more serious betrayals and criticism from its own ranks than Christianity has. Yet, there stands the church of Jesus Christ in strength and vigor, poised for ever-new adventures of faith and love, for advances and exploits in new territories, and for penetration and transformation of culture, society, and mind. Unconquered and ever conquering, it is being led on from faith to faith and triumph to triumph, as Paul exclaims: "Now thanks be unto God who always leads us in His triumph in Christ and manifests through us the sweet aroma of the knowledge of Him in every place" (2 Cor. 2:14).

As it was in the times of Elijah when the Lord had a remnant of considerable size that had not bowed the knee before Baal, and as it was at the time of Christ when a faithful remnant awaited His coming, so it has been throughout the centuries of the Christian era. Total darkness has never befallen the entire body. There always has been a remnant loyal to the gospel and its Lord. The Lord has always preserved some witnesses to bear testimony to the truth. This body within professing Christendom constitutes the church of truly regenerated people that Christ is building.

THE CHURCH AS THE CHURCH OF GOD

The Scriptures bear ample testimony to the fact that the church is the church of God. The church is not a human institution or organization. It cannot be built by techniques and methodology alone. It is principally an organism that was born by the Spirit of God on the day of Pentecost (Acts 2). It is not a natural phenomenon of history; history as such did not give rise to it. In providence God set the stage in history for its coming and its rapid expansion (Gal. 4:4), but history did not originate it. There is no natural way to explain the presence of the church in this world. It is a divine creation, a mystery, a new man appearing on the scene (Eph. 2:10, 15), because God acted in history.

Pentecost is a divine miracle, a heavenly intervention. God in and through the Holy Spirit invaded humankind and interrupted the regular course of history in a supernatural, unprecedented manner and called the church into being. Discontinuity in this manner is as much a fact in history as continuity is thought to be. God broke through and brought forth the church of God. It was an instant church, originating historically in one great and miraculous act of God in a specific place and at a specific date—it happened in Jerusalem at Pentecost (Acts 2), a Jewish Old Testament festival. Forever the church remains the church of God, "being built together to become a dwelling in which God lives by his spirit" (Eph. 2:22).

In many ways the *natural phenomena* of the church—profession, form, structure, membership, ritual, observances, celebrations—take on the form of the environment, culture, and society with modification and enrichment. Not so the pneumena—its soul and spirit, its confession, ordinances, function, mission, and purpose. *Not the world but the Bible sets the agenda for the church.* It is the sovereign prerogative of the gracious Lord to prescribe its membership, nature, mission, purpose, progress, and destiny. *Here is the ultimate law of church growth:* It rests in the Lord. "I will build My church," He sovereignly declares in Matthew 16:18. Because of this, church growth will always contain an element of mystery that defies all human penetration, analysis, and definition and that casts us back on the Head of the church in prayer, trustful waiting, and patient labors (1 Cor. 3:6–8). Also because of this, the supreme Shepherd never has committed His flock completely and totally to the undershepherds. The church is not owned nor absolutely managed by humans (Acts 20:28). Whenever human ownership or absolute management has been attempted, internal disruptions and secessions have resulted. The Holy Spirit cannot be socialized, dominated, domesticated, or acculturated. He breaks forth, as history demonstrates, and creates His own environment. The church belongs to God and flourishes only in a divine climate. Unhesitatingly, convincingly, and uniformly the Scriptures ascribe the church to God as the following statements and metaphors indicate.

The church of God	Acts 20:28; 1 Cor. 1:2; 10:32; 11:16, 22; 15:9; 2 Cor. 1:1; 1 Thess. 2:14; 2 Thess. 1:4; 1 Tim. 3:5, 15
The temple of God	1 Cor. 3:16–17; Eph. 2:20–22; 1 Tim. 3:15
The household of God	Eph. 2:19
The building of God	1 Cor. 3:9; Eph. 2:20–22
The flock of God	John 10; Acts 20:28; 1 Peter 5:2
The people of God	Heb. 4:9; 1 Peter 2:9–10
The bride of Christ	Matt. 25:6; 2 Cor. 11:2; Eph. 5:22–32
The church of Christ	Matt. 16:18; Rom. 16:16
The body of Christ	Eph. 5:23–32
The people of my possession	1 Peter 2:9
The new man	Eph. 2:14–15
The church of the saints	1 Cor. 14:33
The royal priesthood	1 Peter 2:5, 9; Rev. 1:6; 5:10
The church of the first-born	Heb. 12:23

The statements, metaphors, and designations above have great implications and far-reaching significance. Let none dare to manipulate, dominate, exploit, mislead, or mismanage the church of God. Certainly it were better for that person never to have been born. The righteous wrath of God will be upon them for time and for eternity.

From the above list, we see that the church is divine in its eternal election, in its purchase and redemption, in its possession and belongingness, in its design and purpose, in its destiny, and also in its origin and historical realization.

The church has been brought forth for good works that God Himself has prepared beforehand (Eph. 2:10). Thus creation-miracle and work-purpose are beautifully linked together. Paul intimately relates the church to God in and through the Holy Spirit by speaking of it as the "dwelling of God in the Spirit" (Eph. 2:22).

From Scripture we learn the deeper meaning of the relationship of the Holy Spirit to the church.[3]

- He gave birth to the church on the day of Pentecost (Acts 2:1–41).
- He indwells the church as the temple of God (2 Cor. 6:16; Eph. 2:21–22).
- He enables the church to be the church of God and bear the fruit of the Spirit (Rom. 5:5; Gal. 5:22–23; Phil. 1:11; Col. 1:10).
- He cares for the church by raising up for it the needed and qualified personnel to guide and nurture the church (Acts 20:28; 1 Cor. 12:28; Eph. 4:11).
- He empowers the church in life and ministry and qualifies it in its task (1 Cor. 12:1–30).
- He leads the church in its great missionary enterprise (Acts 13:1–4).
- He counsels the church on difficult issues (Acts 15:28).
- He sustains the church in all suffering and persecution (Acts 4:23–31).
- He will continue to build the church, consummate it, and present it to the Bridegroom as a bride holy, blameless, and beyond reproach, "the church in all her glory, having no spot or wrinkle or any such thing; but that she should be holy and blameless" (2 Cor. 11:2; Eph. 5:27; Col. 1:22).

God alone has the property rights to the church. Because it is God's, He alone proposes, composes, imposes, and disposes. Never will He surrender His right as owner and possessor of the church, nor will He totally delegate His authority to human beings to manage the affairs of His church, though they may do their utmost to draw such power and authority to themselves. The church has no resources of its own. Its life and dynamism are not self-existing factors that can be generated. All that the church is, has, does, and becomes is due to the fact that it is divine in origin and possession and that the Holy Spirit is at work. It is the church of God.

THE LOCAL CHURCH

These great and glorious designations must be brought down, however, to our level and situation. What is the church in its local setting? It may be defined simply as a group of believers gathering at specific times around a common Lord for the proclamation of the Word of God, for fellowship, edification, worship, observance of biblical ordinances, and discharging of specific functions and duties to each other and to the world.

A more comprehensive definition would be this: A local church is that ordered body of professing baptized believers who, on the basis of common experiences of the Lord and convictions about the Word, in the bond of mutual love and understanding, in the interest of common concerns and causes, and for the purposes of mutual spiritual benefits and fellowship, assemble themselves together according to the Word of God, and under the guidance and direction of an elected or appointed leadership conduct worship services in an organized and orderly manner, observe the Lord's ordinances, perform such functions as they deem advantageous to themselves and their community according to the Word of God, and discharge such other responsibilities as they judge their duty before God and man.

The basic qualities of a biblical local church expressing the functional nature of the church may be summarized in several statements:

> The church is the gathering together of baptized believers.
> The church is an ordered (structured) body of believers.
> The church is a united body of believers.
> The church is a brotherhood of believers.
> The church is a disciplined fellowship of believers.
> The church is a witnessing fellowship of believers.
> The church is a proclaiming and serving fellowship of believers.
> The church is a worshiping fellowship of believers.[4]

Elton Trueblood speaks of the true church as "The Company of the Committed."[5] Bishop Lesslie Newbigin entitles his lectures on the nature of the church as *The Household of God* and discusses the church under the following subtitles: "The Congregation of the Faithful"; "The Body of Christ"; "The Community of the Holy Spirit"; "Christ in You, the Hope of Glory"; "Unto All the Nations."[6]

Church growth takes place in local situations. It is here that membership increases and decreases. Here the members live, learn, serve, fellowship, thrive, suffer, and die. Here they make their contribution, share their joys, and celebrate their victories, or become a burden and liability to their congregation and to the Lord. In all reality the local congregation becomes the manifestation of the church universal.

THE BIBLICAL SIGNIFICANCE OF THE LOCAL CHURCH

I. Generally, the local church has a threefold ministry to perform:
Upward in worship and adoration, praise and intercession
Inward in mutual care and edification, education and discipline
Outward in evangelism and service, instruction and reproof

II. Particularly, the local church is defined in the following terms:

1. The local church is God's institution to cultivate within its membership true worship and spiritual service (John 4:23–24; 1 Cor. 3:16–17; 6:19; Eph. 2:19–22). It is the *Temple* of God.

2. It is God's institution to preserve His revelation and unfold His eternal purpose and salvation in Christ Jesus (Eph. 1:6, 9, 12, 14; 3:10; 1 Tim. 3:14–15). It is the *Pillar and Support* of the Truth of God.

3. It is God's institution to cultivate true fellowship and mutual care among the children of God (Acts 2:42–47; 4:32–33; Eph. 2:20–22; 1 John). It is the *Household* of God.

4. It is God's institution to edify and perfect the saints of God (Acts 20:27–28; Eph. 4:11–16; 1 Peter 5:1–3). It is the *Priesthood* of God.

5. It is God's institution to admonish the unruly and to discipline the impenitent professing Christians (Matt. 18:15–17; 1 Cor. 5:11; 2 Thess. 3:6–15; 1 Tim. 5:19–20). It is the *Schoolmaster* of God.

6. It is God's institution to bear the weak in faith, to care for the ill in the faith, and to restore the erring ones in the faith and life (John 15:1–7; Rom. 15:1–15; 1 Cor. 3:9; Gal. 6:1; Col. 2:16–23; 1 Thess. 2:7–16). It is the *Vineyard* of God.

7. It is God's institution to proclaim the gospel and evangelize the world (Matt. 5:13–14; 28:18–20; Mark 16:15–16; Luke 24:45–49; John 20:19–23; Acts 1:8). It is the *Witness* of God.

8. It is God's institution to function in this world as a conscience and judge of culture and movements. It is the Salt of the earth and the Light of the world (Matt. 5:13–16; Phil. 2:14–16; 1 John 4:1). It is the *Prophetic Voice* of God.

9. It is God's institution to demonstrate before the world the Virtures of the "Father of mercies" (2 Cor. 1:3), the Servanthood of the Son (Mark 10:45), and the Presence of the Spirit of Grace (Heb. 10:29) in loving, unselfish, and sacrificial service to needy humankind (Matt. 5:16; Gal. 6:10; Phil. 2:15–16; 4:5; 1 Peter 2:9). It is the *Servant* of God.

4

Church Growth as
the Work of God

Because the church is the church of God, so church growth, both qualitatively and quantitatively, is the work of God. Our Lord emphatically expresses this truth in the first reference to the church in the New Testament: in Matthew 16:18 He majestically declares, "Upon this rock *I will build my church*"; then He adds the wonderful prediction, "and the gates of hell shall not prevail against it" (KJV). Just as Genesis 3:15 has been known in the terms of *Heilsgeschichte* as the protevangelium of the glorious salvation of God, objectively wrought by Christ Jesus and subjectively realized by the gracious operation of the Holy Spirit and faith in Christ as Savior and Lord; even so Matthew 16:18 may well be spoken of as the protevangelium of the glorious building program of God as manifested in the church of Jesus Christ.

Four components are clearly set forth in this building program of Matthew 16:18. They are:

- the foundation of the church: Jesus Christ Himself, the rock, is the foundation and chief corner-stone (Isa. 28:16; cf. 1 Cor. 3:11; Eph. 2:20; 1 Peter 2:6–8).

- the builder of the church: Jesus Christ Himself is the builder.

- the enemy of the church: The gates of hell strive against it.

- the endurance of the church: The church will endure and prevail.

Thus, from the very beginning of the church our Lord emphasized that church growth is the work of God.

Other New Testament passages continue this tone and reaffirm this assertion. Mark informs us at the end of his Gospel that the apostles "went out and preached everywhere, while the *Lord worked with them,* and confirmed the word by the signs that followed" (Mark 16:20). Even more pronounced is Paul's consciousness that church growth is the work of God. He writes: "I planted, Apollos watered, *but God was causing the growth*" (1 Cor. 3:6–7). Paul reminded the Corinthians that the church is God's cultivated field and His building (1 Cor. 3:9). Peter also used this figure: "You also, as living stones, *are being built* up as a spiritual house for a holy priesthood (1 Peter 2:5). Luke's record confirms all this: "*The Lord was adding* to their number day by day those who were being saved" (Acts 2:47). Indeed, church growth, qualitatively and quantitatively, is the work of God (Col. 2:19).

The Work of the Godhead in Church Growth

Although the Bible does not spell out in definitive terms an economy of operation within the Holy Trinity, yet such an economy is implied in the words of our Master in John 14–16. From the Scriptures can be deduced a certain order and relationship in the operations of the Godhead. Our Lord made repeated statements of His relationship to the Father: He had been sent by the Father; He was doing the will of the Father; the doctrine He proclaimed was not His own but the Father's who had sent Him; He could do nothing of Himself; and the Father was greater (in office) than He was (John

5:30; 7:16; 8:28–29; 10:25–26; 10:37–38). Similar words describe the Holy Spirit's relationship to the other Persons of the Godhead: He is sent by the Father and the Son (John 14:16, 26; 15:26; 16:7; Acts 2:33; 5:31–32); He will witness concerning the Son (John 15:26); He will glorify the Son (John 16:14); He will take what belongs to Christ and disclose it to the disciples (John 16:25).

The statements of the operations within the Godhead must not be interpreted to mean that the Son and the Spirit are essentially less than God or inferior to the Father. We must distinguish between functional order and essential personality and being. In essential personality and being there is absolute equality and coeternity; in office and function, however, there is coordination as well as temporary subordination.

In relation to salvation this economy within the Trinity may be summarized as follows: the Trinity designed the plan of salvation, the Father covenanted it, the Son procured it, and the Holy Spirit executes it. Although such a division may seem to impose a human scheme on the divine mystery, the statements referred to earlier from John's Gospel and the words of Paul in Ephesians 1:3–14 seem to support such a description. To state this truth of the operations of the Godhead more fully: the Father sent the Son into the world to become the Savior of the world (John 3:16–17). The Son came and in obedience gave His life as a ransom for many (Mark 10:45). He reconciled the world to God by becoming the propitiation for the sins of the whole world (2 Cor. 5:18–21; Phil. 2:5–8; 1 Tim. 2:3–6; 1 John 2:1–2). Therefore, He was highly exalted and given a name above every name (Phil 2:9–11). On the day of Pentecost the Holy Spirit was poured forth by the Father and the Son beyond measure and for a specific mission. He now operates in this world in an unprecedented and blessed manner. He was sent as the Paraclete for the Godhead into the world (John 14:16, 26; 15:26; 16:7). Looked at from this Trinitarian perspective, we can see that the era of the church is uniquely the age of the Holy Spirit.

Paraclete is the official designation of the Holy Spirit in His operations since Penetcost. The word *Paraclete* is difficult to translate and define because of its many-sidedness and richness in meaning and implications. It is used in classical Greek as well as in the Septuagint. As Paraclete the Holy Spirit is the representative, the barrister, the executor, the realizer—the person of the Godhead responsible for the divine plan and purpose of the ages, and the administrator of the divine affairs in this world. Griffith Thomas speaks of Him as the "Executive of the Godhead."[1] He is the presence of God in the world who operates and/or overrules all things, directly or indirectly (i.e., by His permissive will), according to the strategy of the Trinity. He is the divine agent who builds the church of Jesus Christ. He leads the church and this world to a blessed consummation in the full realization of the kingdom of God.

Because of such far-reaching operations and their implications for the ministry, the church of Jesus Christ needs to study carefully and comprehensively the work of the Holy Spirit. His operations and particularly His functions in our age in relation to the church of Jesus Christ and the evangelization of the world are unfolded in the New Testament. In this book we must limit our study to His work as it relates to church growth.

THE HOLY SPIRIT AND HIGH POTENTIALITY

In the Old Testament the Holy Spirit was present in man for official purposes—qualifying people for special duties, responsibilities, and functions—but not in the full official capacity as the Paraclete, the Helper, the Comforter in the New Testament sense. There is a new depth in the ministry of the Holy Spirit since Pentecost.

Griffith Thomas remarks that

> in the New Testament there is an entire absence of all cosmical relations of the Holy Spirit such as we find in the Old Testament. This contrast between the two parts of Scripture calls for careful attention. The New Testament revelation of the Holy Spirit is associated solely with redemption, and the wider doctrine of the direct relation of God to the world is expressed by the Logos, the Second Person of the Trinity (John 1:9; Col. 1:16–17; Heb. 1:2–3a).[2]

And again he writes:

> The New Testament, as we observed, never associates the Holy Spirit with God's action in nature, but only with the redemptive work of Christ for and in man. The sphere of the Spirit is definitely spiritual, and His activities are spiritual also. There may be analogy, but there is certainly no identity between the presence of God in nature and the Holy Spirit of God in the believer.[3]

Must we conclude from this that the Holy Spirit is in no way operative in humankind as a whole? To this I cannot yield. It would seem to me to contradict the immanence of God, and immanence is more than omnipresence. In the words of Griffith Thomas: "Immanence is intended to teach that God is everywhere present and active in nature, ceaselessly at work in history, and spiritually present with and in man."[4]

The Holy Spirit gave birth to the church as a new creation on the day of Pentecost. As the divine Paraclete He builds, preserves, and expands the church and will lead it safely to its eternal destiny after it has fulfilled its mission. The great Pentecostal event, however, is not exhausted in the Holy Spirit's ministry in the church and the believer. Christ explicitly informs us that He will convict the world (John 16:8–11).

How, then, are we to consider the ministry of the Holy Spirit since Pentecost in relation to humankind? I take it for granted that the Holy Spirit continued His ministry of revelation and inspiration to complete the New Testament. I accept the position that He continued His cosmical relationships and activities as indicated in the old economy. It is difficult for me to conceive that Pentecost in any way weakened or altered such relationships. However, what about humankind and history?

Because the great Pentecostal outpouring of the Holy Spirit has made this the age of the Holy Spirit, we can and should expect an *intensification* of the work of the Holy Spirit in the world as a whole. It is evident that He is creating in humankind a deeper conviction of sin, of righteousness, and of judgment (John 16:8–11); a greater awareness of the presence of the divine (John 1:9); and a hunger and thirst for the Word of God (Amos 8:11–14). On one side, all this manifests itself in greater restlessness, in intensified religious activities and movements, in searchings, undefined yearnings, messianic anticipations, and anxious inquiries. On the other side, the kingdom of this world is bracing itself against the intensified operations of the Holy Spirit, as seen in sharpened antireligious movements and activities: atheism, occultism, demonism, Satanism, philosophical scientism, secularism, pseudo-Christian movements, anti-God operations in political structures, and legislation forbidding conversion to Christianity. The world is set in sharp contrast, with irreconcilable polarities.

The Holy Spirit is not merely ushering in an *age* of missions. He is also graciously creating an *atmosphere* of missions in which the church can operate. This atmosphere of missions is the soil for whitened harvest fields. Let us then consider this gracious operation of the Holy Spirit from two points of view: the making of high potentiality, and historical events and high potentiality.

1. *The making of high potentiality.* Our Lord used parables, symbols, and metaphors to depict life situations in a graphic and realistic manner. On several occasions, when describing the spreading of the Good News He had brought, He used the analogy of the soil and the seed, sowing and reaping, and the whitened harvest fields.

Having observed the spiritual plight of the people of the land on His numerous tours through the villages of Galilee, He instructed His disciples to pray for laborers to be sent forth by the Lord of the harvest. Perhaps to their surprise He remarked: "The harvest is plentiful, but the workers are few" (Matt. 9:37). Changing the metaphor somewhat as He went through Samaria, the Lord said to the disciples, "Do you not say, 'There are yet four months, and then comes the harvest'? Behold, I say to you, lift up your eyes, and look on the fields, that they are white for harvest" (John 4:35).

That our Lord's description of a whitened and plentiful harvest field was accurate became evident somewhat later. When the believers were scattered from Jerusalem (Acts 8:1), they returned to these same territories of Galilee and Samaria with a testimony of the crucified and resurrected Lord; and there they saw churches multiply

(Acts 9:31). Philip witnessed a mighty revival in Samaria (Acts 8:5–25). Peter saw great multitudes from the Jerusalem area and even total communities respond to the gospel message (Acts 5:14–16; 9:35, 42). Paul, winding up extensive preaching tours through Asia Minor and Greece, wrote to the Corinthians from Ephesus: "A wide door for effective service has opened to me" (1 Cor. 16:9). Though the disciples did not seem to be aware of it at first, the Lord had His harvest fields—high potential people—who were ready to respond to the message of God.

In another parable using the same analogy, our Lord said: "The kingdom of God is like a man who casts seed upon the ground; and goes to bed at night and gets up by day, and the seed sprouts up and grows—how, he himself does not know. The earth produces crops by itself; first the blade, then the head, then the mature grain in the head. But when the crop permits, he immediately puts in the sickle, because the harvest has come" (Mark 4:26–29).

Five elements are involved in reaping the harvest: (1) the proper seed must be sown; (2) a man is required to sow the seed; (3) time is needed for the seed to sprout, grow, and mature; (4) proper seasons are important; and (5) a man with a sickle must be prepared to do the harvesting. All five elements are important. Above all, however, Christ emphasizes the proper seed and the ready laborers. As in regeneration the Word of God is the only proper seed the Holy Spirit employs (James 1:18; 1 Peter 1:23), so in the preparation the Word of God is the necessary seed through which spiritual awareness can be created in man. Therefore, "sow your seed in the morning, and do not be idle in the evening, for you do not know whether morning or evening sowing will succeed, or whether both of them alike will be good" (Eccl. 11:6).

The same Lord who uttered the words of a whitened and plentiful harvest directed His disciples to think of the world as the field of labor (Matt. 13:38), commanding them to go into all the world, preach the gospel, and make the message of God's redeeming acts in Christ available to every nation and creature. He did not tell them however, that all the world would immediately be a whitened harvest field. As His followers we must therefore discern between the world as a *mission* field and the already whitened *harvest* fields where a plentiful harvest is ready to be garnered in. How, then, are mission fields converted into harvest fields—or high potential areas? What is Christ's position?

Our Lord answered this question specifically when He told His disciples: "In this case the saying is true, 'One sows, and another reaps.' I sent you to reap that for which you have not labored; others have labored, and you have entered into their labors." The result would be: "that he who sows and he who reaps may rejoice together" (John 4:36–38). The Lord implies, then, that without previous diligent labors there would be no plentiful harvest. Paul further elaborated this principle: "Now this I say, he who sows sparingly shall also reap sparingly; and he who sows bountifully shall also reap bountifully" (2 Cor. 9:6). Diagram 2 illustrates this truth.

Church Growth Factors

Whitening the Field

Convergence of Preparatory Factors

Convergence of Operational Factors

Harvesting the Field

One sows
Others labor

Another reaps
You enter into their labors

Diagram 2

From these Scriptures it seems that there are no naturally prepared whitened harvest fields. Humanity is not naturally prepared for spiritual truths, nor do natural experiences prepare individuals for spiritual reality. The law seems to be absolute: "That which is born of the flesh is flesh" (John 3:6). "A natural man does not accept the things of the Spirit of God; for they are foolishness [meaningless, empty] to him, and he cannot understand them, because they are spiritually appraised" (1 Cor. 2:14). Individuals are dead in trespasses and sins (Eph. 2:1) and love darkness more than light (John 3:19).

Natural history, sociology, and psychology do not have the spiritual dimension and vitality to create in people spiritual awareness, to cause them to perceive spiritual needs, to motivate them to seek spiritual remedy. Only the Holy Spirit can cause spiritual awakenings.

The Bible is emphatic in attributing spiritual realities and experiences to God alone. He only is the source of all true spirituality. He gives repentance (Acts 5:31). Just as faith is a gift of God (Eph. 2:8), so are eternal life and divine adoption gracious bestowals of God (Rom. 6:23; 8:15; John 1:12). Only God can regenerate and justify the sinner (John 1:13; Rom. 4:5, 17). All spiritual experiences are effected by the gracious operations of the Holy Spirit and His Word as individuals believe (John 3:5; Titus 3:5; James 1:18; 1 Peter 1:23). It is in the Holy Spirit that we find the only and sufficient source and cause for high potentiality.

How does the Holy Spirit create fields white to harvest—or high potentiality? How do such spiritual effects arise? How do people begin to reach out for spiritual reality and to yearn and search for it? How are they brought into a state of readiness to respond to the gospel message?

Admittedly, there is a broad realm of mystery that no human mind will ever penetrate, for we are dealing with supernaturalism invading and encountering individuals in their natural state. However, from the Scriptures we do know that in all soteriological operations the Holy Spirit binds Himself to persons and to *means—the Word of God*—to bring about His purposes. It is unsafe and nonbiblical to loosen soteriological operations from the presence of God's people and/or the Word of God written. Monism, Hegelian idealism, and mysticism do so freely, but not theistic realism and biblical evangelicalism. That is why our Lord has much to say about the *sower* and the *seed* in His parables (Matt. 13:3–9, 18–23; 13:24–30, 36–43; Mark 4:26–29). Paul also places much emphasis on preaching, evangelizing, and proclaiming; and John emphasizes witnessing.

That the Holy Spirit uses people and the Word is forcefully illustrated in Acts. The Ethiopian eunuch; Saul of Tarsus; Cornelius, the centurion of Caesarea; and Lydia of Thyatira—all experienced the grace of God that culminated in conversion. Each of them had been graciously prepared, in that a ready mind had already been created. The Ethiopian eunuch was reading the Scriptures and had been to Jerusalem in search of truth and reality. Saul had studied the Old Testament; though he had received wrong interpretation and a faulty theology, he had been drinking from the right source. Also, he had been sufficiently in contact with New Testament believers to be acquainted, at least superficially, with their position. Cornelius was in Caesarea (Palestine); he is called a "God-fearer," an expression that is indicative of his relationship to the synagogue. Lydia had met Paul in Philippi at the place of worship. Thus all these had been under the impact of the Word (seed) and people (sowers).

Preparation does not, however, depend on length of time of previous exposure. It may come suddenly because of the intensity of an experience or the impact of circumstances, as with the jail keeper in Philippi. Any extended previous exposure to the Word of God or people of God (Jews) is highly improbable in his case, for there seems to have been no synagogue in Philippi. It is possible that he had observed Paul and Silas being accused, beaten, and thrown into jail. It is even probable that he had asked them why they had come to Philippi. His question—"Sirs, what must I do to be saved?"—seems to imply some acquaintance with the gospel of salvation or at least with the deepest concerns of Christianity. Paul's answer would have had little spiritual significance if the jailer had not had some exposure to the gospel.

The parables and the testimonies of the early church, then, demonstrate when high potentiality—whitened harvest fields—can be expected. On the basis of theological deduction it can be said that there is no area in the world where there are no people who sooner or later will be ready to respond to the gospel if the seed is sown in sincerity and "watered" by tears and prayer (Isa. 55:11; Ps. 126:5–6; Eccl. 11:6). God's purpose is to gather His church from among *all* nations, tribes, and people; and His command to the church is to evangelize and disciple all nations. This command presupposes that there are or will be people among all nations who will respond to the gospel and that the Holy Spirit will make the Word effective in their lives. The church must in faith claim this fact and courageously and sacrificially act upon it.

2. *Historical events and high potentiality.* What about many historic events and movements—do they not also prepare the way for the gospel? It is true that our Lord uses ordinary historical events and circumstances and extraordinary personal and national experiences—such as social upheavals, cultural disintegration, philosophical movements, natural calamities—in the process of creating high potentiality. History and the varied experiences of life do play an important role. They are meaningful in the universal rule of God. They may constitute the *proper seasons* in which the Holy Spirit uniquely intensifies His presence and operation, but they are not the *seed* out of which high potentiality is born. They may provide the circumstances through which the Holy Spirit loosens people from their moorings—the social and religious traditions, structures, and mores that enslave them. Within the hearts and minds of individuals, within total societies and nations, the Holy Spirit may create yearnings, an attitude of hope, a mood of anticipation, a readiness for change, even a demand for change so intense that either a drastic reformation of society will come about or a revolution will break up the existing structure.

It is necessary, however, to distinguish between *readiness for change* and *spiritual readiness.* To confuse those issues betrays not only theological blindness but also psychological blundering. Though intimately related, spiritually whitened harvest fields are not the same as psychological and social moods and circumstances. Readiness to change—a mood of hope and anticipation—is a general psychological and social phenomenon, as standard texts in sociology and social psychology clearly indicate. Circumstances of whatever nature do not by themselves create spiritual high potentiality. They may provide the social atmosphere—the soil—that can be transformed into high potential harvest fields. However, unless such situations are fructified by the presence of Christians and/or the Word of God, the transformation into a condition of high potentiality for the gospel will not take place.

Two contemporary experiences clearly illustrate the difference between readiness for change and spiritual readiness. The failed political coup in Indonesia in 1965 resulted in one of the great harvests for the church of Jesus Christ. Literally thousands of people have been gathered in, and the end is not yet. This was not so in Bangladesh or in Pakistan after the recent war that gave Bangladesh independence: in neither country has there been significant ingathering into the church of Jesus Christ. Why such difference? It is simplistic to say that it was not the Lord's time for Bangladesh or Pakistan. To imply that the Lord is less interested in saving Bengali and Pakistani people than the Indonesians is a serious misjudgment that comes close to indictment. The reason cannot lie in God; with Him there is no partiality. The reason must lie somewhere else. While I do not pretend to be able to give an absolute answer, I do believe that over Indonesia we can write in much bolder letters the words of the Master: "Others have labored." A study will quickly show that the Netherlands Bible Society and in the last several decades the Indonesian Bible Society have poured hundreds of thousands (if not millions) of copies of the Bible, New Testaments, Gospels, and Scripture portions into East and Central Java. This has never happened in a similar degree in Bangladesh or Pakistan. In addition, East and Central Java have witnessing communities of believers. In Bangladesh and Pakistan neither the Word nor the people of God were present as they are in Indonesia.

Observations of experiences such as these together with scriptural deductions lead us to this conclusion: when historic circumstances that produce psychological and social readiness to change coincide with the presence of the Word and people of God, a condition of high potentiality results and a plentiful harvest can be anticipated.

If this conclusion is correct, most areas of the world can be looked on as high potential areas. Certainly we live in times of high potential. A readiness to change—in fact, a demand for change—is evident almost universally. And the sowing of the good seed is widespread. Mass communication has enabled the church of Jesus Christ to scatter the good seed of the gospel over most of the globe during the last decades. Never before has the Good News reached the masses of people as it does today. It is therefore not surprising that we are experiencing unprecedented response to the message of God's saving grace in Christ Jesus. This is, indeed, harvest time, a time of abundant ingathering. But as in Christ's day, the laborers are few. "Pray ye therefore the Lord of the harvest, that he will send forth laborers into his harvest" (Matt. 9:37, KJV), a harvest He has graciously prepared for Himself. *We need a harvest mentality, a harvest theology, and a harvest missiology.*

The Bible commands us to go into all the world and preach the gospel. God "desires all men to be saved and to come to the knowledge of the truth." Because of this Jesus Christ "gave Himself a ransom for all" (1 Tim. 2:4, 6). The Bible clearly teaches that the church of Jesus Christ is to be composed of representatives from among all nations (Rev. 5:9). Consequently we can expect that the Holy Spirit will bring about a readiness to respond to the gospel message among all nations, tribes, and people. It is not for us to decide how and when this is to be done. Our business is to labor, witness, and seek until we find people prepared by the Holy Spirit for the gospel message. In some places the masses will come while in other places only individuals will respond. This was the experience of Christ and also of Paul. In Antioch and Ephesus the multitudes responded. In Athens only a few individuals came. However, the few counted. History records that soon a healthy church grew up even in Athens. The results rest with our Lord who, in and through the Holy Spirit, is the Lord of the harvest.

THE HOLY SPIRIT AND *HEILSGESCHICHTE*

The Bible leaves no doubt that the Holy Spirit in some ways relates to all of humanity (Gen. 6:3; Job 32:8; 33:4; Ps. 139:7; 2 Thess.

2:6–7). He is the immanence of God in this world, the executive of the Godhead. Thus He relates to all history. Humanity is neither totally forsaken nor totally autonomous. In the end, the Holy Spirit is working out the plan and purposes of God. The times of the nations and their bounds are in His control.

The immanence of the Holy Spirit raises some crucial issues. If the Holy Spirit is present and operative in all of humanity and if high potential times and people are the result of His ministry and movings, we may justly ask: To what degree is God operative in the world? What must we conclude about the *Missio Dei* in this world *outside* of the church and *apart* from the written message of God? Does His immanence apart from revelation in the Word suffice for salvation? Does His immanence constitute all history, *Heilsgeschichte,* or salvation history?

1. Heilsgeschichte *and general history.* A diligent inquiry into the Bible leads us to an important distinction in the operations of the Holy Spirit. On the one hand we learn of the *global* or general operations of the Holy Spirit, ministries that extend to all peoples and make themselves felt in all history. On the other hand we find the *soteriological* operations that are limited in their initial application to divinely chosen recipients but are not limited in their intent. The first type of operations results in general history, the second creates *Heilsgeschichte.*

I am aware that contemporary philosophy and theology claim that all history is alike and that there is only *one* history. I am aware also of the attempt to interpret the history of Israel as a model and type of God's operations in the history of the nations, with the Exodus as the great model of divine liberation. But such ideas are human inventions projected upon the Old Testament. They do not harmonize with the total thrust of the Old Testament and the interpretations of its content, history, and purposes by such men as Stephen, Peter, and Paul. These men single out the history of Israel as unique and distinct from all other history. According to their interpretation, the history of Israel is salvation history in a peculiar manner and no other history equals it.

The distinction between the global operations of the Holy Spirit in general history and the soteriological operations in *Heilsgeschichte* is confirmed in passages such as Romans 1:18–2:16; 9:4–5; and Ephesians 2. What are the historical implications of Paul's statements in these and similar passages and of the claims he makes for Israel and her history?

In Romans 9:4–5 Paul lists eight distinctive blessings for Israel that were not shared by the nations of the world. In Ephesians 2:12 he enumerates five blessings that temporarily had been withheld from the nations. If it should be argued that it would be natural for Paul as a Jew to make such claims for Israel, then it must be remembered that it was the same Paul who persuasively argued for the present equality and unity of all people in Christ Jesus and consequently in the church of Jesus Christ (Eph. 2:11–22; Col. 3:11). Not only did he argue for it, but he also suffered for it (Acts 13:44–50; 14:2, 4–5; 17:5, 13; 22:21–22; 24:1–9) and eventually was martyred for the gospel.

The New Testament also declares emphatically that the nations created for themselves a religious dilemma of tragic consequences. Therefore their history is marred and marked by social and moral decay and religious degeneration (Rom. 1:18–32; Eph. 2:1–3).

All history, therefore, is divided into *Heilsgeschichte* and general history. *Heilsgeschichte* in the biblical sense begins with the call of Abraham, continues through Old Testament Israel, and is perpetuated in and through the church of Jesus Christ.

2. Heilsgeschichte *and Israel.* It is an undeniable fact of history that Israel was instrumental in preserving ethical monotheism in the world. Her emphasis on theism rather than pantheism, and the doctrine of creation in contrast to emanation, laid the theoretical foundation for regarding the cosmos not as semi-sacred in itself but as the natural created order made subservient to humans (Gen. 1:26, 28; 2:15). Israel also gave to the nations of the world a linear perspective of history that gives meaning and purpose to the universe and history. The rest of the world regarded history as cyclical and therefore without a future and a goal. Well does van Ruler express it: "The whole idea of history takes its rise from Christian theology, from the gospel and its proclamation, from God's revelation in Israel

and in Jesus Christ. Revelation has made existence historical."[5] The promises given to Israel became the source of anticipation and hope within humankind to be realized in history. In addition, Israel gave to the world a book, the Bible, which is the fountain of the highest moral ideals for every aspect and relationship of life. The Ten Commandments in their moral grandeur tower over any ethical code man has ever dreamed of. The idealism of Jesus as expressed in the Sermon on the Mount (Matt. 5–7), the realism of Paul, and the Christian mysticism of John are riches immeasurable. Finally, Israel was the nation from whom Jesus Christ the Savior of the world came to provide life, idealism, salvation, and hope for all people. Remove from the world the benefits derived from the Hebrew heritage and its outworkings and the whole world would be impoverished beyond measure and repair. *Heilsgeschichte* is a historical reality.

Heilsgeschichte does not deny that high ethical standards, beautiful cultural values, great and mystical insights, benevolent movements, and noble ideals have come out of general history. Great reformers, noble patriots, prominent statesmen, sacrificial philanthropists, wise philosophers, and influential religious leaders have arisen and made wholesome impacts on all people. Human beings are neither beasts nor devils. They are still made in the image of God, though now broken and marred. They may still delight in being good according to human standards and in doing good as they perceive it. *Heilsgeschichte* gladly concedes all this. At the same time it makes some astonishing claims:

(1) God has related Himself to individuals in covenants and made Himself known by acts and words to a particular people of His own sovereign choice—the people of Israel—in a unique way. The Old and New Testaments declare that God uniquely interposed in human history when He called Abram in Ur of the Chaldees, led him out into Canaan, gave to him clusters of promises, and entered into a unique covenant with him and his descendants, Isaac and Jacob. There is nothing parallel to this in all history. We may comb the history of the nations as carefully and comprehensively as we wish, but we will not find anything to compare with the covenants of God

with Israel—Abrahamic (Gen. 15:1–21; 17:1–14), Mosaic (Exod. 19–23; Deut. 29; 30), Davidic (2 Sam. 7:1–29)—and the promises and prophecies deposited in the Old Testament. In various covenants with Israel God grants His people a land, assures them of a history, reveals to them a system of laws of a most astounding nature, and establishes for them a system of worship unequaled in all the world.

(2) The Holy Spirit through revelation has committed to this chosen people specific religious and spiritual truths, ideals, values, concepts, laws, and institutions that are not known to humankind in general and therefore must be proclaimed in all the world. Some of these truths are: the doctrine of the Trinity, creation in an absolute sense, revelation, incarnation in the biblical sense, divine substitution in atonement, resurrection, justification by faith, regeneration in the biblical sense, bodily resurrection, personal glorification, the church as a living organism of eternal substance, consummation as a historical realization. These truths were given to a mediating people not merely for possession and preservation but for worldwide proclamation, because in these truths the God of heaven and earth is addressing all peoples.

(3) God has but one way of salvation, which is found only in the historical, crucified, resurrected, glorified Jesus of Nazareth who is the promised Messiah, the eternal Son of God, who was "promised beforehand through His prophets in the holy Scriptures, . . . who was born of the seed of David according to the flesh, who was declared with power to be the Son of God by the resurrection from the dead, according to the Spirit of holiness, Jesus Christ our Lord" (Rom. 1:2–4). There is only One who is in truth the Logos of God and who truthfully declared: I am the Bread of life, the Light of the world, the Door, the good Shepherd, the Resurrection and the Life, the Way, the Truth, and the Life (John 1:1, 4; 6:35, 48; 8:12; 9:5; 10:7, 9, 14; 11:25; 12:46; 14:6). *Heilsgeschichte* categorically denies that all roads (religions) are the same and lead to the same goal, the same mountaintop, the same God.

Heilsgeschichte makes these claims without hesitation, argument, or elaborate apology. It confronts individuals with these truths and leaves it to their moral sense and judgment to accept or reject the claims and thereby determine their eternal destiny—fellowship with God in glory or doom with the lost and perishing.

3. Heilsgeschichte *and the church.* The New Testament authors know themselves to be in line with the prophets of old in writing Scriptures. Inspired by the Holy Spirit they report soteriological events and record revelational truths about spiritual and eternal verities of highest and crucial importance to humans. They are convinced that without them we cannot discover our way back to God, attain salvation from sin and lostness, and find meaning and purpose in life.

Heilsgeschichte has its most able exponent and ardent defender in the apostle Paul. His Book of Romans is the greatest summary of historical facts and *Heilsgeschichte.* The following is an outline of Paul's views:

(1) The whole universe is the creation of God. It manifests God, is under His sovereign rule, and is responsible to Him (Rom. 1:18ff.).

(2) The whole human race is an organism created in Adam. The organic unity of the entire human race is never questioned in the Bible. Paul firmly holds to it and builds on it (Rom. 5:12–21).

(3) In Adam the whole human race fell and became sinful and depraved (Rom. 5:12–21).

(4) The whole human race followed a course of sin and therefore became guilty and corrupt in every aspect of life, particularly so in religion (Rom. 1:18–3:23).

(5) In order to provide a true revelation of Himself and a way of salvation for the world, God created *Heilsgeschichte* in the midst of world history, and thus operated in and through a mediatorial people and system to prepare for the coming of the true Mediator between God and humans, the Man Christ Jesus (Rom. 9–11; 1 Tim. 2:1–5).

(6) The whole human race was represented in Christ in His incarnation, life, death, and resurrection; and in Him salvation was provided for all people not only by substitution and representation but also by identification (Rom. 5:12–21).

(7) God has provided only one way of salvation—the way of justification by faith in Jesus Christ. This holds true for both Jews and Gentiles (Rom. 3:21–5:21).

(8) The salvation of God has tremendous historical, social, and moral implications for the individual, the church, and society (Rom. 12–16). It will eventually liberate the total created cosmos (Rom. 8:19–23).

(9) God's way of salvation is not discovered by the individual. It comes by revelation, and it must be communicated from the revealed Word of God. Faith comes by hearing and hearing by the Word of God (Rom. 10:8–17; 16:25–26).

(10) Paul knew himself called of God and separated to the gospel of God to bring people and nations to obedience of faith (Rom. 1:1–5; 16:25–27). This was his apostleship; for this he labored, always pressing onward into new mission territories. For this he prayed, solicited the prayers of others, and enlisted companions and colaborers; for this he suffered and sacrificed all he had; and in this he gloried (Rom. 11:13, 25; 15:15–21).[6]

No one has ever made greater claims for Christ, the kingdom of God, the salvation of God, and the church of God; and no one has ever challenged others more than Paul does in his epistles. From him we learn the true meaning of *Heilsgeschichte.*

In the New Testament and in faithful commitment to it, the church of Jesus Christ continues in the stream of *Heilsgeschichte* in a functional manner. Like Israel, the church was sovereignly *chosen* by God and *called* to Him. It was *redeemed* by His gracious gift in His blessed Son. It was *enriched* by a new covenant, by immeasurable and inexhaustible promises, and by unimaginable prospects and glorious hope of eternity. And it was *endowed* with divine qualifications for life and service in the coming of the Holy Spirit. All this has been bestowed on the church that it might love God and serve Him joyfully in His benevolent plan and purpose for humankind.

The church is not an end in itself: it is to be God's bridge to the world. It is called to a mediating ministry between God and the world of nations, mediation not in the sense that Christ is the Mediator between God and the person (1 Tim. 2:5), but as a mediating agency in proclaiming the gospel of Jesus Christ (1 Peter 2:9–10).

The church then—that is, the presence of God's people and/or God's Word—is important both in the creating of high potentiality and in the mediating of salvation by means of the gospel of our Lord Jesus Christ. It is out of the church's soteriological significance that concern for church growth springs. Church growth interest and endeavors are not rooted in religious imperialism, the aggrandizement of the church through expansion or multiplication, or in blind loyalty and devotion to the church. Biblical concern for church growth evolves from identification with God who seeks the salvation and welfare of humanity and has chosen and called the church to be His mediating agency in this holy pursuit. It is only this role that justifies and sanctifies church growth motivation and brings a blessing to all humanity. Church growth? *Yes!* But church growth with a purpose, that the church might be the salt of the earth and the light of the world (Matt. 5:13–16). Only thus is the church truly part of the stream of *Heilsgeschichte.*

THE HOLY SPIRIT AND WORLD HISTORY

The Bible faces us with facts, not with theories and philosophy. It informs us that God the creator has never, as the deists avow, withdrawn from His creation. The pages of the Old Testament provide the documentation. In the person of the Holy Spirit He has always been present in the world of nations in natural blessings and national judgments. As creator and covenant-keeping God, He has never totally absented Himself from history (Gen. 9:8–17; Acts 14:17).

The Bible does not set forth all the details of world history or a full exposition of a philosophy of history, but it does furnish a general framework and principles for such a philosophy. Certain facts are very evident: (1) God has always had His hand over the affairs of the nations; (2) He is King of Kings and Lord of Lords, an "everlasting King" (Jer. 10:10; 1 Tim. 1:17); (3) He is the Sovereign of the universe and in Him reside final authority and power (Matt. 28:18; Pss. 83:18; 103:19); (4) governments are ordained of God and therefore are accountable to Him (Rom. 13:1–7); (5) He is able to set them up and to remove them (Jer. 27:5; Dan. 4:25); (6) He sets their times and their boundaries (Deut. 32:8; Luke 21:24; Acts 17:27). (7) He has a benevolent mind toward all nations and His loving kindness is everlasting (Pss. 106; 107; 118). World history is not devoid of the presence of God.

These facts gave the prophets of the Old Testament authority to address the non-Israelite nations. In the name of the Lord they spoke boldly to the affairs and the sins of these people (Isa. 8:1–8, 10–34; Ezek. 25:1–32:32; Amos 1:3–2:3; et al.). Also, God used the nations as His agents to bring judgment on Israel and Judah. He called Nebuchadnezzar "my servant" (Jer. 25:9), and spoke of Cyrus as "my shepherd" (Isa. 44:28–45:4; cf. Ezra 1:1–11; 3:7). He spoke to Pharaoh, Nebuchadnezzar, and Belshazzar about national affairs and warned them before their own destruction (Gen. 41:1–44; Dan. 2:1–45; 4:4–27; 5:5–29). God has never left Himself without witness (Acts 14:17). He does hold "the whole world in His hand." God is the ever-present and everywhere present God (Ps. 139). The affairs of all humanity are in His hands and are His concern. Because of this, humanity in general is able to share in numerous blessings of the Lord; as the kindness of the Lord leads to repentance, the blessings increase (Rom. 2:4).

Consider this list of the benevolences of God as they are imparted through the gracious ministries of the Holy Spirit in our age to humankind as a whole:

(1) The Holy Spirit in benevolent concern for order and the advancement of human beings gave to the nations the institution of government whose responsibility before God is to seek the physical, material, social, and moral welfare of the people (Rom. 13:1–7; 1 Tim. 2:1–4; 1 Peter 2:13–17).

(2) The Holy Spirit does not permit nations in their madness to annihilate each other. God has assured the human race continued existence (Gen. 8:20–22), and human beings are not permitted to destroy themselves though they may have the mind and at present the capability to do so. The Holy Spirit sets limits to their activities, power, and brutality (2 Thess. 2:1–8).

(3) The Holy Spirit restrains wickedness from overwhelming humankind and leading it into total disbelief and total spiritual blindness and darkness. Absolute blackout does not cover humanity, at least not to the degree that salvation becomes impossible (Matt. 24:22; 2 Cor. 4:3–6; 2 Thess. 2:3–10). Satan would delight in destroying in people the capability for salvation. The Holy Spirit prevents this and preserves humans in a savable condition. This holds true of the individual as well as of humankind as a whole.

(4) The Holy Spirit has sent times of unusual religious stirrings and yearnings to cause people to search for the true and living God (Acts 17:22–34). It remains a mystery of religious history that such men as Lao-tzu and Confucius of China, Mahavira and Gautama (Buddha) of India appeared within a century of each other, preceded somewhat by Zoroaster of Persia (Iran). Such religious stirrings are neither purely human nor solely historical. They can be accounted for ultimately only by the global operations of the Holy Spirit. History of religion abounds with illustrations of similar stirrings, though perhaps on a lower level.

(5) The Holy Spirit inspires, supports, and reinforces humans in their efforts to make life and culture more livable, more humane, more noble, more ideal. God is not indifferent to how people live and how they are being treated. The cultural mandate of God—the creation order of God—(Gen. 1:26–28; 2:15) is still in force and human beings are held accountable for their attitude toward that mandate and their efforts in its realization. God is a God of beauty, order, and goodness. This goodness is partially expressed in enabling humanity to develop a richer culture.

(6) The Holy Spirit preserves a sense of religiousness in human society. Within the human personality the "ought," the "categorical imperative" (Kant), the conscience serves as monitor. Humans cannot rid themselves totally of a conscience, try as they may. Humanity also retains the sense of eternity, a God-awareness and God-dependence. Though possibly unable to define these inner existences, the human creature is aware of a destiny beyond life and of a power beyond the self. While a person may not engage in the *practice* of religion, the *sense* of religiousness remains. Because the

human personality cannot come to rest in itself, the person is continually an inquiring and seeking being, a creature on the way.

(7) The Holy Spirit rules and overrules affairs in the world of nations to open doors for the preaching of the gospel of Jesus Christ. The Lord assured the church at Philadelphia that He had set before them an open door and that He holds the key of David to open doors as He wills, doors that no man can shut, and to shut doors that no man can open (Rev. 3:7-8). Paul urged the church at Colossae to pray that God would open to him a door for the Word, so that he might speak forth the mystery of Christ (Col. 4:3).

(8) The Holy Spirit is present in the world to create high potential times and people as we discussed earlier. Without His immanence there would be no whitened harvest fields or spiritual awareness and readiness, no matter what efforts the church would put forth.

(9) The Holy Spirit is present in world history to gather out from among the nations a people to the Lord, the ecclesia, as the Triune God ordained from before the foundation of the world (Acts 15:13-14; Rom. 11:25; Eph. 3:1-12). He convicts people of their sins and draws them to Jesus. He regenerates them so that they become adopted children of God and members in the household of God. He indwells His people and baptizes them into one body, the body of Christ Jesus. He seals them to the day of redemption as heirs of the kingdom of God. He equips and uses them as His instruments and agents to accomplish His purpose in the world where they serve Him as the bridges of God.[7]

These are some of the ministries the Holy Spirit is rendering in world history. God has never left Himself completely without witness. He who made the world and all things in it *is* Lord of heaven and earth. And though He does not dwell in temples made with hands, He is immanent and is not far from each one of us. He is present so that His creatures might seek Him, perhaps grope for Him and find Him (Acts 17:22-31). God is neither totally hidden nor completely silent. The problem lies with human beings who will not hear and seek Him in order to repent and find Him. Humanity wants to be autonomous, to have no other lord than the self. The following diagram shows this tension.

MAN, THE CULTURE MAKER

Man is not Holy or Righteous, nor is he Neutral; yet he is Human

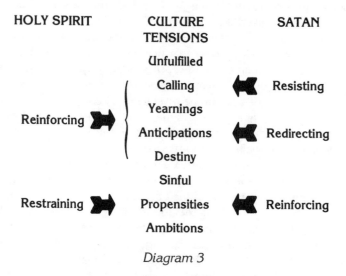

Diagram 3

WORLD HISTORY AS A BATTLEFIELD

General world history is more than the theater of operations of the Holy Spirit. It is an arena of a tremendous world-wide battle between the forces of light and of darkness. While we are assured from Scripture that the Holy Spirit is present everywhere, we are also assured that He is *not* present in all events, systems, institutions, structures, and movements of humanity. The Holy Spirit is not the only force operating in this world. There is a second kingdom—the kingdom of this world—that asserts itself in every possible way and seeks to expand its domain to embrace the total world in all its aspects. It makes every attempt to become a world culture of total dominance. In fact, John informs us that "the whole world lies in the power of the evil one" (1 John 5:19).

The Bible speaks in plain language of a *second person* who is known as Satan, adversary, devil, dragon, serpent of old (Rev. 20:2).

He is "the god of this world" (2 Cor. 4:4), "the prince of the power of the air" (Eph. 2:2), "the power of darkness" (Col. 1:13). He is like a roaring lion, who seeks to devour his prey (1 Peter 5:8). We are informed of rulers, powers, world forces of this darkness, and of spiritual wickedness in the heavenly places (Eph. 6:12). We are warned against the cunning strategies, devices, and schemes of the devil (Eph. 6:11). The Bible tells us that he is deceiving the nations and leading them astray (2 Thess. 2:1–12; Rev. 20:3). He has evolved a world system (Col. 2:8, 20) that blinds humankind. These words depict stark reality; and human history offers the most convincing commentary on these truths. The "conflict of the ages" (Anno Gaebelein) is a horrible reality.

These descriptions and designations cannot, according to Scripture, be ascribed to human agencies. The belief that if we succeed in changing the human scene, personnel, systems, structures, and institutions, then victory will be won and utopia will gradually evolve is not true. Behind all the evil of this world there is a master mind who is Satan himself. We are the tool and instrument but not the source and the power of evil. Satan will attempt to penetrate and dominate any system we may devise and institute. He outschemes all attempts we make to free ourselves from bondage. Were it not for the presence and gracious operations of the Holy Spirit in global dimensions, human history would be a veritable hell. We would be led to destroy all humanness in the individual, society, and culture, as well as every possibility for spiritual awakening.

History is not an even flow, gradually evolving the kingdom of God. Nor is it a process of dialectic that gradually but surely brings about utopia. General history has left behind it a blood-stained path, strewn not only with human corpses, but also with heaps of ruins telling of bygone civilizations, cities, and people. And back of it all as the ultimate cause and inspiration is Satan, the enemy of God and deceiver of us all.

Georg F. Vicedom, in considering the kingdom of God and "The Other Kingdom," describes the latter in realistic terms:

> It is not our purpose here to develop a satanology or to explain the origin of evil. We are merely speaking of a fact.

Assuredly we are here faced with a mystery. The Bible speaks of a devil without offering explanations as to his ancestry. It speaks of him as a reality; he is the foe of God and mankind. The realm of the devil has to be overcome (Mt. 4:3; cf. Luke 4:5). It is subject to the prince of this world (Jn. 12:31; 14:30; 16:11). Because his realm unites all antigodly powers in itself, it is a consistent whole (Mt. 12:26; cf. Luke 11:18). The prince of darkness misleads men, moves them to disobedience, and tries to withdraw them from God's control (Eph. 6:11; 1 Pet. 5:8). He is the foe of the kingdom of God and thus of its mission, against which he is constantly working (Mt. 13:39; Luke 8:12). While God through His Spirit gives power for a new life which pleases Him, the devil transmits to those who are his the power of evil (Jn. 8:44; Rev. 13:2ff). Therefore in the last analysis it is he who misleads mankind to sin and continually turns men into rebels. Actually he exercises dominion in a manner understandable to mankind against the background of sin. With his realm he is God's adversary. That is why Jesus understood the lordship of God and the purpose of His sending to be this that the works of the devil must be destroyed and the prince of this world must be judged (1 Jn. 3:8; John 16:11).

To this we must cling even at the risk of being ridiculed as fundamentalistic. One who does not take these facts into consideration is unfit to carry out the assignment of God. . . . In the last analysis the religions are also to be understood from the viewpoint of their connection with this other kingdom. While they may contain much good, it is embedded in evil and covered over by evil. Satanic powers hostile to God are at work in them. Only the person who realizes this can experience the properly compassionate judgment about pagan man who is imprisoned in these religions.[8]

It is in the light of such revelational and historical facts that the opposition to the gospel and the church of Jesus Christ must be seen. Here is also the explanation for attempts by well-organized forces to shut out the gospel from vast territories and masses of people. The power of darkness seeks by every possible means to keep out all light from God.

On the other side of the "conflict of the ages" are the mighty victories of the Holy Spirit in preserving humanity and in creating high potentiality for a plentiful harvest of souls. This miracle is our present evidence that greater is He who is in us than he who is in the world (1 John 4:4). Therefore we are confident, for our hope is from God (Ps. 62:5). He is *Lord!* And as sovereign Lord He will build His church and the gates of Hades will not prevail against it. He does restrain the evil one, and He does create high potentiality for His church to expand. World history is not a madhouse. It is an arena, a battlefield between the forces of darkness and the forces of light. Its final outcome is sure. The Bible foretells that in the Parousia Satan and all his hosts with all their systems, institutions, and power structures will be destroyed by Him who rides on the white horse, who is called "Faithful and True," "The Word of God," "The King of Kings and Lord of Lords" (Rev. 19:11–21). This victory will liberate the world not only from social and economic oppression and exploitations, but from religious bondage as well. It will set people free in the true sense of the word to hear the Word of God and the gospel of our Lord Jesus Christ. As a result entire nations will turn to the Lord in repentance, faith, and love and will serve and worship Him who alone deserves to be honored. The *eschaton* will break forth and its glory brighten as never before. His kingdom will break through in greater fullness and its hiddenness will be made manifest. That all this is rooted in Calvary is evident in that the Conqueror is none other than the *Lamb.* The Parousia of our blessed Lord is as much a scriptural doctrine as His incarnation, death, and resurrection. He comes in triumph for judgment and salvation to manifest the hidden kingdom of God in truth and righteousness. This is the bottom line of the "conflict of the ages."

Part Two

Biblical Principles
of Church Growth

5

Church Growth and the Primary Means of God

In Part 1 we looked at the theological foundations for church growth—the relationship of ecclesiology to other doctrines and the role of the Holy Spirit in the work of God. The Holy Spirit, the Paraclete, is central in the Book of Acts. He is the ultimate cause of church growth. Spiritual work can be accomplished only by the Holy Spirit. In the kingdom of God the pronouncement is conclusive: "Not by might nor by power, but by My Spirit, says the Lord of hosts" (Zech. 4:6).

However, the Holy Spirit employs agencies, means, and instruments to accomplish His works. At least in part the operations of God are within the realm of the natural and human. In chapter 4 we looked at two agencies of the Spirit in preparing whitened harvest fields—individuals and the Word. In Part 2 we shall more fully explore these two instruments of God's work. A third instrument is the church of God. The role of the church in church growth will be developed in Part 3. The relationship of these three instruments—

the message of God, the servant of God, and the church of God—is pictured on the following diagram.

Church Growth Dynamics

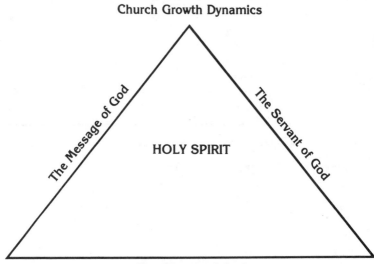

The Church of God

Diagram 4

THE HOLY SPIRIT AND THE MESSAGE OF GOD

There exists a mystic-realistic relationship between the Word of God written and the operations of the Holy Spirit. This is evident from the fact that the same effects are ascribed to the Holy Spirit and to the Word of God: regeneration (John 3:5; Titus 3:5; James 1:18; 1 Peter 1:23); sanctification (John 17:17; Rom. 15:16; 2 Thess. 2:13; 1 Tim. 4:5; 1 Peter 1:2); divine leading (Ps. 119:105; Rom. 8:14); assurance and understanding (Rom. 8:16; Col. 2:2; 1 John 2:20, 27; 5:13). Christ states: "It is the Spirit who gives life; the flesh profits nothing; the words that I have spoken to you are spirit and are life" (John 6:63). Our Lord and the apostles are our examples in using the Word of God. They revered it, believed it, preached it, and expected results from it. Chapter 6 more fully explores the message of God.

THE HOLY SPIRIT AND THE SERVANT OF GOD

The New Testament clearly implies that the Holy Spirit has a special relationship to the servant of God. This is beautifully illustrated in Acts. The Pentecostal phenomena and experiences needed a person—Peter—to expound them. The Samaria revival demanded an evangelist (Acts 8:5–25). The Bible-reading Ethiopian eunuch needed Philip to guide him into the truth and bring him to Christ (Acts 8:26–39). The learned, pharisaic Saul needed Ananias to deliver the message of the Lord (Acts 9:10–17). The God-fearing Cornelius had to send for Peter to point the way into the fullness of the salvation in Christ (Acts 10:22–48). The cities of the Roman Empire had to wait for Paul to bring the gospel to them, as Paul's vision in Troas indicated. The man of Macedonia called to him, "Come over and help us!" Thus the servant of God serves as a special instrument or agent of the Holy Spirit.

While the apostolic band, including Paul, are unique in the history of the church in their experience, authority, and position, the emphasis on the servant of God in the work of God does not cease with the disappearance of the apostolic band. While the apostles are distinct in their *office* as apostles of Jesus Christ, they are not totally distinct in their *function* as servants of Christ. Paul clearly states that God set some in the church: first apostles, second prophets, third teachers; after that the different functionaries and supportive ministries (1 Cor. 12:28). Similarly he writes to the Ephesians: "He gave some apostles, and some prophets, and some evangelists, and some pastors and teachers (Eph. 4:11).

These are not people above the church or outside of the church. They are people of and in the church but their ministry is not solely to the local congregation or determined by a local congregation. They have been uniquely touched by the Lord and set apart in and given to the church.

God has seen fit throughout biblical and church history to touch some individuals, to call them out and use them in His own work in a specific way. There have been brilliant and not so brilliant, prominent and not so prominent, gifted and not so gifted individuals. But God has chosen people as instruments to advance His cause.

What kind of people has He used? In chapter 7 we will look at the apostolic band.

THE HOLY SPIRIT AND THE CHURCH OF GOD

The New Testament also teaches that the Holy Spirit is related peculiarly to the church of God that is His temple, His habitation through which He operates (Eph. 2:21–22). He dwells in His fullness in His temple—the church. He resides in all His holiness, with all His love, wisdom, power, and gifts in the church. Thus the church is to serve Him as the body of flesh served Jesus Christ. In the Old Testament God dwelt in the Temple; in the Gospels He tabernacled in a body of flesh, and now He lives in the church.

The biblical basis of the church was discussed in Part 1. In Part 3, chapters 8–13, we will look more closely at the fitness, the form, the function, and the focus of the church.

6

Church Growth and the Message of God

It is impossible to overemphasize the importance of the Word of God in the work of God, particularly in evangelism and church growth. Emotionalism, personality cults, personal experiences, methodology, and techniques must not be permitted to minimize the Word. The symbolism used to describe the Word is rich and instructive. The Word is like a *hammer* that breaks the rock in pieces (Jer. 23:29); it is the *sword* of the Spirit that pierces and divides asunder—separates, evaluates, judges (Eph. 6:17; Heb. 4:12); it is a *fire* that sifts and sanctifies (Isa. 4:4); it is the *good seed* that the sower plants in the field and from which he expects a great harvest (Matt. 13:3, 19; Isa. 55:11). The Word is the Spirit's only means to regenerate people and to make them into children of God (1 Peter 1:23; James 1:18). It is His means to cleanse them, to nurture them to maturity, and to transform them into Christlikeness (John 15:3; 17:17; Col. 3:16; 1 Peter 1:22; 2:2). The presence of the Holy Spirit in the Word makes the Bible a living and all-inclusive book.

The Bible is given by revelation and written by inspiration of God and is "profitable for teaching, for reproof, for correction, for training in righteousness that the man of God may be adequate, equipped for every good work" (2 Tim. 3:16–17). The Bible in totality is God's message to meet spiritual needs (see diagram).

The Message of God

God-originated and oriented

Word-rooted

Christ-centered

Conscience-bearing

Eternity-awakening

Diagram 5

RELEVANCY OF THE MESSAGE

Paul admonishes Timothy to study to show himself approved to God "a workman who does not need to be ashamed, *handling accurately* the word of truth" (2 Tim. 2:15). The passage implies that not all words are equally suited and applicable at all times, on all occasions, and to all people. While all the words are equally true, they are not equally appropriate. A funeral sermon may be absolutely true to the text and correct exegetically, but it does not fit a wedding situation. We are called not to throw the Word of God at people but to communicate a divine message to their needs. It is the workman's solemn responsibility to study the Word of God in order that he might have a *relevant* message in a time of need, crisis, and opportunity.

In all humility we must learn to make a distinction between the *Word of God* as written and the *message of God* as personally perceived and proclaimed. The Word of God is an *objective reality,* infallibly inscripturated in the Bible. The Word as it came to us through *revelation* from God and by *inspiration* of the Holy Spirit was recorded for posterity in a written form (2 Tim. 3:16; 2 Peter 1:19–21). It is the Word of God in all reality and it remains such. It is the true and full revelation in objective form.[1] The message of God is the *subjective reality* of the Word of God as it comes to us by the *illumination* of the Holy Spirit. While the message derives its nature and content from the objective Word, it does not necessarily exhaust or comprise the total meaning of the Word in that it is purposively designed by the Holy Spirit to meet a specific need or situation. Also the message—both the comprehension and the communication of it—filters through human limitations, such as the presuppositions, experiences, prejudices, and comprehending and communicating abilities of the interpreter.

The Word of God as objective reality is absolute, final, authoritative, and infallible. The message as subjectively received, perceived, formulated, and proclaimed is humanly conditioned and limited. We must in honesty and humility constantly keep this distinction before us in all our interpretation and proclamation. If we say, This is what the Word says, then we ought to quote it accurately. If we only paraphrase it, we ought to say in humility, This is what the Word says *to me;* this is the message it conveys *to me.* After all, the message may be true and assuring to me in as far as I have apprehended it, but it may not be the totality of the truth contained in the Word. We continue to search the Word, not only to correct ourselves, but also to enlarge and enrich our understanding.

The exhortation to search the Scriptures for a relevant message must be heeded in evangelism and church growth, particularly in cross-cultural, cross-psychological, and cross-religious gospel proclamation. Not every message will arrest the attention, engage the mind, win the hearing and consideration, convince and convict the conscience, draw out the heart in earnest yearnings, and move the will of the hearer to decisive action.

The Word of God is rich in its manifold messages to the human heart. While it reveals the eternal counsel of God, it does not confront the unregenerate person with such a comprehensive message. God addresses the individual with a message that is appropriate to the situation and that has a definite purpose. The person must be arrested, must consider his sinful ways, must become aware of his helpless and hopeless condition. God confronts each one everywhere with the command to repent of sin and believe in Jesus Christ, to receive forgiveness of sins and inherit the kingdom of God (Acts 2:38; 3:19; 5:31; 14:15; 16:31; 17:30; 26:18, 20).

To accomplish this purpose, our message must be people-related. This calls for a study of the concepts that are used in modern missiology, such as rapport, conceptualization, configuration, contextualization, conflict, and conversion. The student is advised to consult standard works on communication. In our study here we shall content ourselves with a few practical suggestions.

CONTENT OF THE MESSAGE

Christianity is a historical phenomenon. The firm position of all the apostles and the writers of the New Testament is that Christianity is a historical religion, not a religion born of ideas and ideals. Christianity can be described in terms of real persons, time, space, and acts. God was manifested in the flesh—*person;* Christ was born when Caesar Augustus was emperor in Rome and was crucified when Pontius Pilate was Rome's representative in Jerusalem—*time;* Christ appeared and labored in Palestine—*space;* Christ performed deeds of mercy, died according to the counsel of God, and was raised up again by God—*acts.*

Pentecost is also a historical reality. The Holy Spirit descended from heaven—*person;* on the Jewish day of Pentecost fifty days after Passover—*time;* at Jerusalem—*space;* transforming the apostles and those with them into fearless witnesses—*acts.*

There is more to the historicity of Christianity, however. In Christianity God is seen operating *in* and *through* history. B.C.—A.D. becomes a dividing line of historical significance. God breaks into history, changes its course, and uses it to accomplish His purpose and desired end. He is Lord in the true and full sense of the word. Thus, history must eventually serve His time schedule and goal.

Christianity, therefore, must be distinguished from philosophy, ideology, mythology, and tradition. In Christianity we have *Heilsgeschichte*—actual salvation history—and not religious saga, devotional commitment, or religious, intuitive insight. Though I quote J.C. Hoekendijk with reservations, yet he pinpoints this fact:

> There is a noteable [sic] lack of personal stories in the apostolic preaching. It is constantly affirmed that in the Kerygma a history is proclaimed of which all men are ignorant until it is announced as a revelation, things that "eye hath not seen, nor ear heard, neither have entered into the heart of man" (1 Cor. 2:9). All witness that neglects or minimizes this character of revelation is useless, for it is disobedient and unfaithful.[2]

What, then, was the unique message of the apostles in their evangelism and church planting ministry? There are several prominent emphases. For clarity's sake I state it first in outline:

1. In Christianity God is the great and merciful Initiator.
2. God is the great and gracious Actor; history is the theater of His actions and salvation is the purpose of His actions.
3. The supreme act of God in Christ Jesus was in fulfillment of the Old Testament.
4. In Christ Jesus God offers to humanity a free salvation.
5. Neglecting or rejecting the gracious salvation of God in Christ Jesus draws awful consequences for time and eternity.

1. *In Christianity God is the great and merciful Initiator.* He reaches down to needy humanity. In all other religions of the world humans reach up in search for reality and salvation. The "But God" rings through in apostolic preaching. God broke through and entered history: He loved the world; He acted in the interest of the world; He sent His Son to procure salvation. God broke through on the day of Pentecost and poured out the Holy Spirit. Therefore the multitude on the day of Pentecost heard the apostles proclaim "the mighty deeds of God" (Acts 2:11) and not the great discoveries or illuminations or intuitions or scientific insights of men. This beautiful and emphatic theocentricity forms the substratum of all apostolic proclamation.

2. *God is the great and gracious Actor; history is the theater of His actions, and salvation is the purpose of His actions.* In Chris-

tianity God is the Subject, the Actor, the Operator. In more than one hundred references in Acts alone God is spoken of as the initiator and operator on behalf of mankind. The gospel of God flows from God. This theocentricity in Acts is at first quite startling, yet it is purposive. It belongs to the configuration of the message and led to the all-important power encounter in the lives of the people. The Book of Acts is a theo-Christocentric book with God as the great and benevolent but also the just and righteous Actor. His activities are evident in at least five ways:

(a) God is presented as the Creator of all things (Acts 4:24; 7:50; 14:15; 17:24). He is the Lord of all existence and the God of all humans. Therefore He is not a respecter of persons (Acts 10:34–35). He is the God of the cosmos and therefore the supreme and only true God.

(b) God is present and active in history. He has permitted the nations to follow their own course (Acts 14:16) and to develop their own culture, institutions, philosophy, and religion (Rom. 1:18–32). But He has determined their times and set their boundaries (Acts 17:26). This action accounts for the rise and fall of empires and the decay and vanishing of cultures and even of religions.

In the stream of this general history God created *Heilsgeschichte* (see also chapter 4). The Book of Acts shows God intervening in history and relating Himself to a sovereignly selected people, Israel. He called Abraham (Acts 7:2–3) and gave him the covenant (Acts 3:25; 7:8, 17). He was uniquely the God of Abraham, Isaac, and Jacob (Acts 3:13, 25; 5:30; 7:32; 13:17; 22:14; 24:14). He exalted the people (Acts 13:17) and magnified and manifested Himself in their history (Acts 13:17–23). He sent His word to the children of Israel (Acts 10:36). He made special promises (Acts 2:39; 3:22–23; 7:5, 37–38; 13:23, 32; 26:6–7). He revealed His plans to Israel (Acts 1:16, 20). At present God calls all individuals everywhere to repent and be converted (Acts 17:30), and He will in an appointed day judge the world in righteousness by the man Christ Jesus (Acts 17:31). Thus all the world will know that God is God, because He is present in history.

(c) God has spoken through the prophets. "Thus saith the

Lord" is the peculiar stamp and seal of God upon the Old Testament. Peter refers repeatedly to the prophets (Acts 3:18, 21). He speaks of Joel (Acts 2:16), of David (Acts 2:25), of Moses (Acts 3:22), and of Samuel (Acts 3:24). Paul asks Agrippa a startling question: "King Agrippa, do you believe the Prophets? I know that you do" (Acts 26:27). We are informed more than twenty-five times that Paul spoke of the Word and expounded the Scriptures. He lectured from it, dialogued over it, reasoned from it, and persuaded people by means of it. In the Scriptures the apostles found God's answer to humanity's sin problem. They discovered the promises about Christ: His suffering, His resurrection, His enthronement, His Saviorhood, lordship, and messiahship. The Word as revealed in the Old Testament was their authority in proclamation, for God had spoken with present and abiding effects.

(d) God was present in Christ Jesus. While God is proclaimed to have been the Creator of all things, the supreme Governor of all history, and the Initiator of *Heilsgeschichte,* the supreme act of God focuses and culminates in Christ Jesus our Lord. The Book of Acts is emphatic that God was in Christ and that in the rejection of Jesus Christ, the Jews sinned grievously against their God. Note God's presence and action in and through Christ Jesus. God anointed Him (Acts 4:27; 10:38), was with Him (Acts 10:38), did miracles through Him (Acts 2:22; 10:38), proclaimed peace through Him (Acts 10:36), sent Him to bless and convert Israel (Acts 3:26; 5:31), raised Him from the dead (Acts 2:24, 32; 3:15, 26; 4:10; 5:30; 10:40; 13:30, 37; 17:18, 31), glorified Him (Acts 3:13), exalted Him and seated Him at the right hand of the Father (Acts 2:33–34; 5:31). Thus God was not only manifested and magnified in Christ Jesus, but He also fully and completely justified and vindicated Christ in all His claims.

(e) God has magnified and exalted Jesus Christ. He has made Him Lord and Christ (Acts 2:36), exalted Him to be Ruler and Savior (Acts 5:31; 13:23), designated and ordained Him as Judge (Acts 10:42; 17:31). He has made Him the source and sole Mediator of the gift of the Holy Spirit (Acts 2:33), of healing (Acts 3:16; 4:10; 9:34; 16:18), of salvation (Acts 4:12), of blessings and conversion (Acts 3:26), of repentance and forgiveness of sins (Acts 5:31; 13:38–39).

And all this is conditioned by faith in Jesus Christ (Acts 3:16; 9:35, 42; 10:43, 11:17; 13:39; 16:31).

Thus in rejecting Christ Israel had committed a fourfold sin: it had practically denied its own *Heilsgeschichte* significance; it had voided its own promises and prophecies; it had defied the God of the fathers; and it had aborted its own salvation and blessings. Only repentance and radical conversion could remedy the situation and bring back the salvation and the Savior of God (Acts 2:37–39, 3:19–21, 4:8–12; 5:29–32; 10:43; 13:38–41).

3. *The supreme act of God in Christ Jesus was in fulfillment of the Old Testament.* The anticipations, prophecy, typology, predictions, and promises are yea and amen in Christ (2 Cor. 1:20, KJV). Jesus of Nazareth was the long-awaited Messiah of Israel and the desire of all nations (Hag. 2:7, KJV; Acts 2:22, 32–36; 3:18–26; 9:20–22). He was the seed of the woman (Gen. 3:15; Matt. 1:18–23; Luke 1:26–38; Gal. 4:4), the seed of Abraham (Gen. 17:19; 22:18; Acts 3:25; Gal. 3:16), a prophet like Moses (Deut. 18:18; John 7:40; Acts 3:22; 7:37), the seed of David (2 Sam. 7:12–13; Ps. 89:3–4; Acts 2:30; 13:23; Rom. 1:3), the suffering Servant of Jehovah (Isa. 53; Acts 8:32–35), the Son of Man (Dan. 7:13). He was to convert Israel, bring in the times of restitution of all things and the times of refreshing, and through Israel bring back the nations to God and lead them into the fullness of the blessings of God.

4. *In Christ Jesus God offers to humanity a free salvation.* In His death and resurrection Christ has provided forgiveness of sins, justification from all condemnation, newness of life and immortality, membership in the household of God and the kingdom of God, and fellowship with Him in time and eternity. Such salvation, however, must be appropriated by faith—faith accompanied by repentance and forsaking of sin and by obedience to God (John 3:16–18; Acts 2:26–28, 38; 3:19; 5:31–32; 10:43; 13:38–39; 15:9, 11; 16:31; Rom. 3:21–5:21; 6:23; 2 Cor. 5:11–21; 2 Tim. 1:10; 1 John 2:1–2).

5. *Neglecting or rejecting the gracious salvation of God in Christ Jesus draws awful consequences for time and eternity.* The preaching in the Book of Acts is based on the fact of the lostness of all human beings. Though it is not directly taught here as it is in

some other portions of the Bible, this condition is implied in the emphasis that all persons need salvation and that such salvation is found only in Christ Jesus (Acts 4:12; 8:12, 35; 9:20; 10:36; 13:38–39; 16:31; 26:23; 28:23). All deserve to be under the wrath of God and will experience His wrath in full unless saved from it through Jesus Christ. All need salvation from death and eternal judgment and condemnation (John 3:36; Acts 3:23; 13:41; Rom. 1:18–3:20; 2 Thess. 1:5–10; Rev. 20:11–15).

These main points, then, form the core of the preaching of the apostles. When preaching to non-Jewish audiences, however, the apostles varied the emphasis of the message to be meaningful to their listeners. Luke records two such events: Paul's addresses in Lystra and Athens (Acts 14:14–18; 17:22–31). As a wise communicator, Paul began his messages with topics familiar to his audiences. He also omitted some of the themes found in messages to the Jews: he does not refer to the Scriptures or the Old Testament, to the God *of the fathers,* or to the historical fact of the rejection of Christ. Although Paul keeps his messages within the framework of revelation, his emphasis is on God the Creator and Sustainer, the God who is not hidden altogether, who expects people to search for Him and turn to Him in repentance, and who has appointed a day of judgment when Jesus Christ will be the judge.

The abrupt ending of the messages indicates that both were interrupted and remained unfinished. It would be interesting to know how Paul would have concluded his preaching. However, these messages do instruct us in Paul's tone, approach, and initial emphasis in communicating to non-Jewish audiences. The configuration differs from the messages to Jewish audiences (cf. Acts 13:16–43). In the next section we will treat the issue of adapting the communication according to the audience as well as the purpose to be achieved.

The brief outline given above does not, of course, cover the totality of apostolic teaching. The apostles also taught the eternal purpose of God and the consummation of the kingdom of God; the great doctrines of salvation and the church; and personal, family, and church ethics. They warned about the dangers of the Christian life, doctrinal aberrations and heresies, spiritual laxness, legalism, and syncretism.

The biblical message of salvation and evangelism, however, has a clear focus and a much narrower frame. It is not a comprehensive defense of the gospel, a polemic of doctrine, or a system of apologetics. It is the proclamation of the gospel in the strictest sense of the word and deals principally with God's saving act in Christ Jesus and the individual's faith relationship to Christ, the Son of God. It is important to distinguish between *kerygma* and *didache* in the New Testament even if precise lines of division cannot and should not be made in a dogmatic manner. We have not proclaimed God's saving message unless we have set forth, first, Jesus Christ crucified for our sins and raised again for our justification and life (Rom. 4:25; 6:23; 2 Cor. 5:21) and, second, our need to repent of sin and believe in Jesus Christ.

This message was the core of apostolic evangelistic preaching. It was the kerygma of the early church. The church was founded on it, rested in it, grew and prospered by it. The message is refreshing, simple, and relevant. It arrested the attention of the people; it engaged their interest, pricked their hearts, and convicted their consciences; it gripped and drew them; it smote, converted, and transformed them. In some it aroused anger, opposition, brutality, and persecution. By the power of the message others were steeled to suffer heroically and continue persistently, boldly, and patiently in the way of the Lord. In our day, as in days of old, this same message is proclaimed, believed, accepted, debated, despised, disputed, rejected.

COMMUNICATION OF THE MESSAGE

Life is filled with failing, frustrated or partly succeeding COMMUNICATION.[3]

At a conference in Tokyo, Japan, a Shinto expert from the government center of communication addressed more than three hundred representatives who had gathered from all over the world. In his closing moments he stirred our minds with a tremendous challenge: "You Christians claim that you have a message which every man, woman, and child should hear. When will you wake up and communicate it in a manner that they will hear and understand it? When and how do you expect to reach the masses of mankind?" That is the challenge that confronts the Christian communicator. Yes, we have a message, a divine message. When and how will we communicate it?

1. *The nature of communication.*

(a) Communication is a complex interaction between speaker and listener, advocate and receptor. While it has the elements of encoding and decoding, transmitting and confirming, it is more than a combination of these elements. Principally communication is an encounter, an intelligible dialogue, a give-and-take experience.

Hendrik Kraemer teaches us to distinguish between communication *to* and communication *with* or between.[4] The first is like delivering goods to the door of another and leaving them there. It is a mail carrier's business. The job is complete when the goods have been delivered. The second is like baking a cake and inviting neighbors in to share the cake as friends in loving conversation.

Communication in the true sense of the word takes place when there is a meeting of mind with mind, of heart with heart—*it is intelligible meeting.* Communication is an encounter of one mind with another mind, of one meaning with another meaning—*it is meaningful interaction.* Communication is an impartation of living ideas, evoking mental and emotional responses—*it is a response-evoking invasion.* Thus communication involves hearing, understanding, encountering, and responding as well as speaking and delivering. The ideal encounter, which is the true meaning and intended aim of communication, is in fact a rare occurrence. It is a priceless experience.

(b) Communication is not only interaction, it is also a *process.* It implicitly confesses a given solidarity. The communicator takes a stand *in* the world, and as a part of the world, of the other (identification). The communicator finds a basis, creates a common platform on which an encounter or a dialogue can take place (commonality). Communication is not a boxing match or a debate to out-do, overcome, or overpower an opponent. It is a meeting of friendly neighbors to discuss issues of common concern. It may also be a meeting of deadly enemies to discuss seriously a possible reconciliation and a resolution of differences without resorting to violence.

The process of communication consists of (1) the *perception* of an object, (2) the *association* of perception with related impressions already stored in the mind, (3) the *interpretation* of such impressions in the light of previous experiences, (4) a mental *formulation* of ideas, (5) *verbalization* of such ideas in intelligible symbols (words), and (6) the *transmission* of them from the perceiver to a receiver. The receiver in turn perceives the symbols, relates them to already possessed ideas, interprets them within a personal frame of reference and against personal background and experiences, and formulates them into ideas. Only to the degree that ideas of the receiver correspond to the original ideas has communication been successful.

(c) Communication is also an art and a gift. In his catalog of spiritual gifts in 1 Corinthians 12:4–11 Paul includes communication gifts (v. 10). In Christian service, communication involves both the gift of enablement by the Spirit of God and the art and technology of an appropriate symbolism.

2. *Presuppositions for effective communication.*[5] In the natural realm effective communication presupposes linguistic-rhetorical capability and psychological rapport. These are like two arches that span the gulf from mind to mind. In the spiritual realm effective communication also presupposes in addition to the above the ministry of the Holy Spirit.

The spiritual aspect of communication is expressed in the word *illumination*. The Holy Spirit lifts the veil and opens the spiritual eyes, ears, and heart to permit the divine light to shine in (Acts 16:14; 26:18; 2 Cor. 4:6). Humans are blind by nature to spiritual reality and are totally dependent on the Holy Spirit to penetrate and illumine their darkness. At the same time, the individual is exhorted in the Word: "He who has an ear, let him hear what the Spirit says" (Rev. 2:7, 11, 17, 29; 3:6, 13, 22).

The linguistic aspect of communication can be expressed in one word: *symbolism*. Words, thought-forms, imagery, metaphors, illustrations, even gestures, combine to form a modified drama.

The psychological aspect of communication is best expressed in the word *rapport.* Not until rapport has been established does the possibility exist for successful communication and transmission of ideas, concepts, and meanings from mind to mind. Rapport leads to empathy and to interpenetration of minds and experiences. Rapport facilitates communication by building an intimate and sympathetic relationship. The communicator's first responsibility and effort must be to build rapport.

Rapport rests on (1) respect for the individual as an individual, (2) personal friendship and common bonds, (3) an understanding of and appreciation for the mental make-up of the receiving person as conditioned by culture and by social relationships.

(1) Respect for the individual as an individual. To respect the individual as an individual is not an easy matter even in one's own social and cultural milieu. The problem is magnified in cross-cultural communication. This respect is comprised of several elements:

- denying to self every conscious and subconscious feeling of superiority and readily admitting the "otherness" of the mental characteristics of the receiver.
- freeing oneself from the evil of making generalizations such as: This is the way the people of India (or Latin America, Africa, Germany, America, etc.) are. Generalizations betray immaturity and are unfair, cruel, and crushing. No one is just a "generalization"; each person is an individual. It is a mistake to lump many individuals together under one stereotype, for there are notable differences even among those who are apparently alike.
- learning respect for personal feelings. Feelings may be expressed in different ways in different cultures, but they are nonetheless a real, determining factor of the individual personality.
- understanding culturally conditioned and defined sentiments—other ways of thinking, doing, and behaving: other culture patterns, value systems, and relationships.

- building up the other's sense of personal importance. This can be achieved by remembering names and addresses, by delegating responsibilities, and by giving public recognition of services rendered and achievements attained.

(2) Personal friendship and common bonds. Rapport demands that the individual be treated not only as an individual but also as a personal friend in whose welfare the communicator is deeply interested and whose relationship is coveted for mutual benefit and enjoyment. Personal friendship presupposes the following common bonds:

- *mutual understanding.* This does not necessarily mean agreement in all matters, but it does mean knowledge of the other's differences and acceptance of such disagreement.
- *common tastes.* There are certain likes and dislikes all people share, such as a liking for honesty, openness, and kindness.
- *common interests.* In contemporary terms we speak of interest groups, that is, people who share interests and concerns in common causes, projects, people.
- *mutual assistance.* A friend can be relied on for help in case of need, whether material, physical, or spiritual.
- *mutual admiration.* Friendship is not given to negativism, censorship, and criticism. Friends see values in each other and find positive stimulation in each other.
- *mutual accessibility.* Friendship includes an openness of mind and heart for each other and times of sharing and fellowship.
- *mutual confidence.* This is the bond of true neighborliness and trust and appreciation.

Such mutuality is a rare commodity in an age and culture of extreme individualism and technocracy. People appear more like machines, sometimes with bolts and screws so loose that the machine may come apart, and sometimes wound too tight with tensions and anxieties. Everyone rushes home to get away from everything and everyone, to be alone and to be left alone. Thus there is a great need for personal friendship for successful communication.

(3) An understanding of and appreciation for the mental make-up of the person as conditioned by culture and by social relationships. Human beings like to think they are rational creatures, seldom realizing that rationality is relative. Beings are rational in relation to the culture and society by which they have been conditioned. Thus they behave differently because they think and feel differently. While individuals from different cultures may not agree, they can learn to understand the reasons for differing opinions and to appreciate each other despite disagreements. Only thus can rapport be maintained and communication really take place.

In summary, illumination by the Holy Spirit (spiritual aspect), an accepted and understood symbolism (linguistic aspect), and rapport (psychological aspect) are necessary presuppositions of effective Christian communication.

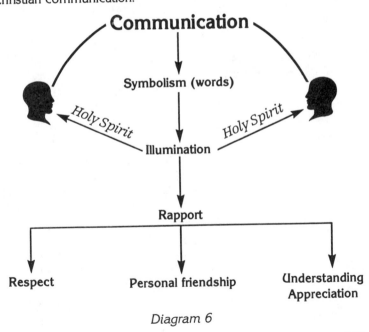

Diagram 6

Communication

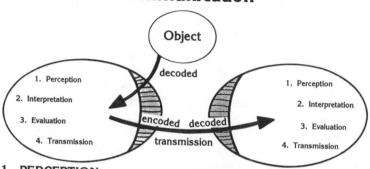

1. **PERCEPTION**
   It is decoded to my mind conditioned by previous experiences.

2. **INTERPRETATION**
   It is integrated into my previous knowledge
   —given meaning

3. **EVALUATION**
   It is reformulated in the light of my total knowledge
   —given value

4. **TRANSMISSION**
   It is then encoded and transmitted with my meaning and my value system and within my code system

Diagram 7

3. *Principles of gospel communication.* If the gospel is to be accepted, it must be communicated in an intelligible, meaningful, appealing, relevant, and persuasive manner. Only as the gospel is understood at least in part and as it is seen to meet certain needs, will it attract the people. The communication of the gospel will be most effective when known principles of communication are observed. Here are seven such principles.

(1) *Communication must be conceptually intelligible.* In the Gospels we read that "the common people heard him [Jesus] gladly" (Mark 12:37, KJV). Something in His communication won a hearing and held the attention of the people.

To be conceptually intelligible the gospel must be communicated in a language that is *understood*. To do so, necessitates, of course, a thorough knowledge of the language of the common people. There is a considerable gap between the language of the scholar-theologian and that of the people of the land and the streets. Paul used the koine rather than the classical Greek in the proclamation of the gospel and in the writing of his epistles because he wanted to be understood more than admired. This principle raises some serious questions regarding the usage of such mediums as lingua franca, trade languages, the language of the schools, and theological and ecclesiastical jargons in the communication of the gospel.

The gospel must be communicated also in a language that is *meaningful.* Words are only symbols of meanings. Meanings, however, are relative. Thus words are not absolute in their content and meaning. A word may project different images on different minds and even transmit opposite meanings to different people. The communicator must know the meanings the receivers assign to particular words. Paul is an excellent example. He knew the mind and vocabulary of his readers well enough to write his letters accordingly. A study of the vocabulary choices in various Pauline epistles and their appropriateness to the reader Paul had in mind is a profitable lesson in communication. That adherence to this principle is essential for evangelism and church growth is borne out by a survey of the great movements among the various tribes and people: seldom have tribal and community movements toward Christianity taken place unless the gospel was presented in the language of the people. (Into this matter of meaningfulness comes also the question of "dynamics equivalents" in Bible translations and communication. Because this is a much-debated matter we shall not enter into it here.)

(2) *Communication must be formally appealing.* The Word is given. It is settled in heaven. The word of the gospel remains eternally unchanged, but the form in which it is presented must change with the age and culture. This principle was fully recognized by Paul: he explicitly stated it in 1 Corinthians 9:19–23; he applied it in his message in Acts 17:22–34.

Well does R. E. O. White say: "The ceaseless mental endeavour [must be] to translate the unchanging truth into the changing thought-forms and living terms of successive generations, without for a moment betraying the everlasting gospel, or compromising the essential and inescapable offence of the cross."[6]

One of the issues arising out of this principle is the advisability of translating the Scriptures into cultural dynamics or equivalents of the various peoples and tribes of the world. How much latitude can be allowed and yet remain totally loyal to the Bible as the Word of God given? The fact of the phenomenal sales and broad market appeal of *Good News for Modern Man* and *The Living Bible* seems to support the need for paraphrased editions. The archaic language of the King James Version does not communicate well to the present generation.

The principle of communicating in an appealing form is clearly illustrated in the Bible. The Bible contains the following *forms,* among others, in the presentation of the eternal truth:

- historical biography in the Old Testament;
- typology of Christ and the plan of salvation in the Old Testament;
- symbols and metaphors of great truths in the Old Testament, such as the potter and the potter's wheel (Jer. 18:1–6) and the dry bones (Ezek. 37);
- dreams and visions and their divine interpretation, such as in the Book of Daniel;
- parables, proverbs, and terse statements, such as Christ used to present the gospel in a Hebrew garb;
- syllogism, such as Paul used in writing to the Romans.

A study of the language of the ancient church creeds reveals the influence that language has had on the theology of the West. What will theology be like when it is clothed in Asiatic dress and put into Asiatic thought-forms, or African thought-forms, or Latin American thought-forms? In order to be appealing the gospel must be garbed both in the vocabulary and the thought-forms of the people and illustrated in the imagery and culture-pictures of the people.

(3) *Communication must be psychologically adapted.* All peoples possess a unique mentality and psychological temperament

and mood. They live in a specific psychological climate. Although all the factors that make up a people's psychology and that account for psychological differences may not be fully understood, it is quite certain that there are psychological differences—differences in mood, sensitivity, perceptivity.

Such differences can be observed, for example, in different styles of church services—Anglican, Roman Catholic, American Black, Presbyterian, and Pentecostal. These vary from area to area— America, Europe, the Arab lands, the Orient, Africa, Latin America. Each grouping and each individual within the group can be described psychologically as pragmatic, rationalistic, esthetic, moralistic, dogmatic, agnostic. It may well be that various denominations appeal to various psychological make-ups.

These psychological differences cannot be ignored if communication is to be acceptable and appreciated. The human being is not pure reason or pure spirit, but is a psychological personality.

(4) *Communication must be culturally related.*[7] Language is only one of several major cultural expressions. While it is the primary vehicle for the communication of the gospel, there are other socially accepted and understood channels of interrelationship and intercommunication. (See following diagram.)

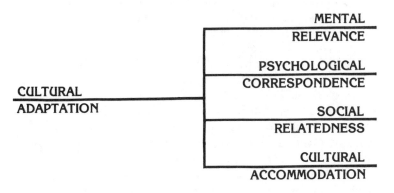

Diagram 8

To be transmitted effectively, the gospel must be communicated along socially natural and accepted channels. In every society there is a "canal system" of communication. It is this canal system that the communicator must discover. If the gospel is to penetrate society and to reach the individual, it must navigate along channels of the group or society. In general this channel leads from the father to the family, from the elders to the people, from the chief to the tribe, from the head man of the village to the people of the village, and so forth.

The Scriptures record examples of household evangelism and conversions, and community movements. This century provides examples of village movements, people movements, tribal movements. Are national movements possible? Is it possible to find channels that will communicate to men and women of socially functional importance who could become the means of access to total communities and nations? Have we imperiled the impact of the gospel by making it too individualistic and by ignoring social and functional power structures and channels in our communication? Is God less interested in great movements today than He was in the days of the New Testament? In a time of "mass psychology" and mass networks of people, is it possible to move masses of people to seriously consider the gospel and then lead them to personal faith in Christ? Perhaps we have become too fearful of large movements. Perhaps we have too exclusively expected that only individuals will turn to Christ. We need to ponder these issues and find scriptural and historical answers for them.

Not only must communication move along socially accepted channels, it must also establish "points of contact" in the mind and culture of the people. A sound pedagogy begins with what is familiar to the pupil and leads on to the new and unfamiliar. It is well to follow this principle in communicating the message of the gospel. The approach Christ used when He preached in Galilee (Matt. 13) differed greatly from His conversation with the learned Nicodemus or with the Samaritan woman (John 3; 4). Nor did Paul use the same approach when speaking in a Jewish synagogue as when preaching in Athens on Mars Hill. Both Christ and Paul began with points of contact in the religion, life, and culture of their audience.

Points of contact can be found in various world religions. E. Stanley Jones believes that points of contact can be found in Hinduism. He writes: "In the hand of the mummied forms and customs of Hinduism I think there are five living seeds: (1) That the ultimate reality is spirit. (2) The sense of unity running through things. (3) That there is justice at the heart of the universe. (4) A passion for freedom. (5) The tremendous cost of the religious life."[8]

Huston Smith gives the following vivid descriptive information about Buddhism: "The First Noble Truth is that life is *dukkha,* usually translated 'suffering.'"[9] The thought is that at the core of all human life there is misery. Smith continues:

> *Dukkha* means pain that seeps at some level into all finite existence. The word's more constructive overtones suggest themselves when we discover that it is used in Pali to refer to an axle which is off-center with respect to its wheel, also to a bone which has slipped out of its socket. In both cases the picture is clear. To get the exact meaning of the First Noble Truth, we should read it as follows: Life in the condition it has got itself into is dislocated. Something has gone wrong. It has slipped out of joint. As its pivot is no longer true, its condition involves excessive friction (interpersonal conflict), impeded motion (blocked creativity), and pain.[10]

Isn't this description reminiscent of the tragic aftereffects of the Genesis 3 experience? Is it possible to lead Buddhists back to Genesis 1 and 2 and show them humanity's state before the tragedy? I have personally tried it with very positive results.

Although I differ in points of theology with Jones and Smith, they are pointing a way to search for possible points of contact in the mind, culture, and religion of the people we seek to reach with the gospel message.

To be culturally relevant, communication must be related also to the world and life views of the people. The ancient text must find meaning in the present context. When text and context are brought together, contextualization takes place. Contextualization distinguishes itself from and goes beyond pure exposition and exegesis. In the simplest form contextualization means that God is addressing the person in the context of that person's life situation. God meets the individual with instruction, reproof, and correction, perhaps also with encouragement and power, with promises and warnings, with blessings and judgments.

The contextual situation may not only apply to the individual but may also relate to the church. For example, the text in the seven little letters in Revelation 2 and 3 speaks through the messenger of the church to the total congregation with illumination, instruction, and warnings as well as with promises. A text may speak likewise to families, employers and employees, to governments, and to nations and total societies. Contextualization reaches as far as the text allows and the situation demands.

(5) *Communication must be religiously relevant.* Religion is designed to meet certain specific needs. Natural religion is basically pragmatic. It is expected to do something for people that they cannot do for themselves. It is to be their ally in a world that threatens to overwhelm them. In general, dogma plays a minor role. The principal question is, What will religion, God or the gods, spirits or demons, fetishes or charms do for the people in their needs and aspirations?

If the gospel is to be presented in a meaningful manner, if it is to appeal to and attract the people, it must be presented in practical, dynamic terms.

- The gospel must become a power encounter. It must encounter and overcome specific evils that are destroying or threatening people, such as diseases, drought, and war.
- The message must relieve people of fear of spirits and death. The anxiety complex or *angst* is real and deep in the minds of the people of any society. The sense of lostness and emptiness is universal. What answers and security does the gospel message provide?
- The message must provide a framework for a world and life view that explains the beginning and the consummation of history and that breaks the dismal cycle of birth and death in which most people believe themselves to be helpless and hopeless victims.

- The message must stir up the dim, mostly subconscious, awareness of a deep, spiritual need—a hunger for God, a desire for forgiveness of sin, a yearning for eternal certainties, and an escape from sure judgment to come. All people live with eternity in their heart, and they cannot escape it, no matter how fast and how far they may run. Eternity trails and haunts them.

To be religiously relevant, then, the gospel message must emphasize the spiritual context of a given people. In Latin America emphasis on the lordship of Christ and the presence of the Holy Spirit as life realities is making the greatest impact. In India stress on the forgiveness of sins and peace with God attracts the greatest attention and draws most people. In Indonesia the people reach out for safety and security in Christ Jesus in the midst of life's uncertainties and dangers. In East and Central Java the truth of the mystic union with Christ constitutes an effective bridge to the Javanese fascination with the mysteries. In Africa the cry is for life, freedom, and equality. Thus there seems to be a message-key that opens the door to the ear, the heart, the mind, the conscience, and the will of the person. It is for the communicator to find that key.

(6) *Communication must be divinely authoritative.* The messenger proclaims the message of God in the deep confidence that the individual is a being made in the image of God, is related to God, is in need of God, and by the grace of God is enabled to respond to the call of God.

- The proclamation is made in divine authority and "Thus saith the Lord" rings through the message with real conviction.
- The proclamation is directed to a person's deepest spiritual needs in the full assurance that the gospel is able to meet those needs.
- The proclamation is made in the consciousness that the Bible is absolute in defining spiritual needs, that it is self-authenticating in the conscience, and that it is able to overcome stubborn resistance.
- The proclamation is made in love and authority to challenge

individuals in their deepest perversion as guilty sinners before God. It calls on them to forsake their false gods and their path of self-redemption and self-righteousness. It urges them to return to God in repentance from sin and to accept the offer of salvation in Christ Jesus who alone is Savior and Lord. Here is the deepest encounter of God and the person—the divine conviction of the resistant conscience. This is the most serious conflict that the proud mind, the stubborn will, and the self-seeking, self-justifying heart must face. The sinner must relinquish his own lordship and forsake his own religious systems, and now accept by faith what God offers in free grace through Christ Jesus and by the Holy Spirit. Here is the real power encounter between God and the individual and between God and Satan in the soul of a person. The final conflict is a question of authority: Is God or Satan or the human person the final authority? Is the individual an autonomous being or a created, submissive being? Because of the ultimate consequences of this issue, the message must be proclaimed in authority—the authority of God.

(7) *Communication must be made in the confidence of the Holy Spirit.* In the end, the preaching of the gospel is not merely one individual facing another. It is not one person confronting or arguing against another. It is the Holy Spirit in the Word of God encountering the individual, facing the sinner. He is the real Communicator, Interpreter, Illuminator, Persuader. He is the One who transforms the gospel into a personal message, who illumines and convicts the heart and conscience of the individual (Isa. 55:10–11; John 16:7–15). Our confidence is not in our own art of communication or the strength of our arguments but in the living witness of the Holy Spirit in and through the preaching of the Word of God.

7

Church Growth and
the Servant of God

Let us return for a moment to the figure in chapter 5 that illustrates the relationship of the Holy Spirit to "Church Growth Dynamics" as a triangle whose three sides are the message of God, the servant of God, and the church of God. Thus far we have emphasized the mystic-realistic union of the Holy Spirit with the Word of God written and the proclamation of the message of God to humans.

The Holy Spirit is also united to the servant of God. He indwells and uses all believers (John 7:38–39; 14:17, 23; Rom. 8:9, 11; 1 Cor. 3:16; 6:19; 2 Cor. 1:21–22; Gal. 3:2, 5; 4:6; 5:22, 25; Eph. 2:22; 5:18). He also singles out specific individuals whom He qualifies and uses in an extraordinary way and for a particular purpose in the kingdom of God (Acts 9:15–16; Gal. 1:15–16; 1 Cor. 12:28–30; Eph. 4:11). The Bible and history are commentaries on this fact.

While it is true that the selecting and qualifying of His peculiar vessels is the sovereign operation of the Holy Spirit, yet it is also true that human response to the working of the Holy Spirit is necessary.

Individuals are moral and responsible beings, endowed to respond to or oppose, accept or reject the gospel, and they are enabled to submit to or resist the operations of the Holy Spirit. Paul's admonition to the Christian not to nullify the grace of God (Gal. 2:21) must be taken seriously. To live a life empty of true meaning and void of true fruitfulness is contrary to the provision, the will, and the pleasure of God. It is possible even in the most difficult circumstances and despite serious handicaps to live a life full of the Holy Spirit (Acts 7:55), laden with fruit of righteousness (Phil. 1:11) and "filled with the knowledge of His will in all spiritual wisdom and understanding [and to] walk in a manner worthy of the Lord, to please Him in all respects, bearing fruit in every good work and increasing in the knowledge of God" (Col. 1:9–10).

The apostles of Jesus Christ may, indeed, be characterized as "bearing fruit in every good work." In them both the sovereign choice of God and their faithful response were fulfilled in Christ's words: "You did not choose Me, but I chose you, and appointed you, that you should go and bear fruit and that your fruit should remain [abide]" (John 15:16). Let us look more closely at the characteristics of this core of Christ-trained men. What are their qualities and qualifications for bearing not only much fruit but *abiding* fruit, the fruit that is the church of Jesus Christ and that has endured.[1]

The Apostles Were Men Who Had Been Called by Christ and Were Irrevocably Bound to Him

They had come under the impact and grip of Christ and were unable and unwilling to part with Him. His call—"Follow Me"—had become an irresistible compulsion in them, an almighty magnet in their lives that would not let them go and to which they voluntarily responded and feverishly clung. A beyond-human relationship captivated them, and they were bound morally and spiritually to Him without whom life was empty, meaningless, and impossible. They had heard Christ's call; they had seen the presence of God in Him; they had heard Him pray; they had observed His manner of life; they had listened to Him teach and converse; they had beheld His glory; they had witnessed the power of God go forth from Him in signs, wonders, and miracles. They had cried out: "Thou art the Christ, the Son of the living God" (Matt. 16:16). When He asked, "You do not want to go away also, do you?" there was but one answer possible for them: "Lord, to whom shall we go? You have words of eternal life. And we have believed and have come to know that You are the Holy One of God" (John 6:67–69). Though in the hour of severest test they had been overwhelmed by human weaknesses and slept while He prayed, and fled while He suffered, and denied when He boldly confessed before the highest ecclesiastical hierarchy and Roman court, and fearfully hid when He was crucified, they later wept bitterly because of their cowardly behavior and disloyalty. Humbly they had met in fear and trembling behind locked doors awaiting the outcome of things, hesitatingly yet joyfully responding to the news of His resurrection. They had fellowshiped with Him for forty days after His resurrection and listened to Him speak of the things pertaining to the kingdom (Acts 1:3). They had received the Great Commission, which delegated world evangelization to them, and patiently waited in Jerusalem according to His instruction until the promised Holy Spirit came to qualify them for the great task before them.

That is a brief summary of the course of the men who had been chosen to be with Him and whom He named apostles (Mark 3:13; Luke 6:13). Paul expressively described himself and the disciples as *apostles* of Jesus Christ and *bond-servants* of Jesus Christ, expressing in these two terms their calling and their voluntary commitment.

THE APOSTLES WERE MEN WHO HAD WILLINGLY ENTERED THE SCHOOL OF DISCIPLESHIP WITH NO CONCERN FOR MATERIAL BENEFITS OR PERSONAL GAIN

What was the motivation of the disciples? From the Gospel records it is evident that the school of discipleship conducted by Christ had the most stringent requirements (Luke 9:57–62; 14:25–33). Only one promise is recorded as having been upheld before the disciples: "Follow Me, and I will make you fishers of men" (Matt. 4:18–22). Hearing this specific call and promise, Peter and Andrew, James and John left all and followed Him. The call "Follow Me" was extended to others who also followed Him without reservation on their part and without commitments on His part. Their motivation seemed simply to be personal attraction and a personal relationship.

In fact, instead of holding before them financial or material gains, Christ spoke of self-denial, cross-bearing, hardships, privations, sufferings, persecution, hatred, and death for His name's sake. At the same time, He assured His followers: "My yoke is easy, and My load is light" (Matt. 11:30).

It must not be imagined that no second thoughts ever came to the disciples as time went on and events unfolded. They were human beings, not an angelic host. Mixed motives did arise in them. For example, they disputed among themselves who would be the greatest in the kingdom and who would sit on the right hand side of the king and who on the left. On another occasion Peter came to the Master with the question: "Behold, we have left everything and followed You, what then will there be for us?" (Matt. 19:27). Christ's answer is important. He did not brush the question aside as totally irrelevant or unspiritual and unbecoming. Christ corrects human motives in a different manner. He used this moment of human weakness to substantiate the fact that the great promises of the Lord to Israel stand firm. He also assured the apostles that in the restoration of Israel and the coming kingdom they would have a vital role to play and that their sacrifices for Him would draw a just reward (Matt. 19:27–29). But these things were not to be their concern. The Father holds all times in His hand and His plan is supreme, final, and wise.

The disciples' motivation was transmuted after Pentecost. The question of greatness in the kingdom no longer occupied them. They lived and labored under the impetus of the decisiveness of the act of God in Christ Jesus for the salvation of humanity; the glory and victory of the risen Lord; the Pentecost event and the indwelling Holy Spirit; the transformed view of much of the Old Testament; the imminency of the return of the Lord; the glory, universality, and relevance of the gospel message of Jesus Christ. These great truths seemed to fill their minds and to be their motivating power—particularly in their sense of the urgency of evangelism.

THE APOSTLES WERE MEN WHO HAD BEEN DISCIPLED BY THEIR MASTER*

The Twelve had many lessons to learn. They needed to be disciplined and shaped for a future ministry and leadership. From crude fishermen and other occupations, they had to be converted and molded into disciples, followers, examples, leaders, teachers, apostles. This was a long and difficult route. They were to become true representatives of their Master not only *proclaiming His message,* but also *incarnating His principles* and *reflecting His image.* They were to be men of God, messengers of a glorious gospel, apostles of Jesus Christ, living monuments of His grace and power. His qualities and characteristics were to be engraved in their lives so that people would recognize that they had been with Jesus (Acts 4:13; 1 Peter 2:9).

The fact for us to note is that Christ's chosen (not merely attracted) disciples remained with Him and persisted in the school of discipleship at any and every cost and any and every demand.

---

*I am aware that the word disciple has a *a broad popular usage* in the New Testament. We note that the Gospels use "disciples of Moses" (John 9:28), "disciples of the Pharisees" (Matt. 22:16), "disciples of John" (the Baptist) (Mark 2:18; Luke 5:33; John 1:35). It is also evident that the word disciple in some instances refers to superficial followers of Christ (John 6:66). In the Book of Acts it has various shadings and in some instances means no more than being a believer or professing to be a believer.

In the *teaching of Jesus,* however, it has a deep spiritual and theological content. It is wise, therefore, to look at His teaching rather than at the ordinary usage and casual practice of some individuals or groups. It is evident that the demands of Christ on *His disciples* are most radical and therefore His followers must be people of different quality. His demands are most fully expressed in the "Sermon on the Mount" (Matt. 5–7) and such passages as Luke 9:57–62; 14:25–35; John 8:31–32; 13:34–35; 15:1–25. What the "Law of Moses" was to the disciples of Moses, the "Law of Christ" (the new commandment) is to the disciples of Christ. There is a "Law of Liberty," the "royal law," the new commandment (James 1:25; 2:8; 1 John 2:7–11). The Christian disciple cannot free himself from Christian discipline. However, the radical demands are matched by a radical provision. The Christian believers are disciples not in their own strength but in the strength, wisdom, and love of the Holy Spirit (2 Tim. 1:7).

Therefore, the Lord paid much attention to the training of the Twelve. He had chosen them, after a night's prayer, to be His disciples and to be made into apostles (Luke 6:12–16). A threefold method in this training process is evident from the Gospels.

First, there was His personal example and the impact of His life upon the disciples. They were permitted to observe His total life style, His work, His relationships, His mannerism, His prayer life, His teaching, His ministry of healing and helping, and so on. His life and ministry were like an open book.

Second, there were periods of private instruction. Several gaps in the timetable and chronology imply that Christ sliced out considerable periods of time to be alone with the disciples for special seasons of instruction. In addition, several recorded discourses were addressed primarily or solely to the disciples: the Sermon on the Mount (Matt. 5:1–2); the Olivet discourse (Matt. 24–25); the Upper Room discourse (John 13–16); the high priestly prayer (John 17); and the discourses on the kingdom of God after Christ's resurrection (Acts 1:3). A great deal of instruction was given to them of which the Holy Spirit later reminded them (John 14:26).

Third, the disciples were personally involved in ministries. They were with Christ in His ministries, and they were dispatched by Him on special missions, bringing back to Him their reports (Matt. 10; Luke 10:1–24).

Observation, instruction, participation, delegation—these were the stages in the development of the disciples. A good, thorough resource for further study of this topic is found in A. B. Bruce's classic *The Training of the Twelve.* As I have personally found, such studies can lead to insights and conclusions on discipleship that will touch life on the deepest levels. Discipleship is an inexhaustible concept and never-ending process when it is in accord with the teaching of Christ.

What were some of the lessons the disciples had learned? Most markedly, they had learned obedience and confidence. Following Christ's ascension, they quietly and patiently waited as they had been instructed, without running ahead of God. Though they had been commanded to go into all the world, they had also been told to wait in Jerusalem (Luke 24:49; Acts 1:13). They waited until they were qualified to go.

They did not engage in heated arguments with people. They testified as true witnesses, preached without fear, prayed in boldness and faith, suffered quietly and joyfully. Like their Master, they did not fight for their cause and right, but earnestly prayed and persistently followed their course of duty, insisting that they must obey God rather than men whatever the consequences might be (Acts 4:19–20; 5:29).

They did not permit an antagonistic attitude to develop toward those who were their enemies and oppressors. They remained longsuffering and patient in their ministries, trusting the Lord to make all things right. Their sole concern was to be loyal and true witnesses of the resurrection of their Lord, for in the resurrection the Father had fully and completely vindicated Christ Jesus as His Servant and Son. With this Christ had also been made both Lord and Messiah, Savior and Prince (Acts 2:36; 5:31). In Him alone was the hope of Israel and the hope of the world (Acts 3:17–26).

Such conduct is in marked contrast, indeed, to their former behavior. Had they not frequently been carried away by indignation? On one occasion they had even been prepared to command fire to come down from heaven and consume the Samaritans in reprisal for their inhospitality (Luke 9:51–56). Not so now! Under the tutelage of their Master, they were changed. They were new creatures in Christ Jesus.

THE APOSTLES WERE MEN WHO LIVED AND WALKED IN THE SPIRIT

Walking in the Spirit must not be confused with living in the Spirit. Paul draws attention to a difference in the two in Galatians 5:25. Though he does not define the terms, he makes a distinction when he writes: "If we live by the Spirit, let us also walk by the Spirit." There is no spiritual life apart from the Spirit of life. It is possible, however, to have life in the Spirit but not to walk in the Spirit. Walking in the Spirit means to live in complete submission to and dependence on the Spirit. The apostles knew experientially what it meant to be filled by the Spirit (Acts 2:4; 4:8, 31; 13:9) and expected to find men among their company who were full of the Spirit (Acts 6:2, 3, 5). They knew that such a life was possible only as they lived a life of obedience and in submission to the Lord and dependence on Him (Acts 5:29–32). Indeed, obedience is better than sacrifice. Obedience requires no other and no lesser sacrifice than the sacrifice of self-will.

Bystanders interpreted Pentecost in several different ways (Acts 2:12–13). Peter, however, knew its theological and experiential significance (Acts 2:14–21, 38–39). The life and ministry of the apostles were characterized by dependence on the Holy Spirit (Acts 4:8). They expected the Holy Spirit to single out and discipline the dishonest (Acts 5:1–11). They permitted the Holy Spirit to resolve serious tensions and theological differences in the brotherhood and to unfold His program for them (Acts 15:13–18, 28). The Holy Spirit was a reality in their lives to guide and to minister boldly and wisely in the midst of pressure, tensions, threats, opposition, and suffering (Acts 4:31; 6:5, 10; 7:55). He was their enablement and sufficiency as they lived and walked with Him. Later Paul wrote some tremendous lessons on the Holy Spirit (cf. Rom. 8; 1 Cor. 12–14; the epistles to the Galatians and Ephesians).

THE APOSTLES WERE MEN WHO HAD
SET THEIR PRIORITIES STRAIGHT

There is a divine ordering of priorities both in personal life and in the ministry of the church. Our Lord admonished His disciples to put first things first when He commanded: "Seek first His kingdom" (Matt. 6:33). Paul informed the church of God's order for the ministry: "and God has appointed in the church, first apostles, second prophets, third teachers, then . . ." (1 Cor. 12:28).

In the first part of Acts the apostles administered all affairs of the church. They preached, taught, witnessed, healed, and administered alms (Acts 4:33–37). In chapter 6 a crisis developed. The work was getting too big. A moment of decision had been reached: Either the work must suffer or part of the labor must be delegated to others. The choice was made in the light of divine priorities. Prayer and the preaching of the Word of God must not suffer. Therefore, the care of the widows and the serving at tables must be delegated to others. So that is what was done and the divine priorities were safeguarded (Acts 6:1–7).

The following priorities are evident in the apostles' ministries:

- The apostles put spiritual ministries before social and material services, though they did not permit the latter to be neglected, making adequate provisions for them (Acts 6:1–6).
- They combined prayer with preaching without allowing either to usurp the place of the other (Acts 6:2, 4).
- They put evangelism before all other ministries. All apostles became "missionaries" except James who died an early death as a martyr (Acts 12:2). Thus the word of God multiplied and spread over vast territories (Acts 12:24).

Their evangelism effort was contagious (Acts 8:4; 11:19–21), and the churches they planted became centers of evangelism—in fact, to such a degree that Paul could not find pioneer territory between Jerusalem and Illyricum (Yugoslavia) after some years (Rom. 15:19, 23). As a result, Paul looked toward Rome and from there to Spain (Rom. 15:24, 28; cf. Acts. 19:9, 10, 20, 26; Rom. 1:8; 1 Thess. 1:6–8). There is real progress in the kingdom of God when the priorities of the church are in keeping with the divine order.

THE APOSTLES WERE MEN WHO HAD LEARNED THE VALUE OF TEAM MINISTRIES

Team effort required cooperation, coordination, and subordination. Although relatively little is known of the post-Pentecost experiences and ministries of most of the apostles, Acts has several illustrations of cooperation in the early church. Peter stood up *with* the eleven on the day of Pentecost to deliver his great message (Acts 2:14). It must have been an impressive sight to see these men stand together—a symbol of unity and of moral and spiritual support. Peter and John went together to the temple at the hour of prayer. Luke significantly reports that "Peter, along with John, fixed his gaze upon him [the lame man] and said, 'Look at us'" (Acts 3:1, 4). In another instance, when the rulers and elders released them, Peter and John went to their own company where a great prayer meeting took place (Acts 4:23–31). Thus all the saints cooperated in the ministry of witnessing and suffering. Next Peter and John went together to Samaria (Acts 8:14) and after completing their work went on to evangelize in many villages of the Samaritans (Acts 8:25). Later Peter was delivered from prison and certain death when "prayer for him was being made fervently by the church to God" (Acts 12:5). The apostles were a *band* of co-laborers cooperating in the ministry, not a number of individualists going their own ways.

Coordination was also an important principle in apostolic ministries. There may well be truth in the tradition that the apostles divided the world as far as it was known to them, each receiving his allotment for evangelism. According to tradition they dispersed in several directions. Also, Peter, James, and John, for example, agreed with Paul and Barnabas on a division of the field of labor, thus eliminating possible duplication and conflicts (Gal. 2:9).

The principle of subordination was also important to them. Peter, James, and John were considered pillars in the church (Gal. 2:9). Philip did not object to Peter and John coming to Samaria to see what was happening and the apostles added their ministry to his (Acts 8:14–25). Barnabas was sent to Antioch in Syria to assume responsibility for a ministry begun by others (Acts 11:19–26).

The brightest illustration of coordination and cooperation in the ministry is found in Paul who always was surrounded by a group of co-laborers. Here was teamwork *par excellence*.

The Apostles Were Men With a Message Burning in Their Hearts

Jeremiah, the weeping prophet, permits his reader to sense some of his inner conflicts in his ministry. He writes of his temptation not to speak because he was derided and mocked. However, it became utterly impossible for him to remain silent. He tells the Lord: "Thou hast overcome me and prevailed"; therefore he had to speak. When reproach and derision continued: "But if I say, 'I will not remember Him / Or speak any more in His name' / Then in my heart it becomes like a burning fire / Shut up in my bones; / And I am weary of holding it in, / And I cannot endure it" (Jer. 20:7–9). The experiences of the prophet of old were shared by the apostles. Boldly Peter answered the rulers of Israel: "We cannot stop speaking what we have seen and heard." This inward pressure to speak grew out of obedience to God Himself (Acts 4:19–20). On another occasion he replied to the threats of the rulers: "We must obey God rather than men" (Acts 5:29). These men with a message burning in their hearts and with a determination to obey God rather than men could not be silent. They had to speak.

It is tragic when there are cold hearts with a message that is frozen, or when there is a burning heart without a message. The first results in cold, heartless orthodoxy; the second in a vague mysticism, emotionalism, or heated fanaticism. In the experience of the apostles there was a beautiful blending of a burning heart and a message from God, the instrument and the content. Throughout the centuries the burning message has ignited many and sent them forth with a message burning also in their hearts. This is what we need to meet the challenge to our age of *Wissenschaftliche Theologie* (scientific theology). Only as the message of God burns in the hearts of servants of God will our age of scientism and secularism listen again to the voice of God.

THE APOSTLES WERE MEN WHO COMMUNICATED THEIR MESSAGE WITH PRACTICAL WISDOM AND SPIRIT-ILLUMINATED INSIGHT

It is astounding that simple fishermen were able to stir a whole city with the gospel of Jesus Christ (Acts 5:26–28). No doubt, the impact of Pentecost was tremendous and decisive—the afterglow lingered long and the light shone on. Yet there is a human side to the story.

In the Gospels our Lord accused the leaders of the Jews of not reading the signs of the times. They were neither observant nor discerning. They were steeped in tradition; they could not look beyond their own wall. They were blind to the evident realities of the time. As a result of their blindness, they were not relating to the needs of the people and the challenges of the times and circumstances. This cannot be said of the apostles of Jesus Christ after

Pentecost, for they knew how to reach the people. They knew how to hit their targets. Their message pierced the hearts of the crowd at Pentecost, it drew and convinced multitudes, it angered the fanatics, it perplexed the opposition, it provoked the intelligent to thought (Acts 2:37; 4:4; 5:17; 5:24; 5:34–39). Their message did not dwell on the beautiful, benevolent, and sinless life of Jesus; it did not portray His cruel death on the cross to arouse sympathy and sentimentality. Boldly they spoke of His resurrection and His position as Lord, Christ, Prince, and Savior (Acts 2:36; 5:31).

The apostles prudently adapted their methods to the culture of the people. They communicated their message in relevant and intelligible terms by speaking to the people in the common language of the time. They were communicators, not orators.

Finally, they wisely invested their lives in people rather than in institutions. Therefore their way and message were life-related.

THE APOSTLES WERE MEN OF JOYOUS SUFFERING AND SACRIFICES

Joyous suffering is one of the most evident qualities of the apostolic band. Poverty and suffering could not deter them from placing their lives as living sacrifices on the altar of the Lord. They served Him without reservation, without counting the cost. When they were threatened, they went to their company to pray for greater boldness (Acts 4:21–31); when they were beaten, they departed from the council, rejoicing that they were counted worthy to suffer shame for His name (Acts 5:41). Stephen prayed for his enemies in the midst of a rain of stones that completed his earthly course (Acts 7:60).

Of the many prayers mentioned in Acts, there is no request that the Lord would intervene to prevent persecution and suffering or save them from such experiences. One possible exception might be the prayer meeting mentioned in Acts 12 that resulted in the release of Peter from prison. But even here it is a question whether they prayed for his release or for his steadfastness. The apostles and members of the early church lived too close to the time of the cross to think of Christianity apart from suffering. The shadow of the cross was still on their path. It is not surprising that Peter mentions suffering seventeen times in his writings. He exhorts his readers not to think of sufferings as strange things, but rather as sharing in the sufferings of Christ (1 Peter 4:12–13). Sufferings are part of their calling (1 Peter 2:20–21).

The apostles claimed no right of their own, only the right to proclaim the gospel. For the sake of the gospel they suffered without being hailed as heroes or martyrs. Eventually they laid down their lives in the cause of their Master and for His glory. It is most peculiar that the New Testament remains silent on the manner of their death, except that James is mentioned as dying by the sword (Acts 12:2). The death of the apostles is not allowed to becloud the death of the Master.

Their devotion and dedication were not the result of human resolution or a subjective "Easter-faith". They were not heroes, martyrs, or brave men fighting for a human cause. They were bond-slaves devoted to a *Person* who had captivated their all. They were soldiers in the army of the Lord under the Holy Spirit, the great Captain who was leading the hosts on to victory. In a chorus they would have joined the chant: not to us, but to Thee, our Lord, be glory, honor, and praise! Their stand was exemplified by Livingstone's testimony before an audience in Cambridge. When someone asked the explorer about his sacrifices for Africa, Livingstone replied that only *One* had ever really sacrificed for a cause and that *One* was Jesus Christ Himself. Others could only distantly approximate and vaguely experience the shadow of sacrifice. To this Livingstone added that it was impossible to sacrifice for God because God remains no man's debtor.

From the human point of view the apostles were men of unmeasured sacrifices; from the divine perspective they were the recipients of unmeasured joy, blessings, and glory.

THE APOSTLES WERE MEN WHOSE CONCEPT OF GOD WAS SCRIPTURAL, HISTORICAL, AND PERSONAL

To the apostles God was not shut up in heaven or shut out of history and personal experience. He was present and active and His predetermined plan was overruling all affairs, even the misdeeds of men (Acts 2:23).

More than any other portion in Acts, the prayer in Acts 4:24–30 reveals the existential theology of the apostles. To them God is the Creator of heaven, and earth, and sea, and all that is in them; He is the God over all nations; He is the God of eternity and the eternal counsel; He beholds the threatenings of the enemies; He is the God who upholds His servants and qualifies them to speak boldly and act courageously under pressures and persecutions. Thus He is the living God, the ever-present God, the God who is here and can be known personally. And this was more than theory—this was reality to them. In radical faith they acted, in bold faith they confessed, in joyous faith they suffered, in anticipating faith they prayed—and God acknowledged and responded to their faith. Therefore they boldly declared the mighty deeds of God (2:11).

These, then, are some of the qualities of the men Christ called and God used in times past to magnify His grace, to advance the gospel, to strengthen the church of Jesus Christ, and to bring light to the nations. The apostles actually became what Christ destined them to be when He said: "You did not choose Me, but I chose you, and appointed you, that you should go and bear fruit, and that your fruit should remain; that whatever you ask of the Father in My name, He may give to you" (John 15:16).

J. Sidlow Baxter remarked:

> What God chooses, He cleanses,
> What God cleanses, He molds,
> What God molds, He fills,
> What God fills, He uses.

The apostles and those who followed them are vibrant demonstrations of the truth that God uses Spirit-filled people. They are His primary agents.

Part Three

Four Pillars
of Church Growth

8

Four Pillars Introduced

Church growth does not just happen, it must be made to happen. And this is no easy matter. Church growth is downright hard work. It demands all we are, all we have, and all we are able to marshal. Already Christ had predicted that the gates of hell would be turned loose against it and Paul informs the Corinthians "we are not ignorant of his [Satan's] schemes" (2 Cor. 2:11) to take advantage of every possible opportunity to oppose Christ and the work and worker of God. Church growth is a warfare as well as a method.

A church may have the right message and a faithful and true servant of God and yet remain stagnant and dwarfed. There is no such thing as automatic, spontaneous growth. In the natural world only weeds seem to grow spontaneously. Cultivation is necessary for proper growth and is therefore a biblical concept. Adam and Eve were to cultivate even the Garden of Eden. Paul uses the concept as a metaphor when he refers to the Corinthians as being God's cultivated field (1 Cor. 3:9). Not every church grows, nor can every church be made to grow unless it is willing to meet specific divine requirements for growth. Growth takes much careful and diligent cultivation.

Besides a garden or field to be cultivated, the church can be looked at as a building. "I will build my church," Christ assures His disciples (Matt. 16:18). Paul tells the Corinthians that they are "God's building" (1 Cor. 3:9). Peter reminds the believers that they, "as living stones, are being built up as a spiritual house" (1 Peter 2:5).

This spiritual building has four sides of equal dimensions. These four sides can be labeled fitness, form, function, and focus. Or the church can be seen as resting on four pillars that reach down to the primary rock formations and uphold the building in the midst of storm and stress—natural quakes, cultural convulsions, and satanic attacks. The gates of hell have not prevailed and will not prevail against it. The church rests securely on the Rock of Ages.

This metaphor of the church as a building resting on four pillars will provide the framework for the discussion of church growth in the remaining chapters of this volume. The Book of Acts can be outlined to show the church developing in this pattern:

Pillar One: Fitness	—the church as a qualitative community	Acts 1:1–5:42
Pillar Two: Form	—the church forming an adequate and serviceable structure	Acts 6:1–7
Pillar Three: Function	—the church reaching out in aggressive evangelism in the local communities	Acts 8:1–12:25
Pillar Four: Focus	—the church concentrating its ministry on aggressive world evangelism	Acts 13:1–28:31

Not until all four pillars are evident has the church reached the standard of a New Testament church and entered the full New Testament order and purpose. Without anyone of the four pillars the church remains dwarfed, paralyzed, or immature.

The following diagrams also illustrate the outline of Acts in relation to church growth. The first figure shows the four equal sides of the building; the second illustrates the progressive unfolding of the church.

The Church Four-Sided

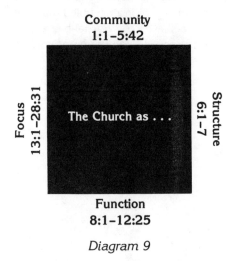

Community
1:1–5:42

Focus
13:1–28:31

The Church as . . .

Structure
6:1–7

Function
8:1–12:25

Diagram 9

The Church in Acts
PROGRESSIVE UNFOLDING

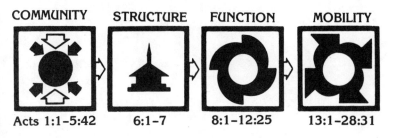

COMMUNITY	STRUCTURE	FUNCTION	MOBILITY
Acts 1:1–5:42	6:1–7	8:1–12:25	13:1–28:31

Diagram 10

This progressive unfolding of the church does not conflict with the emphasis in the leitmotif verse (Acts 1:8) that Jerusalem, Judea, Samaria, and the uttermost parts of the earth must receive equal and simultaneous attention and ministries. We must allow for the fact that the believers needed time to be formed into a church before Christianity could become a dynamic and united movement for its Lord. This forming and organizing occupied the church in its initial years. Once this was achieved the gospel-bearers fanned out over the then-known world according to the command of their Lord.

9

Pillar One—
The Fitness of the Church

The fitness of the church is measured by its moral and spiritual quality, not by an activist methodology or a pragmatic technology. Paul exhorts the churches to walk worthy of the Lord (Col. 1:10), worthy of God (1 Thess. 2:12), worthy of their calling (Eph. 4:1), and worthy of the gospel of Christ (Phil. 1:27). These exhortations have tremendous implications. The church is in this world as a divine demonstration of the manifold grace, wisdom, and power of God (Eph. 3:10, 20). It is a sign of the kingdom of God.

Peter also speaks of the spiritual calling of the church. He reminds the believers that "You are a chosen race, a royal priesthood, a holy nation, a people for God's own possession, that you may proclaim the excellencies of Him who has called you out of darkness into His marvelous light" (1 Peter 2:9). Just previous to this passage he has exhorted them: "But like the Holy One who called you, be holy yourselves also in all your behavior; because it is written, 'You shall be holy, for I am holy'" (1 Peter 1:15–16).

Worthiness or fitness is not the natural state of humankind or of the church. *Positionally,* the church is perfect in Christ Jesus (Col. 2:10); *conditionally,* it must be made perfect through the ministry of the Holy Spirit (1 Thess. 5:23–24; Jude 24–25). The church of Jesus Christ is a congregation of people characterized by spiritual qualities. These qualities are developed as the church places itself under the Holy Spirit and under the instruction of the Word of God (Acts 2:42).

Pentecost sets the pattern. Peter preached the gospel (Acts 2:14–36); and admonished the audience to repent, believe in Jesus Christ, and be baptized (2:38). The people received the message, obeyed the word, were baptized as a public confession of repentance and faith, and were added to the church of Jesus Christ (2:41). This was the initial transaction—their conversion and their entrance into the church of Jesus Christ. This church unfolds itself from here most beautifully.

The early church began as an assembly of people who were learning, fellowshiping, and praying together (Acts 2:42). There was no formal confession, doctrinal statement, constitution, structure, or standard of behavior for membership. Initially the church had to take on the character of Him who brought it into being, who forever claims it as His own, who resides in it and presides over it. Its purpose was and is to serve, to be a vessel fit for the Master's use. As a community under the Holy Spirit, the assembly must be holy as He is holy.

The church, then, is a quality community. To be a growing and multiplying church it must first be a fit church. What were the qualities of the early church? Diagram 11 lists nine, which will be amplified in the rest of the chapter.

A CHURCH MUST EXPERIENTIALLY KNOW THE PRESENCE OF THE HOLY SPIRIT

The church had been divinely designed to be the habitation of God in and through the Holy Spirit (Eph. 2:20–22; 3:16–19). This became a reality on the day of Pentecost. The company of believers were united into a holy temple and "filled with the Holy Spirit" (Acts

QUALITIES OF THE CHURCH

1. **A church** **must experientially know the presence of the Holy Spirit.**
2. **A church** **must be united by a common faith.**
3. **A church** **must submit itself to a God-ordained leadership.**
4. **A church** **must be molded into a unified, functioning community.**
5. **A church** **must train its members in the school of discipleship.**
6. **A church** **must proclaim a clearly defined and relevant message.**
7. **A church** **must continue in prayer.**
8. **A church** **must live in the realm of miracles.**
9. **A church** **must suffer and sacrifice joyfully.**

Diagram 11

2:4) as the temple of Solomon had been filled with the presence of God (1 Kings 8:1–11; 2 Chron. 5:1–14). From that time the temple of wood and stone gave way to the spiritual house built out of living stones and the sacrifices of animals were replaced by spiritual sacrifices (1 Peter 2:5). Thus the "household of God, which is the church of the living God, the pillar and support of the truth" (1 Tim. 3:15), functions in and by the Holy Spirit and exists for His operations. This is experientially demonstrated in the church of the Book of Acts.

The church freely acknowledged the presence and authority of the Holy Spirit and intimately lived and dynamically operated in Him. Its dependence on the Holy Spirit was natural and complete. The church, indeed, became the habitation and temple of the Holy Spirit. The Book of Acts might well be titled the Acts of the Holy Spirit in and through the church. Theologically speaking, it may be more correct to say that the church was so yielded to the Holy Spirit that He could fully and completely work out His plan and purpose in it.

There are fifty-four references to the Holy Spirit in this book. His superintendency is felt in every chapter and in every incident. The manifestation of the Holy Spirit is evident not only on the day of Pentecost, but also later in Samaria, in the home of Cornelius, and in Ephesus. The manifestation took the form of speaking in tongues and loosening the lips in praise and the proclamation of the gospel of Christ. His power is revealed in signs and miracles, in healings and deliverances (see Acts 5:12–16). His convicting and convincing ministry is made known in multitudes of conversions. His sanctifying impact is seen in the transformation of lives, in the unification of believers, in the liberality of all who came into the fellowship of the church, in the transformation of their value system—they turned from the material to the spiritual—and in the power that was released in answer to their prayers. The Holy Spirit came in power, wisdom, holiness, and love, setting people free to serve the living God, to form a new community, to create a new way of life, and to proclaim a new message (see Acts 4:23–25). The Holy Spirit gave boldness, authority, and power in preaching and in witnessing, joy and endurance in suffering and martyrdom.

The need for the presence of the Holy Spirit was acknowledged when the apostles called the multitude together and charged them to "select from among you, brethren, seven men of good reputation, full of the Spirit and of wisdom . . ." (6:3). The apostles expected that ordinary church members who were filled with the Spirit of God would be available for service. The seven men listed in 6:5 all knew experientially what it meant to live lives filled with the Spirit. By inference, those who chose them were walking in the Spirit and were thus enabled to discern those men who were truly qualified for the ministry. They had the gift of discernment as Paul mentions in 1 Cortinthians 12:10. This incident bespeaks the spiritual quality of the believers.

From this overview two most important facts can be observed—one doctrinal, the other practical. *Doctrinally,* the Book of Acts shows that the early church clearly acknowledged the Holy Spirit as *a divine Person.* He was not merely a breath of God, an impersonal power, or a benevolent influence. He was the Spirit of witness (Acts 5:32), the Spirit of God, the Paraclete.

Practically, the early church was conscious that the Holy Spirit related Himself to the individual believer as well as to the corporate church. The believers knew that they had been regenerated by the Spirit (John 3:5; Titus 3:5) and that they were baptized into one body, the body of Christ, and sealed by Him (Acts 1:5; 11:16; 1 Cor. 12:13; 2 Cor. 1:22; Eph. 4:30). They had the witness of the Holy Spirit within them (Acts 5:32; Rom. 8:16); and they were living, walking, and praying in the Holy Spirit (Gal. 5:25; Eph. 6:18; Jude 20) as well as being strengthened by His intercession (Rom. 8:26–27). This was more than theory to them; this was a life reality. They knew that the Holy Spirit was dwelling within them. He filled, guided, emboldened, enlightened, empowered, and sustained them. He filled them with joy unspeakable and full of glory (1 Peter 1:8). He was their sufficiency in life, ministry, witnessing, evangelizing, suffering, martyrdom.

He spoke (Acts 8:29), He caught Philip away (Acts 8:39), He bade Peter to go to Cornelius (Acts 11:12), He singled out missionaries (Acts 13:1–4), and He forbade Paul to enter Asia and Bithynia at a certain moment of time (Acts 16:6–7). They also believed that He could be lied to (Acts 5:3) and that He could be resisted (Acts 7:51).

The Holy Spirit was an ever-present life reality to the believers of the early church. And He was fully acknowledged and obeyed as the Leader and Superintendent of the church and the individual.

A CHURCH OF BELIEVERS—A COMMUNITY—MUST BE UNITED BY A COMMON FAITH

The apostolic church was a community of believing people. Faith is the hallmark of all New Testament saints. Without faith it is impossible to please God, the writer to the Hebrews informs us (Heb. 11:6); and Paul argues in Romans that righteousness comes by faith only (3:21–4:25). This had been so in the Old Testament dispensation, it was so in the time of Jesus Christ, and it remains so in the New Testament. It is the unifying quality of the people of God of all ages (Heb. 11:1–12:3).

At first reading we may be somewhat surprised that the noun *believer* appears only once in Acts (5:14). It is not found at all in the Gospel of John. The verb and cognitive forms are predominant and are found fifty-eight times in Acts. This preponderance of the verb form is highly significant. It signifies that belief in the New Testament sense is not a passive state of mind. It is not a mere *assent* of the mind; it is a *consent* of the total personality. It is not merely intellectual but is volitional and emotional as well. The verb, particularly in the present tense, implies a continuous movement toward the object of faith, a dynamic life of decision and action, and conscious, deliberate involvement.

The content of the faith of the early believers is based on historical identification and facts. Acts is a book of evangelism in which identification and facts are more important than theory and theology. Christianity is a historical, factual religion in contrast to intuitive insights, mythology, elaborate theories, and even ideologies and theologies.

The object of their belief was the historic Jesus of Nazareth, a man approved of God (Acts 2:22; 10:38). He was known by many titles: Jesus Christ of Nazareth (3:6; 4:10), Christ the heir to the throne of David (2:30), the Holy and Righteous One (2:27; 3:14; 7:52), the Lord (signifying an identity with the Old Testament Jehovah, 2:34; 7:60; 8:25; 9:5, 10, 13, 15, 17; 11:16, 21, 23), Lord and Christ (2:36), Son of God (9:20), Prince of life (3:15), a prophet (3:22), a stone (4:11), the holy Servant Jesus (3:13, 26; 4:27, 30), a Prince and a Savior (5:31), Son of Man (7:56), Christ (the promised Messiah of the Old Testament, 9:22), the One of whom the prophets testified (2:25–35; 3:18, 21, 22, 24; 4:11, 25–28; 10:43). Such designations were not a vain bestowal of titles or a heaping up of honors in an attempt to make a favorable impression. They expressed His essential qualities, divinely apportioned offices, experiential relationships, and existential reality. Jesus Christ had biblical, historical, and personal meaning for them. This was not a knowledge in-the-flesh (*Wissenschaftliche Theologie*); this was divine revelation made real in life experiences. Even their enemies perceived that they had been with Jesus (4:13).

Comparatively little is said in Acts about the significance of the death of Christ. We are informed that He died according to the determinate counsel and foreknowledge of God (2:23, 36; 3:13, 15;

4:10, 27, 28; 5:20; 7:52; 10:39), and Philip identified Him with the Suffering Servant of Isaiah 53 (8:32–35).

In contrast to the above, *the resurrection of Jesus Christ is emphasized.* It is made the central event in the life of the Lord. The reason for this emphasis will be discussed later. Interestingly, the Resurrection is continuously described as an act of God. God had acted, raised Him from the dead, and fully vindicated Him (2:24, 32; 3:13, 15, 26; 4:10, 33; 5:30; 10:40). The apostles had been made uniquely *the witnesses of the resurrection of Jesus Christ* (1:22; 2:32; 3:15; 4:33; 5:32; 10:39, 40).

The present and future ministry and status of Christ is referred to in several significant statements as we have shown before.

The historic Jesus was not the total substance of their belief, however. They were no Christo-monists. Their Christology and their soteriology had a broad framework derived from the Old Testament. Although the kingdom concept does not receive a major emphasis, they did believe in and preach the kingdom of God.

They believed in God as the living God, the God who is present in history, who is the main Actor in history, either directly or indirectly, through Christ or the Holy Spirit. The result of this article of their faith was that divine interventions in history were not amazing surprises to them. Miracles were not novelties or shocking phenomena. They were realities of life and history to be expected from a God who is present. They knew of a supernaturalism that was free to act within the universe without destroying the natural order, because God was the Creator of all things (4:24).

The early believers also saw Pentecost as an event brought about by God (2:17). The Holy Spirit for them was not merely a *breath of God or divine influence.* They knew Him as a Person. Attributes, activities, and relationships which are ascribed to Him are personal and can be attributed only to a person.

It is a marvel how Pentecost swept away traditional monotheism in its monadic, judaistic form and made room for faith in the Trinity. Righteousness by works gave way to righteousness by faith in Christ Jesus; legalism made room for freedom in the Holy Spirit of God; and ritualism and symbolism were swallowed up by reality.

The faith of the early believers was in appearance and emphasis a *new faith*. Yet, Christianity had continuity with Old Testament teaching, promises, and anticipations. In every major doctrine, except the mystery of the church, the apostles fall back on the Old Testament. Even the doctrine of the church does not stand in isolation, for it belongs in the broader realm of the kingdom of God in its spiritual qualities, characteristics, essentials, ministries, and purposes. Therefore, while the new faith is unique, it is not unrelated to or isolated from the old.

A CHURCH MUST SUBMIT ITSELF
TO GOD-ORDAINED LEADERSHIP

Communal relationships, mutual edification, efficient functioning, and effective ministries required strong leadership in their initial stages. This leadership was granted to the early church in the apostles. It was at that time that the word *apostles* came into prominence. The Twelve became the acknowledged leaders and ministers. They seemingly had graduated from discipleship into apostleship.

The significance of strong and wise leadership at the beginning of a movement is invaluable and is not sufficiently recognized, especially by the American mind. Americans are constitution minded. A constitution, however, is no substitute for personal leadership. God uses individuals. Setting a clear goal, persistently pursuing the goal, and providing an energetic and inspiring example are the invaluable elements of leadership necessary in laying the foundation of a work. The early church had no New Testament to give directives. Leadership, therefore, was bound up in those persons whom Christ had chosen and trained. Unique authority was vested in them to lay the foundation of the church. They were not the foundation—that is in Christ Jesus (1 Cor. 3:11). They were foundation layers (1 Cor. 3:10–11; 2 Cor. 10:8; 13:10; Eph. 2:20).

From the beginning, therefore, leadership was purely functional. Nothing is said of structure until Acts 6. The church functioned as an organism rather than as an organization. This manner of functioning under a God-ordained leadership was natural and necessary to develop responsible, mature members of the community. Later, local congregations modified and elaborated the system of organization. But even then structure remained subordinate to the function of the church—to its order, purpose, and relationships. No permanent pattern can be established conclusively and defended exegetically. A fuller exposition of structure follows in chapter 10.

A CHURCH MUST BE MOLDED INTO A UNIFIED, FUNCTIONING COMMUNITY

The church was a brotherhood in operation, a new and model society, a new community in progress. It was a community of *unity* functioning in harmony and with one accord, being of one mind, one soul, one heart (1:14; 2:46; 4:24, 32; 5:12; 15:25). It was a community of *liberality,* freely sharing its substance (2:44; 4:32, 34–37). It was a community of *fellowship* in word, prayer, and deed (2:42, 44; 4:24, 32). It was a community of *equality;* a congregation; a body of belivers, of disciples, of brethren (4:32; 6:2–3; 9:19, 26, 30).

Palestinian and Hellenistic Jews and proselytes were living, praying, learning, fellowshiping, worshiping, praising, and celebrating the Lord's Supper in harmonious company. Well-to-do people freely and voluntarily shared their substance with people who had material needs. Members of the priesthood and the most common people were keeping company and forming one community. Soon the church expanded and the Samaritans were acknowledged as fellow believers, eventually joined by Gentile believers. Their homogeneity consisted in their common humanity, common spiritual possession. common need of a Savior, common experience of salvation and the forgiveness of sins, common loyalty to the risen Lord, common instruction in the Word of God, common devotion to the church, and common purpose.

The social and geographical range of converts introduced by Luke in the Book of Acts is most impressive. A partial listing includes such personalities as Barnabas, a wealthy Levite from Cyprus (4:36–37); Stephen, a Hellenist, a man of learning and comprehensive knowledge (6:5, 8–10; 7:1–53); the Ethiopian eunuch of great authority (8:27); Saul, a prominent Pharisee and scholar (9:1ff.); Cornelius, a Roman centurion of Caesarea (10:1–48); Simeon, Lucius, Manaen, the latter of royal descent, from Antioch (13:1), Sergius Paulus, a Roman proconsul of Paphos (13:6–12); Lydia, seller of purple, of Thyatira (16:14–15); a jailer of Philippi (16:27–34); chief women of Thessalonica (17:4); Dionysius, the Areopagite, of Athens (17:34); Aquila and Priscilla of Pontus (18:2); Crispus, the chief ruler of the synagogue in Corinth (18:8); Apollos, an Alexandrian Jew of stature and ability (18:24–28); Publius, leading man of Malta (28:7–10); Stephanas of Corinth (1 Cor. 1:16); Luke, a Greek physician (Col. 4:14); and Philemon of Colossae (Philem. 1–2). This impressive list of personalities in early Christianity is the more astounding in light of the fact that the original band, the apostles, belonged to the common people of the despised Galileans.

What can be learned from such a list? First, the gospel as the power of God unto salvation, if proclaimed in purity, simplicity, and the power of the Holy Spirit, can reach up the social scale as well as down. The gospel is not limited to the social level of the proclaimer. It operates according to the origin, content, and intent of the message rather than according to the social position of the bearer of the message. The gospel, when fully preached, cuts vertically through society. It must not be limited to the flow of horizontal and pyramidal relationships of natural society. The Book of Acts shows that it finds prepared and responsive hearts in all strata of society. Such heterogeneity in the Christian community is especially important at the beginning of planting the church in a country or larger community, in order to prevent the impression that Christianity is a religion for one social class and for a few selected individuals.

Second, the gospel liberates. On one hand it liberates the person from former moral, social, and religious bondages. On the other hand it binds and relates the liberated person to a new Savior and God and to a new society, community, and family.

Christian liberation, however, must not be confused with social separation or isolation, dislocating and dissociating individuals from their groups, communities, or societies. Christian liberation is primarily an experience and process that frees the mind and innermost being of the personality. It is spiritual, psychological, philosophical, and religious, as well as social. Individuals are freed from the dominance of corporate society, though not necessarily from their relationships in society. True spiritual liberation transcends physical and social isolation. The Christians of Jerusalem did not physically separate themselves from Judaism and form their own colony. They remained in the city and filled Jerusalem with their doctrine until the number of the disciples was very great (5:28; 6:7). They were liberated but not isolated.

By the indwelling Holy Spirit the individual is inwardly liberated to become a whole and autonomous being—socially, morally, religiously. Truly liberated people are able to make their own decisions, develop a personal sense of responsibility, enjoy their own spiritual privileges in Christ Jesus, and permit the Holy Spirit to develop within them the fruit of the Spirit. Only when individuals experience the meaning of Romans chapter 8 will they be liberated from the social and religious evils of the community. Only then can they grow in grace and in the knowledge of the Lord Jesus. Only then will they be able to become followers of the Lord within the community and be witnesses among their own people.

Third, the gospel creates equality and unity among the membership of the new community. They have been purchased, cleansed, and bound together by the blood of Jesus Christ (Eph. 2:11–22). In Christ individuals are made new (Eph. 2:21–22), they are made one (Eph. 2:11–18), they are made equal (Eph. 2:19–20), they are made holy (Eph. 2:21–22). They are all members of the same household. In the words of Paul: "There is one body and one Spirit . . . one hope . . . one Lord, one faith, one baptism, one God and Father of all . . ." (Eph. 4:4–6). The New Testament emphatically insists on the unity and equality of all believers in Christ.

In order to establish the unity and equality of believers of different social, national, and religious backgrounds, the Holy Spirit manifested Himself in the same manner on several occasions. At Pentecost the phenomena—the sound from heaven like a rushing mighty wind, cloven tongues as of fire, speaking in other tongues (2:2–4) —verified the presence of the Holy Spirit. As the giving of the law had been substantiated by signs and wonders (Exod. 19:16–19), so the coming of the new Lawgiver was accompanied by signs and wonders. But the Feast of Pentecost was attended only by Jews and proselytes. What about Gentiles? Could they be admitted to the church of Jesus Christ without becoming Jewish proselytes first? What would be their position and status in the church? The principle of equality and unity had to be established by the presence of the same signs and wonders, the same phenomena. This happened first in Samaria and somewhat later in Caesarea in the house of Cornelius. It is in the light of the principle of equality that these instances must be interpreted.

Only such evidences could have persuaded the Jews to hold their peace, to glorify God, and to acknowledge that God had also granted repentance and life to non-Jewish people (see Peter's report, Acts 11:15–17). Nothing short of the repetition of these phenomena could have moved the Jewish Christians to extend the hand of fellowship to the non-Jewish believers. Even such evidences were not sufficient to convince all of them. A certain partyism continued to keep some of them in bondage (Gal. 2:11–14). The Judaizers continually harassed Paul, and against their error the Epistle to the Galatians is directed. Because of this problem the Jerusalem conference was convened (Acts 15:1–29). Religious prejudices based on experienced privileges are difficult to overcome and even more difficult to eradicate.

One other rift in the church of Jesus Christ had to be bridged— the gulf between the Petrine churches and Pauline churches. Since, Paul insisted, the signs and wonders of an apostle had accompanied his ministry and he was not inferior to the most eminent apostles (2 Cor. 12:11–12), his churches should have equal status with the churches of the other apostles. The external evidence for their equality is again found in the phenomena of the Holy Spirit. At the church in Ephesus the same phenomena were experienced when Paul laid his hands on the people as had been evidenced in the experience of Peter (Acts 19:1–7; 8:17). Also in Corinth the Spirit had manifested Himself through the ministry of Paul in signs, wonders, and miracles (2 Cor. 12:12).

Thus the principle of equality and unity was divinely established by the manifestation of the Holy Spirit alike to Jews, Samaritans, and Gentiles and to the churches of all the apostles. God wills His church to be one and its members equal in Christ Jesus. The church, therefore, must ever strive toward this ideal even though it dwells in the midst of imperfect humanity, and social and cultural cleavages and tensions. This indeed is wrestling with flesh and blood.

That such melting and molding together into the *biblical ideal* did not come about without struggles and tensions in not hidden from the reader of Acts (Acts 6:1; 10:9–18; 15:1–29). Serious debates and even dissensions occurred (Gal. 2:11–14). For the most part, however, the Holy Spirit prevailed, the Christ-ideal triumphed, and a model community of spiritual unity was created. The following diagram shows the characteristics of this united community.

**Characteristics
of the
Apostolic Church**

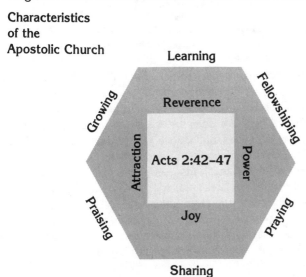

Diagram 12

Does the biblical ideal of unity demand that the church be cast into *one* mold or assembled in *one* flock in order to be the *one* church of Jesus Christ and to demonstrate Christian *unity* in the body of Christ? Such a conclusion would not be a realistic reading of the Scriptures. Spiritual unity does not necessarily demand social and cultural fusion nor does it disannul or dissolve all linguistic, social, cultural, and psychological differences. These are realities of life that the Lord has permitted to arise in the course of history and that the Holy Spirit seems to respect in His operations.

While spiritual unity does not necessarily do away with social and cultural heterogeneity, the gospel of Jesus Christ most certainly judges and instructs us to do away with prejudices, enmity, pride, and exclusiveness. It breaks down the wall of separation due to birth, position, profession, wealth, religious background, race, or national- ity. These attitudes poison and disrupt Christian fellowship, appre- ciation, and brotherliness in the family of God. Christian love gladly acknowledges all believers in Christ as members of the household of God and the body of Christ—all equal in Christ; all united in the Spirit; all one in calling, purpose, position, and destiny; all worthy of equal care, honor, respect, and dignity. This is depth-unity in Christ and through the Holy Spirit.

However, for practical reasons, social, cultural, and psychological distinctions may well be recognized and respected *on a voluntary basis.* As in the natural realm "birds of a feather flock together," so in the human family. There is a social mutuality that, though not nec- essarily Spirit-created, does not violate the bond of the Spirit or grieve the Spirit. Therefore, people of like psychologies, social strata, cultural milieu, racial backgrounds, occupational level, and even more, ethnic and national heritages, will more readily gravitate to- gether, will understand each other better, and will fellowship more easily. The natural bonds of mutuality, sanctified by the Holy Spirit, will link them together in a most intimate and natural way; and a "people-feeling," much like a family-feeling, will bind them into a functional unit for fellowship and service.

This natural drift should not be discouraged. It is not necessarily evil or sub-ideal, though it may easily become so when exclusivism and pride motivate people to design and promote such separation. The Bible does not seem to encourage such separation, nor to judge or forbid it. In fact, it may be argued that at least a temporary accommodation was accepted and practiced by the apostles. Possibly the two-level meetings—in the temple and from house to house—did serve this purpose, at least partially and temporarily. Perhaps the main instruction and the great, general celebrations took place in the temple where all believers joined together, while in the homes the more intimate fellowship was fostered. Possibly the more socially related met for edification, sharing, and evangelism in the houses where they felt most at home. That such may degenerate in partyism and separatism is evident in the church at Corinth (1 Cor. 11:17–22).

To mold a church into a unified functioning community is no easy matter. It is however, our Lord's ideal and must remain the ideal and striving of the church.

A Church Must Train Its Members in the School of Discipleship

The first five chapters of Acts show that the apostles followed the method of their Master in making disciples—instruction, observation, participation, and eventually delegation in actual ministries. In the beginning instruction dominated the ministry. The word *teach* is emphatic in the first chapters (Acts 4:2, 18; 5:21, 25, 28, 42). The early church recognized the value of teaching and indoctrination (Acts 2:42). apostles believed in the impact and molding force of the Word of God and therefore followed the instruction of their Master in "teaching them to observe all things" (Matt. 28:20, KJV).

The apostles found it necessary, however, to adapt the training to a larger and growing group. So in the making of disciples several significant *changes* are introduced.

1. *A first change is the new order.* The church as the new community of God becomes the divine institution for training in discipleship. It may well be stated that it was *in the church, by the church,* and *for the church* that such training took place. It was recognized that true spiritual training for maximum growth and usefulness must take place in the fellowship of the saints so that both their vertical relationship to God and their horizontal relationships to each other may develop simultaneously in healthy and wholesome balance.

151

2. *A second change appears in methodology.* Training in discipleship takes place on two levels. It is recorded that the believers met daily *in the temple* to hear the apostles rehearse the life, words, and works of Christ; the Gospels are the evidence for this and Luke speaks clearly about it in Luke 1:1–2 (cf. Heb. 2:3–4). Further they heard the apostles expound the great truths of God's Word as given in the Old Testament (Acts 3:22–26). In addition to meeting in the temple, they met in small *house groups* for more detailed instruction, fellowship, sharing of needs, and evangelism (Acts 2:46; 5:42; 20:20). Both levels are essential to true growth in grace and in the knowledge of Jesus Christ. Both methods were approved by the Spirit and were richly blessed in the early church. They have continued to be used throughout the history of the church.

3. *A third change is found in the new nomenclature indicative of a new relationship.* The term *disciple* is still used but it is waning in usage. Whereas in the Gospels it is found 238 times, Luke employs it only 30 times in Acts. It is never used by the apostles, nor is it found in the Epistles. Several words seem to take the place of disciple. The Christians are known as *believers,* indicative of their personal faith relationship to Jesus as Savior and Messiah; *brethren,* suggestive of their equality and fraternity as members of the same family; *followers,* expressive of their walking in the way and footsteps of Jesus Christ and descriptive of their life style with Jesus Christ as their example; *saints,* connotative of their position of separation and unreserved commitment and devotion to Jesus Christ as Lord and Master.

The absence of the word *disciple* in the Epistles does not imply that the disciples lowered the standards of the Christian life or the ideals of church membership. The content of Christian discipleship is fully preserved throughout the New Testament. Peter reminds his suffering readers that "you have been called for this purpose, since Christ also suffered for you, leaving you an example for you to walk in His steps" (1 Peter 2:21). John speaks of believers walking in the same manner as Christ walked (1 John 2:6). That is true discipleship, reminiscent of Christ's call, "Follow me." Paul writes of being imitators of Christ (1 Cor. 11:1; 1 Thess. 1:6), of having the mind of Christ (Phil. 2:5), of being transformed into the image of Christ (2 Cor. 3:18), of Christ being in us and living in us (Rom. 8:10; Gal. 2:20; Eph. 3:17; Col. 1:27), of Christ being formed in us (Gal. 4:19), of the Holy Spirit dwelling within us (Rom. 8:9, 11; 1 Cor. 3:16; 6:19; 12:12–13; Gal. 3:2; Eph. 5:18), and he exhorts the Christians to live, walk, and pray in the Holy Spirit (Gal. 5:16, 25; Eph. 6:18; Jude 20). Certainly such expressions are realistic synonyms for Christian discipleship.

4. *A fourth change is a new relationship.* Not one of the apostles ever speaks of "my disciples." No man aside from Christ discipled men more effectively than Paul did, yet the word *disciple* never comes from his lips or pen, though editorially Luke once mentions "his disciples" in relation to Saul in his escape from Damascus (Acts 9:25). Paul considered them his brethren, co-laborers, fellow-workers, fellow-soldiers, fellow-sufferers, but never disciples.

There are two probable reasons for the discontinuance of the designation and the change in vocabulary. The term *disciple* was discontinued because of its very general and shallow meaning in the non-Jewish world. It is a common Greek word and means no more than a learner, a pupil, an observer, an underling of a philosopher. This concept is a far cry from the ideal set forth by the Master in the Gospels. The second reason could be that discipleship as defined by Jesus Christ is supremely a relationship-bond. It is a loyalty-attachment and love-commitment to the Person of Jesus Christ first and foremost, rather than a mere adherence to His ideas, ideals, and precepts. Therefore the greatest command is, "You shall love . . ." and Christ's piercing and restoring question to Peter is "Do you love me?" (John 21:15–17). No New Testament discipleship truly expresses Christ's full concept without this depth-relationship to Jesus Christ. Many have fallen in love with the ideals of Christ and upheld His principles and precepts without becoming really attached to Him by faith. Consequently, they have never entered His school of discipleship and committed themselves to Him.

Every relationship, method, or designation that could possibly hinder the development of this depth-relationship between the individual and Jesus Christ must be studiously avoided. It is here that a serious danger in the one-to-one discipleship training programs is lurking. An unwholesome attachment and dependence is easily formed between disciple and discipler. Small group ministries and church ministries must serve as a balance. God knew what He was doing when He graciously brought the church into being and made it an institution for the perfecting of the saints (Eph. 4:11–16; 2 Tim. 2:2, note the plural). The church is God's school of discipleship training.

The apostles, then, followed the model provided by their Master for training disciples but adapted it to the new situation after Pentecost. The *content* of discipleship training was also important. It was doctrinal (apostles' teaching), edificatory (fellowship with breaking of bread and prayer), and practical (house-to-house gatherings for evangelism, teaching, sharing, observing, praying, 2:42; 5:42).

There were things that were "most surely believed" among the believers and Luke spells them out in his Gospel. The "things" were made sure by "many convincing proofs" (Luke 1:1; Acts 1:3). The author to the Hebrews fully agrees when he writes: "How shall we escape if we neglect so great a salvation? After it was at the first spoken through the Lord, it *was confirmed* (made sure) to us by those who heard, *God also bearing witness* with them both by signs and wonders and by various miracles and by gifts of the Holy Spirit according to His own will" (Heb. 2:3–4).

We have observed already that the faith of the early church had solid theological content. The early Christians came from Judaism and therefore had an Old Testament revelational background. Divine salvation and Messiahship were familiar doctrines. However, they needed a complete reorientation in the mission and ministry of the Messiah, and a life in the Spirit rather than in the law. Thus the apostles stressed not only the life, words, works, and work of Jesus Christ, but also a reinterpretation of the Old Testament. Much of the Old Testament had been fulfilled in Christ and thus was obsolete (Heb. 8:13). Other parts of the Old Testament had been transmuted in Christ (Matt. 5–7; Gal. 3:6–22). Yet other parts still await their fulfillment in the return of Christ (Acts 3:19–26).

The early discipleship training program included the following concepts:

- To be rooted and grounded in Christ; to know the facts, nature, and experience and assurance of salvation—the objective and subjective aspects of the salvation of God.
- To discover a proper perspective of biblical revelation; to know how to study the Scriptures, have a wholesome appreciation for the Word, obey it, and pass its message on to others.
- To know and experience life in the Spirit of the Lord and to walk and serve in His enabling.
- To know true fellowship in the community of the saints and to joyfully, liberally, and generously share in the needs and burdens of others.
- To learn under the Lordship of Christ the true meaning and blessing of prayer, witnessing, evangelizing, and servanthood.

The anticipated results of such training are expressed by the apostles in Acts 6:3. The believers were to become people of honest report, full of the Holy Spirit, and willing and able to accept ministries and discharge them in a responsible and efficient manner. That not all would reach that level simultaneously is implied in the charge that the church is to "select from among you" seven men with such qualifications. The quality of the training is demonstrated by Stephen, the staunch defender of the faith and noble martyr for the Lord (6:8–7:60); Philip, the effective evangelist (8:5–40); Barnabas, the wise churchman (11:22–26); and a multitude of willing and effective witnesses and evangelists (8:1, 4; 9:31; 11:19–21).

Disciples cannot be manufactured in a hurry and in mass. It takes time, work, and wisdom. Discipleship is more than skill, zeal, and knowledge; it is a level of spiritual maturity. To this end the church must labor, pray, and in faith anticipate, for it is God's ordained institution to accomplish this end.

A Church Must Proclaim a Clearly Defined and Relevant Message of Divine Revelation

The message is rooted in a historical person, in facts, and in events. We note Peter quoting freely from the Old Testament. So does Stephen, and so does Paul, especially in his messages in the synagogues. It was a Word-oriented message, a message of Good News, a message of hope, and a message of repentance and conversion. (See ch. 6.)

A Church Must Continue in Prayer

Acts 1:14 reads: "These all with one mind were continually devoting themselves to prayer." This centrality of prayer continues throughout Acts and into the Epistles (particularly Paul's). Continual prayer was one of the marks of the early church. Habitually the church was laying hold of God and pressed on in prayer to exploits and victory. Prayer was more than a recital of formulas or a practice of rituals. It was the expression of a kinship relationship, dependence, anticipation, confidence, and assurance, not only in the existence of God, but in His ability to change the course of history and to direct the ways of people. Prayer was also a method of operation to accomplish things that could be accomplished in no other way (12:1–14; 16:22–28). Prayer is a work with and for God and a means to bring about God's work, as well as communion with God, praise and adoration and intercession. We read in Acts of numerous prayer meetings and the believers *continued* steadfastly in prayer (2:42, KJV).

Prevailing prayer must be learned in the school of the Holy Spirit and in fellowship with saints. Therefore, the apostles included prayer as one of the essential and primary lessons of the life of the early church (2:42). The apostles themselves had learned from the Master how to pray. In fact, their only specific request to the Lord in reference to prayer had been, "Teach us to pray" (Luke 11:1). It was not the technique and method of prayer they had desired for themselves, but the *reality* of prayer. They had heard and observed Him and noted something different in His prayer from what they found in the synagogue and in the religious leadership. The Lord withdrew from public ministries for times of prayer (Matt. 14:23; Mark 1:35; Luke 5:16; 9:18; 11:1), and often was out all night in prayer (Luke 6:12). Repeatedly He breathed brief prayers in public before performing deeds of mercy and power (John 6:11; 11:41–42). He prayed in times of crisis as they witnessed in the Garden of Gethsemane and at the cross. His prayer life kindled a yearning in their hearts and lifted them into the presence of the Father. There was intimacy, directness, liberty, and a mysterious reality in His prayer that was new to them. Therefore the request: Teach us to pray! Something had been transmitted to and implanted in them during their own days of training in *discipleship* that they now sought to transmit to and inculcate in the lives of those whom they were making into disciples. Therefore they *continued* steadfastly in prayer.

There are at least eighteen examples in the Book of Acts of God's marvelous answers to their continual prayer. They include the following:

- Prayer gave the apostles unusual boldness in witnessing (3:1; 4:23–33).
- Prayer gave the Christians strength to joyfully suffer and die for the cause of their Lord (7:59–60).
- Prayer led people to be filled with the Spirit of God (8:15–17).
- Prayer brought life to the dead and wrought great miracles (9:36–41).
- Prayer defeated Satan's evil and destructive plans (12:1–17).
- Prayer released the first missionaries for world evangelism (13:1–4).
- Prayer shook the gates of the prison open and led to conversions (16:25–34).
- Prayer gave direction to people in delicate decisions (1:14, 24).

Thus we know something of the prayer life of the early church and find it illustrated in Acts.

The apostles encouraged prayer not only by spoken precept and example as they had learned from the Lord, but also in written letters. James begins his practical exhortations with an encouragement to the believers to "ask God" if they lack wisdom for all the practical demands on their lives. He also assures them that the Lord will hear them if they ask in faith, without any doubting (James 1:5–6). James concludes his epistle with a most fitting illustration and strong admonition to prayer (5:13–18).

In his first epistle Peter has two pertinent injunctions about prayer that need renewed emphasis today (1 Peter 3:7; 4:7). John encourages his readers to ask in boldness and confidence and assures them that God does honor the requests made to Him if asked according to His will (1 John 5:14–16). Jude concludes his brief discourse with the familiar benediction: "Now to Him who is able to keep you from stumbling, and to make you stand in the presence of His glory blameless with great joy, to the only God our Savior, through Jesus Christ our Lord, be glory, majesty, dominion and authority, before all time and now and forever. Amen" (Jude 24–25).

Paul provides the most noble example next to Christ. His prayers for the churches are comprehensive and detailed, full of faith and anticipation. Paul offered definite petitions and intercessions for the spiritual growth of the younger churches: for charity (1 Thess. 3:12), for love and steadfastness (2 Thess. 3:5), for completeness (2 Cor. 13:7–9), for unity (Rom. 15:5–6), for hope (Rom. 15:13), for full assurance of knowledge (Col. 2:1–3), for knowledge of God's will (Col. 1:9–12), for the glory yet to come (Eph. 1:15–21), for the indwelling of the Triune God (Eph. 3:14–21), for continued growth and fruitfulness to the very end (Phil. 1:9–11).[1] Paul's epistles also give several extensive outlines of his prayers for the churches (Rom. 1:8–10; 1 Cor. 1:4–9; Eph. 1:15–23; 3:14–21; Phil. 1:9–11; Col. 1:9–12). Paul's doxologies are refreshing, exalting, and instructive (Rom. 11:33–36; 16:25–27; 2 Cor. 13:14). Paul also exhorts others to pray and requests prayer for himself (Rom. 15:30; Eph. 6:19; Phil. 1:19; Col. 4:3; 1 Thess. 5:25). Paul truly believed in the reality, power, and practice of prayer.

Prayer, then, was a serious and continuous engagement for the early church. It was a practice of laying hold of God, of claiming His promises, of coming to Him as a Father who gladly meets the needs of His children, of standing in the presence of God as true mediators and intercessors, of waiting before Him to act as the Lord of all history. However, the practice of prayer did not come naturally. It had to be inculcated and cultivated. As the early church permitted itself to be led into a life of prayer, the believers experienced marvelous answers to prayer. God did not fail His people. Prayer does accomplish things because it is one of God's main methods of accomplishing His blessed purpose.

A CHURCH MUST LIVE IN THE REALM OF MIRACLES

Miracles were not lacking in the experience of the early church. God was manifesting Himself in a miraculous manner to validate the message that was being proclaimed (Heb. 2:3–4). In a world of pagan philosophies and legalistic religion, miracles were needed to authenticate the new message of God's presence in the gospel of Jesus Christ. Miracles had brought about Israel's redemption out of Egypt, and supernatural manifestations had accompanied the giving of Israel's law, constitution, and institutions. So the Jew held tenaciously to them as sacred and enduring. At the same time, the Jews were so mindful of the judgment of God on them—sending them into captivity for not being faithful in their religious observances and moral and social commitment—that only equally great evidence could establish the divineness of a new order that deviated from the Mosaic order and institutions. Divine authentication of the message was an absolute necessity to turn the Jew from the shadow of typology, promise, and anticipation to the reality that was presented in the gospel of Jesus Christ. How else could the Jews be sure? The circumstances demanded miracles, signs, and wonders (Acts 4:13–16; 5:12–16; 5:33–39; Heb. 2:3–4).

In our day a debate rages around the subject of supernatural phenomena because of the renewed emphasis in the charismatic movement. Without entering into the debate at any length, it seems to me fair to say that the Bible nowhere closes the age of miracles. Therefore to do so dogmatically is to go beyond the Bible. But neither does the Bible promise their continuation nor does the Word encourage one to seek the gift of miracles or expect them to occur. It seems vain to me to argue one way or the other when God has chosen to keep silent. We do well not to circumscribe the sovereign and supernatural operations of God on the one hand, nor to demand their manifestation on the other hand. Simply because our wisdom and expectations deem physical and material miracles necessary does not mean that they must occur. No Bible-believing person doubts that God *can* perform miracles when He deems it wise and necessary; therefore they *may* occur. On the other hand, because God *can* perform miracles does *not* mean that He *must* and *will* perform them.

Citing John 14:12—"He who believes in Me, the works that I do shall he do also; and greater works than these shall he do; because I go to the Father"—as proof of present-day occurrences of miracles exhibits serious superficiality of Bible exposition. But to insist that this passage applies *only* to greater *spiritual* accomplishments of the apostles after the coming of the Holy Spirit seems to betray an unjustifiable narrowness in exegesis. It is a simple fact that miracles have occurred and continue to occur. God is not bound by any of our interpretations.

It is a serious error, however, to make physical and material miracles of continuing major significance to Christianity and the gospel of Jesus Christ. The major issue is the presence and reality of the Lord in the life and ministry of the church. This truth is implied in the words of Christ when He says: "The kingdom of God is not coming with signs to be observed; nor will they say 'Look here it is!' or 'There it is!' For behold, the kingdom of God is in your midst," or "within you!" (Luke 17:20–21). Paul too is quite emphatic when he writes: "For the kingdom of God is not eating and drinking, but righteousness and peace and joy in the Holy Spirit" (Rom. 14:17). The true concern is not the display of strange phenomena, but rather the reality of the presence of God in our lives and ministry. How deep is our consciousness of God? How sensitive are we to the needs of fellow Christians? How sacrificial is our giving for missions? How do our hearts burn for evangelism? How generously do we meet the demands of the destitute and downtrodden? These are the true tests of the reality and presence of the Lord in His congregation. The deepest miracle and the one most keenly and quickly sensed by the world is the miracle of the changed person. That is a miracle difficult to resist and impossible to disprove. The church should covet miracles of transformed lives more than anything else in this world. Attractive, sanctified personalities are contagious and arresting.

God is able to do the impossible and to save not only to the uttermost but also from the uttermost. The challenge of William Carey is still with us: "Attempt great things for God and expect great things from God." The church today suffers seriously from a heart disease which may be called "littleness" and therefore expects but little from God. God specializes in the impossible and leaves the possible to man.

A CHURCH MUST JOYFULLY SUFFER AND SACRIFICE FOR ITS LORD AND THE GOSPEL MESSAGE

Suffering and martyrdom could not silence the overflowing hearts. Their reply to threats was: "We cannot stop speaking what we have seen and heard" (Acts 4:20). "So they went on their way . . . rejoicing that they had been considered worthy to suffer shame for His name" (5:41).

Suffering and martyrdom are not always tragedies. While they are not coveted or sought, they do seem to be a part of the plan and program of God. There are many instances of suffering recorded in the New Testament, and the church has continued to suffer throughout history. Even in our enlightened century more people are suffering for the name of Christ than at any other time. It is not surprising that Asian brothers are speaking of the need for "A Theology of Suffering."[2] Suffering has always been an accompaniment of the gospel of Jesus Christ. The Lord must have a particular purpose in permitting His church to endure so much suffering from others.

It should also be pointed out that sufferings are a method of divine operations. It was the suffering and persecuted church in Acts that scattered abroad and evangelized and churches multiplied. This has remained so. It is peculiar how in times of suffering and persecution the church has grown. It is so today. Behold the church of Russia and China.

Suffering is a way of sacrificing. But sacrificing may be the dedicating of our bodies as a living sacrifice (Rom. 12:1). When actual physical sufferings are not taking place, should not the Christian life be characterized by the liberality and sacrifice of substance to the cause and honor of the Lord and the well-being of humanity? Such sacrifice could become a worthy substitute for physical sacrifice and a genuine demonstration of Christian devotion to the Lord and love for the people. God so loved that He *gave* His Son. Christ so loved that He *gave* His life. The apostles and the early church so loved that they *gave* their lives as living sacrifices in life and in death. Both physical suffering and sacrificial giving are overwhelming demonstrations of the all-sufficiency of the grace of God and the overmastering power of the Holy Spirit. They are divine qualities. At the same time our readiness to suffer and sacrifice demonstrates our value system. Our Lord tells us that where our treasure is there our heart will be. Perhaps it is not unfair to say that where our treasure is there our money and life will go and the degree of our readiness to suffer and to sacrifice for the gospel is a measure of the value we place on the gospel.

These were some of the qualities of the early apostolic church as illustrated on the pages of the Book of Acts. Of course, it is easy to idealize. The point is not that the church was perfect. But the record in Acts gives the impression that the people were willing to be made perfect, to move steadily toward the goal of perfection. It was not a static community, one that defended the status quo or rationalized its position. It was a society in the making, a community being molded, a people moving toward a divine ideal—to become what God wanted it to be. The words of Paul can be aptly applied to the early apostolic church: "Not that I have already obtained it, or have already become perfect, but I press on in order that I may lay hold of that for which also I was laid hold of by Christ Jesus" (Phil. 3:12). Divine fitness seems to have been the deepest ambition of the early church. Under fundamental building principles I indicate how such a church can be produced (chapter 11A).

10

Pillar Two—
The Form of the Church

The metaphor of the church as a healthy plant that *grows* implies an inner urge and dynamic. The figure of the church as a building of God that is being *built* suggests progressive, planned, external operations. These inner and outer forces combine to cause the church of Jesus Christ to expand. To be a quality community does not assure the growth of the church, however. There is an outer factor that is also very important (under some circumstances, perhaps equally important). This is the factor of a relevant structure, or organization. The *form* of the church is *pillar two* of church growth.

Quality and structure must be kept in a healthy relationship and in balance. Neglecting one or the other will prove paralyzing to the church. Chapter 9 spoke about the quality aspect. In this chapter we turn to the structure of the church and its relationship to church growth. I will be using the terms *form, structure, order,* and *organization* interchangeably.

In his book *Followers of the New Faith* Emilio Willems makes the following observation after considerable and careful research in Brazil and Chile:

> A comparative study of the three major churches in Brazil and Chile suggests that their attractiveness in terms of membership is, to a considerable extent, a function of their structure. Apparently preference is given to the egalitarian denominations in which the layman is in control of the church affairs and the individual congregation enjoys complete autonomy. On the whole, Protestantization may be regarded as a selective process in which functional adaptability to the needs and aspiration of the people is rewarded with the highest membership figures and the most proselytic drive.[1]

Such a statement deserves scrutiny. It raises the serious question: "Is church growth actually related to structure and organization?"

The New Testament says relatively little about structure or organization of the church. It seems to be preoccupied with quality-quantity and with function. This could be interpreted to imply the relative importance of these various factors. However, this is not necessarily so. *It could also point to the fact that structure and organization are a natural part of life.* It is evident that no society can live without some measure and kind of order and structure. No group of humans has thus far been found that did not have some kind of order, chain of authority, and role governing it. As society unfolds and enlarges, more and more structure is required and our sophisticated society has wrapped itself up in form until it almost resembles a mummy. Today we speak of *organization man.* We wrestle to free ourselves from the captivity of organization that we have cast about ourselves.

Such overburdening with structure, however, does not eliminate the need for form and order. Man is an organized and organization being and will remain so as long as he is a societal or normal human being. Some form of structure is natural to human life.

THE BIBLE AND STRUCTURE

The Bible is not averse to organization. Structure and organization is inherent in creation and the universe in which we live. The record of the six days of creation shows order, symmetry, harmony, and beauty. Day follows day in logical sequence. The God of order spoke and the creation came forth in order and beauty.

Order is found not only in creation, it is also evident in the life of the Old Testament people of God. The Lord ordered the life and work of humans when He gave them six days to do their business and one day to rest. He organized the religious life of Israel around the tabernacle (place), the holy days (times), and sacrifices (institutions and practices).

Moses organized the Israelites for the journey through the wilderness, and Joshua did likewise for their march into Canaan (Num. 1–4; Josh. 3:1–4:13). David structured the people for worship and brought order and beauty into their worship (1 Chron. 25). Nehemiah organized all manpower to rebuild the walls of Jerusalem (Neh. 3). Our Lord organized the multitudes of five thousand and four thousand before He fed them in groups of fifties and hundreds.

The church, too, is an ordered and organized institution. That it has form and order is evident from the fact that the New Testament repeatedly speaks of the office of overseer (bishop or *episcopos;* Acts 20:28; Phil. 1:1; 1 Tim. 3:2; Titus 1:7; in 1 Peter 2:25 the same word is applied to Christ). There are elders (*presbyters*). This word occurs sixty-six times in the New Testament and is applied to Jewish leaders as well as to leaders in the Christian churches. It is used by all New Testament writers except Jude (some of these references are: Acts 11:30; 14:23; 15:2, 4, 6, 22–23; 16:4; 20:17; 21:18; 1 Tim. 5:1, 2, 17, 19; Titus 1:5). The New Testament tells us that God appointed first apostles, prophets, and teachers in the church, and then the various other functionaries and supportive ministries (1 Cor. 12:28). The New Testament bids the church to obey, submit to, acknowledge, and respect those over them (1 Cor. 16:16; 1 Thess. 5:12–13; Heb. 13:17). The overseers are responsible to lead and spiritually feed (shepherd) the church of God (Acts 20:28) and to take heed to the ministry that they have received from the Lord (Col. 4:17). Both Paul, in the Pastoral Epistles, and Peter outline the qualifications and responsibilities of the overseers and deacons (1 Tim. 3:1–13; Titus 1:5–9; 1 Peter 5:1–4).

The church in the New Testament had structure and order as well as quality. Even the symbols employed to portray the church imply structure: the body of Christ, a royal priesthood, a holy nation, a household, a building, a spiritual house, a temple of God. There is no organism that is not organized. Structure is a New Testament principle without which no New Testament church exists. The New Testament, according to my understanding, does not give evidence for an unorganized church that exists merely as a fellowship.

The principle of structure for efficient and effective functioning of the Christian church begins to emerge in Acts 6:1–7 when the necessity for organization surfaces. A division of labor is necessary in the quality community. There are several stages in the movement toward structure in the Christian church—from being (1) strictly person-centered (the apostles), to being (2) structure-centered (James is the leader), to becoming (3) a pyramidal system (James, the elders, the deacons, the congregation). The multi-level structure replaces the person-centered operation. By Acts 6:1–7 the church has reached the second stage. The apostles have molded and shaped the believers into an initial qualitative community capable of functioning responsibly. Now structure is needed to undergird it and give it form, order, and stability. The organism is forming its own organization; the church is becoming an institution. The structure provides for a division and apportioning of labor and assigning of responsibilities (see diagram 13).

Problems and Tensions

The present-day reaction to organization and structure is not derived from or motivated by the Scriptures. It is a reaction, rather, to over-organizing and over-institutionalizing the church. It is the natural reaction of an organism to a mechanism that does not fit it, to a machinery that stifles the natural functions and legitimate expression of the organism. The organism will also react, however, to the absence of structure and form. Fellowship, as it is often advocated and practiced, is no substitute for organization; and sooner or later the organism will suffer seriously, cease to function dynamically, or progressively disintegrate. There may be some tension be-

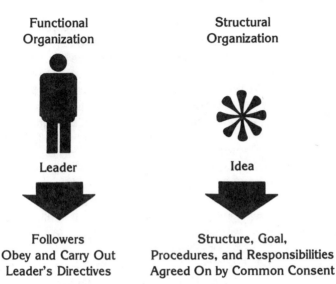

Functional Organization	Structural Organization
Leader	Idea
Followers Obey and Carry Out Leader's Directives	Structure, Goal, Procedures, and Responsibilities Agreed On by Common Consent

Diagram 13

tween functionalism (i.e., organism) and structuralism (i.e., organization), but there is no inherent contradiction. In fact, such tension is wholesome and is indicative that the organism is alive. It is intended to be "creative tension" (Neill). The two belong together. Structure without function is like a corpse. However, an organism of function without structure is like a paraplegic—unable to be coordinated and to move in an orderly manner. In either case, growth or progress is impossible. Thus structure is necessary for the church to function effectively.

While it is true that fellowship is no substitute for organization, it is equally true that much that is called the church today is not really the church of Christ, but is a religious establishment to preserve its own sacred traditions. The traditions are rich in ritualism and symbolism but poor in message; their form leaves the heart empty and dissatisfied. The establishment passes on a snake for a fish and a scorpion for an egg (Luke 11:11–12). It is not surprising that people in multitudes are turning their backs on the religious establishments and are being drawn to functional groups and movements. The church has no one to blame but itself. The world has not weaned away and captured the people as much as the church has driven them away by forsaking the gospel of the Lord of the church. It has robbed its people of the Bread of Life. The complaint of the Lord should be written over the pulpits of many churches: "My people have committed two evils: They have forsaken Me, The fountain of living waters, To hew for themselves cisterns, Broken cisterns, That can hold no water" (Jer. 2:13). Much of Christendom has substituted organized religion for Jesus Christ as the living Lord. It is from this organized religion rather than from Jesus Christ that the people have turned away. Organization never has been and never will be an adequate substitute for organism no matter how beautiful organization may be.

In spite of the dangers of organization, however, it is still true that the church as a divinely created body and institution cannot neglect the New Testament principle of structure, form, and order. This principle cannot be set aside if a group of believers wants to function efficiently and effectively and be the church of Jesus Christ in a specific locale.

HISTORY AND STRUCTURE

Historically, the church has acted as though the imaginative, creative power of God has been either exhausted or arrested in the forms that history and culture, not God, have cast over the church—the episcopalian, presbyterian, congregational, or brethren structures. Has God no other forms, no other structure? He who could populate the earth with hundreds of species of animals and the waters with hundreds of kinds of fish and could beautify the fields with endless kinds of flowers, is He exhausted in these four forms of church structures? In the Melbourne, Australia, botanical gardens the gardener informed us that they had more than 10,000 varieties of trees, shrubs, and plants. God is a God of variety. Perhaps Western Christians will be surprised at the new forms that will eventually emerge in the church of Jesus Christ in the Third World.

The major forms of church structures are a matter of history and culture rather than of revelation and apostolic tradition. They developed in times of serious struggles and stresses in the church, in periods of history when the church was principally on the defensive. Episcopalianism served the church well in the first three centuries in its life-and-death struggles with paganism, Gnosticism, Manichaism, Docetism, and other encroaching enemies and distortions of the gospel. A firm hand and unifying head was demanded even somewhat later in the battles for sound doctrine and the forming of historic creeds. The New Testament books only gradually were disseminated among the churches, then gathered and formed into a canon. In the meantime *men* were needed to guide and protect the churches.

Presbyterianism and congregationalism broke through in the troubled religious waters of the sixteenth and seventeenth centuries. Men of religious convictions and theological insights believed that these new forms were expressions of biblical ideals that had to be recaptured, preserved, and practiced. Episcopalianism had led to the monolithic structure of Rome with a pope dictating not only to the church but to society in all other realms. Neither the Bible nor conscience could be heard in the church. The voice of an earthly church head had replaced the voice of God. Unmodified Anglicanism was not much milder in its hierarchical structure and spirit. Thus the revolt against these systems seemed justified, and presbyterianism and congregationalism came into being. The question may well be raised, however, whether the revolt was really against the systems or against the corrupt men within the systems.

These saints fought their battles valiantly in their generation and at tremendous cost. They were relevant in their own time. The church structured itself according to the demands of the times to preserve itself in bitter struggles, and it practiced certain ideals within a relatively homogeneous culture. The structures have served those purposes quite well. At no time, however, has the church seriously sought to structure itself for an all-out *offensive warfare* against paganism and for the evangelization of its total community and the world. What kind of structure will be demanded to transform and mobilize the church into a dynamic, functioning, evangelizing force in a world of radically different peoples and cultures? This issue needs to be pondered in all earnestness.

THE SERVANT ROLE OF STRUCTURE

Structure or organization can become binding, blinding, blighting. It can ensnare, paralyze, even choke a movement, and become a serious stricture with damaging effects. On the other hand it can be mobilizing, building, ordering, strengthening, channeling, and thus give dynamic, direction, purpose, meaning, and realization to a movement. One of the most serious situations in the structuring of the church is the transplanting of predetermined structures from one movement or culture to another movement or culture, from one people to another people. An equally serious problem is borrowing structures wholesale and permitting them to master rather than serve the organism or movement. When this is permitted to happen, lifelong paralysis or stunting of the natural growth of the organism, the church, results.

The continuous tension between structuralism and functionalism has existed throughout history and is not confined to the Christian movement. Cultural and religious conservatism in the form of traditionalism is a powerful preserver of past patterns and modes and may become a serious stricture to change and advancement. It is a highly resistant power; it is steady and static. It keeps one in captivity to the past and hinders progress, efficiency, and effectiveness. Traditional ways of doing things are easily hallowed by time and made sacred by habit. Structuralism continuously seeks to enthrone itself and dominate functionalism. Some people fear that to let fresh air in may also let fresh demons in. To change may signify disloyalty and irreverence for the ways of the ancients and bring in liberalism and apostasy. Thus structuralism in the form of traditionalism pretends to be the guardian of the sacred and the true.

Functionalism, on the other hand, can be dynamic, as long as it continually enlarges its purpose and improves its efficiency and effectiveness. Inherent in it is the dynamic of expansion. In terms of Christianity it has the world as its focus. It is flexible and adaptable in external matters. It practices prudent accommodation in communication and organization (see diagram 14). Hence as an organism enters *new* cultures and peoples it demands *new* forms, order, and structures in order to remain relevant, indigenous, and psychologically and socially related. In so doing it fulfills its divine purpose and design and only then will the people feel *at home* in the church. As the gospel sets the prisoners free from the guilt and bondage of sin and many of the traditional social and cultural chains of enslavement to walk the ways of God, so the church must be set at liberty to function freely and create its own relevant form and structure. For this purpose religious traditionalism and cultural conservatism in the form of predetermined structures must be guarded against. Otherwise, they easily become the forces to imprison the church and stymie its health and progress.

ACCOMMODATION
THE
RESPECTFUL
PRUDENT
SCIENTIFICALLY
THEOLOGICALLY
SOUND ADJUSTMENT
TO THE
PREVAILING CULTURE
IN
ATTITUDE
APPEARANCE
STRUCTURE
APPROACH
METHOD

Diagram 14

To sum up, then, structure is a New Testament principle and is necessary and important. But it is not all-important. It must take the servant position and play the servant role. What is most important is the nature of an organism or movement that is to fulfill a specific function and accomplish a definite purpose within a given natural environment and cultural milieu and among a people with a unique psychology. To transplant Western-developed church structures and mission organizations to non-Western cultures and people without modifications or transformations, is, therefore, unnatural.

There always will be some degree of tension between function and structure because an organism is an ever-growing and ever-changing entity if it is healthy and strong. Consequently, the structure must be flexible and adaptable, never fixed or restrictive. Functionalism and structuralism are not polarities or enemies, but they must be held in a certain degree of tension with the former always holding the upper hand and being the determining force. This is particularly true for the Christian church, which is the temple of God and in which the Holy Spirit resides and through which He performs many of His functions. Therefore, the form of the church must be granted considerable latitude and freedom, limited only by the precepts and precedents of the Scriptures. History and tradition, no matter how sacred they may seem, must not be decisive. Structuralism must never be allowed to shackle the free operations of the Holy Spirit.

DETERMINANTS OF FORM AND STRUCTURE

The form or organization of a movement is determined by at least five factors: the *nature* of the organism, its *purpose,* its *function,* its *environment* or the immediate milieu in which it is to thrive, and the *psychology* of the people whom it is to serve. Some of these determining factors are absolute and others are relative. The nature of the church is an absolute factor. The immediate purpose and function of the church are relative absolutes. The natural and cultural environment and the psychology of the people are relative factors in determining the structure of the church.

1. *The absolute factor.* The nature of the church never changes.

It is and remains the church of God. It is His by right of creation, redemption, regeneration, adoption, and preservation. Here is an unchanging factor, an absolute. The nature of the church was covered in an earlier chapter.

2. *The relative absolutes.* To designate the purpose and function of the church as relative absolutes may seem unusual, if not paradoxical. Let me explain. The overall purpose and ultimate function of the church are biblically fixed and absolute. As noted before, the church has a three-dimensional function to perform—upward in its relation to God, inward in its relation to itself, and outward in its relation to the world. It has a fixed purpose (Eph. 3:11; cf. Eph. 1:5, 9, 11—purpose is in the singular). Yet within this purpose there are purposes to be achieved (see the outline on the biblical significance of the local church on page 58). The church has function (singular) and functions (plural), purpose (singular) and purposes (plural). While the singular remains steady and absolute because it is ultimate, the plural may be relative because it is immediate. For example, it may be necessary from time to time to shift the configuration of the church by emphasizing a specific function such as worship, adoration, and celebration. At another time the emphasis may be placed on organizing the people for Christian education, edification, fellowship, and discipleship training. Yet on other occasions aggressive home evangelism or community service may be needed.

Each one of these emphases and practices will demand some changes, modifications, and additions in the function, patterning, and configuration of the body in order for it to act appropriately and efficiently. This may involve some changes in organization and structure as it did in Acts 6:1-7. There must be room for flexibility, adaptability, and creativity if the corpus is not to become a corpse. Churches in America have had considerable leeway. This is evident in the several organizations within the local church structure, such as the Sunday school, youth clubs, small group fellowships, home Bible studies, men's meetings, women's meetings. Organization and structure have been adapted to function and purpose where times and circumstances seemed to dictate.

3. *The church and parachurch movements.* Ideally, all Christian

functions should proceed from the church and express the general and integrating purpose of the church. However, various factors have led to the rise of numerous independent and parachurch movements—such factors as rigidity of form or lack of structure; limited vision and hesitation of action by the church coupled with a felt urgency; apparent spiritual needs along with the challenges and opportunities to meet them; and, frankly, impatience and at times a strong impulse to independent action are some of the factors that have called forth independent and parachurch movements. That these organizations are meeting a spiritual and functional need is demonstrated by the strong support they receive from numerous spiritually minded church members. That they are serving a divine purpose is well established by the rich blessings they experience from the hand of the Lord. They are evidence that there were latent functions and purposes in the nature of the church that were called forth by needs and circumstances. However, these functions and purposes could not be expressed in and through the established church either because of lack of adequate structure or because of the rigidity of form. As a result, parachurch groups cut their own channels and pursued their own course because they believed these functions and ministries to be the will and design of the Lord for the people of God.

It behooves a church to watch carefully the signs of the times, to be alert to spiritual needs and opportunities. The church must study the circumstances the sovereign Lord permits to arise and be ready to function as He directs and desires. To do so there must be vision, motivation, readiness, and flexibility. Structure must remain a servant and not hamper demanded functions. Whenever the church does not function as it ought to, God permits other functionaries to arise and do His work. In our times many parachurch movements have arisen as a result of the lack of functions on the part of the churches.

There is, however, another aspect to the presence of parachurch organizations. They may exist for a higher purpose. The Holy Spirit may call them into being to express practically and cross-denominationally the unity of the church of Jesus Christ. He may desire to demonstrate before the world the supra-denominational oneness of the character of the church of God. He may wish to visibly portray the people of God working together in love in the purpose of God. Such possibility must not be discounted.

Parachurch movements face at least *two crucial issues.* First, their calling and ministry could be for a specific mission and time only. When such purpose is fulfilled they may face dissolution. In this they should not feel defeated or dishonored—their mission is done. At this point there arises the serious danger of yielding to the temptation of perpetuation of the organization for the organization's sake. To this parachurch movements must be alert.

Second, it is possible that the church may awaken and ready itself to perform the function that originally caused a parachurch movement to come into being. What position does the parachurch movement then take? Does it hand over the responsibility to the church? Does it integrate with and operate within the structure of the church? This is not an easy matter to answer. History presents some arguments in favor of such integration. However, some serious warnings also stand before us. A recent example of a disastrous integration was the dissolution of the International Missionary Council and its integration into the World Council of Churches.

There are, then, varying purposes and functions of the church within its overall and ultimate purpose. These I have called relative absolutes. The structure is a servant to these functions.

4. *The relative factors.* The relative factors affecting the structure or form of the church are the environment or cultural milieu in which the church thrives and the psychology of the people whom it serves. These factors and the resultant emphasis on indigenization have become familiar in recent years in part because of the new insights gained from studies in the history of missions and in such behavioral sciences as cultural anthropology, sociology, and social psychology. Cross-cultural studies have been standardized to the great benefit of missions. Such emphasis is partially a reaction of nationalism and liberalism to the overbearing Westernism of past centuries. But it does compel the church to evaluate the relationship of the gospel to these factors and their influence on world evangelism.

In fairness to history it must be stated that throughout modern history of missions there have been voices speaking for indigenization or the creation of indigenous churches. "Boden-standige Kirchen" is a well-known German expression and orginated already in 1854 when Karl Graul insisted on it. The idea never died out.

5. *The gospel—its own architect.* The Bible is quite clear that no culture as it has developed and formed itself is fit to incarnate Christianity or serve as a prepared vessel to communicate the gospel unadulteratedly. This was true of the contemporary Jewish, Greek, and Roman cultures. The New Wine demanded new skins. The reality of Jesus Christ and His gospel demanded a new community, a new structure, its own way of life, its own creed or body of doctrine, and its own cultus of worship. Pentecost introduced a new thing into history. This new organism or institution—the church of Jesus Christ—refused to be completely identified in nature, design, purpose, structure, form, and order with Judaism, Hellenism, or Romanism.

While in form the church borrowed and adapted from all streams, it converted, modified, recast, and enriched almost every element it adopted and added new factors to them. The Christian church was not a Jewish synagogue or a Stoic brotherhood, or a Greek academy, or a Roman school of jurisprudence. It insisted on being its own masterbuilder and architect. It was God's unique masterpiece (Eph. 2:10); it had a separate identity (1 Cor. 10:32); it was a distinct community (Eph. 2:15, 19–22), different qualitatively and quantitatively (Eph. 3:6). It was nowhere completely indigenous. It was a community of pilgrims and sojourners with citizenship in heaven (Phil. 3:20; 1 Peter 1:1). wwhenever the church sought too close a relationship with the prevailing culture, evil befell it; it died in accommodation or Christo-paganism. The gospel of Jesus Christ is the great nonmixer (Hammer).

6. *The gospel and accommodation.* Over-accommodation seems to have been the mistake of Judaistic Christianity in the centuries that followed Pentecost. James relates a most serious situation when he tells Paul: "You see, brother, how many thousands there are among the Jews of those who have believed, *and they are all*

zealous for the Law" (Acts 21:20). This statement was made a number of years after Acts 11:1–18 and the conference of Acts 15 had taken place. The Jerusalem Jewish Christian community was not able to liberate itself from Judaism and the Law. Neither could the Jewish church liberate itself from a static, nomadic, stringent monotheism and break-through to a biblical doctrine of the Trinity. Their doctrine of Christology remained hazy, weak, and became sectarian. The Epistle to the Hebrews clearly implies that Jewish Christians were facing the dangers of accommodation. The eventual result was that the Jewish Christian community shrunk to insignificance, without spiritual dynamic and missionary outlet. The communities of Arabia, Babylon, and Persia were evidence of this. In the second century they became petrified Christian societies, sometimes identified as Jewish and sometimes as Christian communities. The remnants died a natural death in the desert of Arabia. The rich Jewish Christian churches of Babylon and Persia fared no better. They dried up because they did not permit Christianity to create its own doctrine, way of life, worship and culture. Their relationship to Judaism became their downfall and inevitable death. Accommodation may become a serious trap to the gospel of Jesus Christ and to the Christian church.

7. *The gospel and Christo-paganism.* The church in Corinth is an example of the way into Christo-paganism. Every ill that is mentioned in Corinthians was a carry-over from society. Many socially sanctioned and religiously endorsed cultural traits and practices were taken over by the church—such practices as partyism, litigation, socially approved and religiously endorsed adultery in the temple courts, participation in sacrificial meals, ecstatic utterances and speaking in tongues, etc. All of these were traits of contemporary culture and religion outside of the church. The letters of Paul and the "Epistle of St. Clement" (of Rome) to the Corinthians did not change the situation substantially or permanently. Continued indiscriminate adoption of cultural mores resulted in serious aberrations of Christianity and in potential and eventually certain Christo-paganism as it is witnessed today in the Eastern Church, particularly in Ethiopia.

8. *The gospel and Paul's radicalism.* Christians are to have a

separate identity. The Christian life is a new pattern. Paul's fivefold exhortation to the Ephesians *to walk* and *to walk not* (Eph. 4:1, 17; 5:2, 8, 15) constitutes a set of comprehensive directives for the totality of life. On the one hand it proscribes and on the other hand it orders a new way of life, a Christian life style that is different qualitatively and quantitatively. It stands in sharp contrast to the former walk and way of life (Eph. 2:2). It cuts out and cuts across many well-accepted social patterns of behavior and moral standards. It establishes new relationships in personal behavior, family life, and social practices. It is a call not to indigenization but to the bold forming of *a counterculture.* Paul beautifully summarizes in eight positive precepts his Christian ethics: "Finally, brethren, whatever is true, whatever is honorable, whatever is right, whatever is pure, whatever is lovely, whatever is of good repute, if there is any excellence and if anything worthy of praise, let your mind dwell on these things" (Phil. 4:8). In his letter to the church at Colossae he catalogs the traits to *put off* and *put on* (Col. 3:5–14). While this is Pauline radicalism, it is not legalism. It is an expression of the *radical holy nature of the gospel of grace.* Nothing is more holy than the sovereign grace of God and nothing is more righteous than the pure love of God.

Therefore, wherever Christ enters and is enthroned and obeyed, a cultural upset will take place. He leaves no culture as it is. He judges and puts away. He approves and enriches. He accepts and transforms. A church that enthrones Him can never be completely indigenous. It will always live in tension and often in conflict with society and culture; accommodation will always be a serious danger. Spiritual Christians will always seem somewhat radical, different, peculiar. They will be in the world but not of it and often against it. They must live as children of God without rebuke, in the midst of a crooked and perverse nation, among whom they must shine as lights in the world and hold forth the world of life (Phil. 2:15–16).

Accommodation is not the only danger. The church also faces the opposite extreme—it may also become a *holy huddle,* a *ghetto;* it may isolate itself and become a total "Stranger in the Land"[2] to society and culture. It thereby ceases to be the salt of the earth and light of the world. It may hide its light under a bushel of religious separation. Balance and discernment must always characterize a spiritual church.

The strength of early Christianity was derived in part from the fact that the church dared to be the people of God. The early church proclaimed *a new message,* constituted *a new community,* created *a new order,* blazed *a new way of life* (see diagram). It willed, designed, and created its own culture that was mainly a counterculture. It refused to be either absorbed by the prevalent culture or isolated and boycotted from society. The idea of a "hidden kingdom" or "invisible universal church" or "anonymous Christian" would have seemed strange ideas to the early church.

THE CHURCH OF
THE EARLY CENTURIES

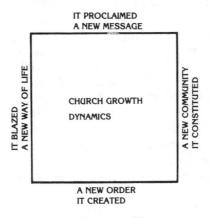

Diagram 15

It demands a great measure of divine wisdom and courage to reflect the holiness and otherness of the church as the people of God and to be a new community in this world. At the same time the church is to demonstrate the servanthood of the church and the relatedness of the gospel of Jesus Christ to the people of the world in their need and spiritual aspirations. Only the Holy Spirit and total obedience to the Word of God can qualify the church in this way.

9. *The gospel and Westernism.* The very tension between the demand for a new and unique form for the Christian church on one hand and the need to relate to the psychological and social milieu of the people on the other hand has led to some criticism of nineteenth- and early twentieth-century missionaries. Why did Western missionaries wrap the gospel message in a cloak of Westernism and plant around the world a church that was shaped by Western culture and relevant to Western man? Were their actions the result of ecclesiastical colonialism, cultural imperialism, or theological *Kultur-Christentum* (culture Christendom)?[3]

Those engaged in contemporary studies must guard against generalizations and refrain from impeaching the motives and message of those early missionaries. There always have been some who could say with Paul: "For though I am free from all men, I have made myself a slave to all, that I might win the more. . . . I have become all things to all men, that I may by all means save some. And I do all things for the sake of the gospel, that I may become a fellow-partaker of it" (1 Cor. 9:19–23). It would be difficult to accuse Robert Moffatt, Hudson Taylor, or Mary Slessor of Westernism. They did not incarnate or export Westernism, and they most certainly propagated indigenization. It would be unfair to accuse such missionary statesmen as Karl Graul, Henry Venn, and Rufus Anderson of lack of concern for indigenization.

Having allowed for such exceptions, it is readily admitted that most missions and missionaries thought basically in Western terms, surrounded themselves in their mission compounds with a bit of Western world, and set up church structures—principles, practices, symbolism, vestments, altar, and buildings—according to Western styles and types. Creeds, confessions, catechism, hymns, music, and educational systems were completely carried over to the mission fields. There seems to have been little attempt to build a typical Asian or African church and indigenize or adapt the church to the various cultures and types of people. As a result, the church has been given a Western coloring, mood, and appearance that have remained binding on it until the present in most places. Although this practice of Westernization seemed at that moment of history expedient and appropriate, it is unfortunate and lamentable if not unjust and unfair. Today we are living in a new world. As a sensitive nationalism, which includes not only national independence but also cultural revival, and a renaissance of ethnic religions develop, the church appears to be a foreign import, a remnant of Western colonialism. Little of non-Westernization is in sight, with the exception that some radical forms of theology, mostly borrowed from Western Europe and America and adapted to particular situations, are replacing the evangelical, pietistic theology of the pioneers.

Caution and humility are needed in evaluating the motives of the pioneers in missions who together with the gospel took with them their Westernism—some good, some not so good. Their sterling character, noble ideals, total commitment to the cause in the midst of opposition and most trying circumstances in the fields of labor, their unreserved loyalty to the Master amid misunderstanding and misjudgment at home, their unwavering fidelity to the truth of the gospel and joyous sacrifice, forbid us to talk loudly or lightly. They served as saints in the sight of God, as servants in the presence of men, as heroes in the face of suffering and trials, many becoming martyrs in the cause of God and mankind. To attach to their names such statements as Western ecclesiastical colonialism or Western cultural imperialism may be deeply un-Christian.

The reasons for their behavior and missionary practices are found principally in their kingdom of God theology and ideology. This was the dominant concept of American and British theology. The tragedy was that their kingdom of God concept was intimately knotted to Westernism in ideology and culture. *Kultur-Christentum* (German theology and missiology) was the leitmotif that prevailed in much of theology, both liberal and evangelical.

10. *The gospel and culture* While Wesleyan Evangelicalism and German Pietism became the major motivating force in most missions, the broad concept of the kingdom of God formed the frame of reference within which missions operated. World evangelism included culture building—built according to Western style. The missionaries did not clearly distinguish between gospel and culture. Their theology and ideology were faulty in this matter but not

their zeal, motivation, and intention.

The above approach accounts at least in part for Westernism in the mission compounds, in the forming and structuring of the church, in the educational institutions, in the social institutions and provisions, as well as in the medical programs. All had the stamp of Westernism because the lines between Christendom and Christianity, the church and the world, the gospel and culture, were blurred and confused.

Although Westernism has burdened the church with many strange cultural accretions and seems to have hindered the free flow of the gospel in many places, let it be said emphatically that Westernism is not necessarily the handicap and perhaps not even the main hindrance of church growth that it is made to seem. It would be difficult to find a group of churches in all the Orient that is more Western than the churches of Korea are—Presbyterian, Methodist, Baptist, Assemblies of God. Yet they are the fastest-expanding churches in all the Orient, perhaps in all the world. At present they are doubling on an average of every three to five years. This is fantastic church growth. The same can be said about the Java Christian Church in which any Dutch Reformed member from the Netherlands would feel perfectly at home (provided Javanese were understood). Yet of all mainline churches in Indonesia this is the most rapidly growing body. The same may be said about the Lutheran Church related to the Neuendetelsau Mission in Papua New Guinea. This church is not overly concerned about indigenization, yet grows by leaps and bounds. Generalizations should be avoided. They are easy to make but are never safe and are seldom accurate.

Indigenization is healthy when guided by biblical principles and Spirit-illumined insight. It is *one* of the important factors in church growth and in the structuring of the church but by no means the main factor. In the church of Jesus Christ spiritual factors are at work that outweigh all cultural factors. Concern for biblical and spiritual revival must outweigh concern for indigenization if new energy for growth is to come to the church.

Nevertheless, the relative factors are important and should be seriously considered in the molding and structuring of the church. Though they do not equal in value the absolute factors, they are significant if people are to feel at home in the church. In fact, these cultural factors play heavily on the sentiments of people and captivate the humanness in them. Everyone feels more at ease and less threatened in familiar surroundings and with familiar practices.

That organization or structure is necessary to the organism, the church, is supported by the Scriptures and is seen to be emerging in the early church in Acts 6:1–7. In the tension between function and structure, structure must play a servant role. In church growth—in the planting of the church in various cultures—both absolute and relative determinant factors must be kept in mind. These include the nature, function, and purpose of the church, and the natural environment or cultural milieu and psychology of the people. Wisdom and humility are demanded to find God's way in establishing His church in a new culture and among a new people and relating the church properly to culture and the psychology of the people.

11

Pillar Three—
The Function of the Church

Before entering into the study of our present section it would be helpful to refer back to the *outline* on the biblical significance of the church (page 58). A careful study of the designations and symbolism and also some clear pronouncements in the New Testament lead us to the conclusion that the function of the church is multiple. Diagrams 16, 17, and 18 present this multiple function in a vivid manner. A careful balance must be maintained in this threefold function if the church is not to become warped and impoverished. Certainly all three aspects must be emphasized and practiced.

The *upward* reach of the church rests in the fact that God is who He is and that the church of Jesus Christ is His peculiar possession. It owes Him not only obedience and service but also humble and reverent worship. Christ informs us that the Father seeks people to be His worshipers (John 4:23). Certainly He ought to find them in His church. Worship is His due and our privilege and obligation as well as our eternal calling.

The *inward* ministry of fellowship, education, edification, discipline, and structuring is designed to produce that type of qualitative and responsible community as I have depicted it in chapter 9 under pillar one, and the properly structured church as discussed in chapter 10 under pillar two.

The *outward* ministry charts the relationship and responsibilities of the church to the world. It constitutes the major emphasis of our study and magnifies the principal functions and divine focus of the church in our age. It must be admitted that such function and focus are not "natural" to the church. They do not just happen. They must be cultivated. They result only from a *specific quality* of the church (chap. 9), under *careful tutelage* of the church, and by building *specific principles* into the church (chap. 13). It is possible that a church may not be able to achieve the required quality and therefore be incapable of functioning according to the design of the Lord and be focused according to the Lord's pattern and ideal. Consequently not every church attains that maturity of which Paul writes to the Ephesians when he speaks of "the measure of the stature which belongs to the fulness of Christ" (Eph. 4:13). It is possible to miss God's highest and to fail in our calling.

Our task therefore is twofold. *First,* we must study *how* we can build a quality church that will be able to enter into the Lord's design. We must discover and define principles that will guide us in building a quality community, a church that is fit to function according to the purpose and pleasure of the Lord. I believe that Luke in his report guides us in this matter, particularly in Acts 2–5. Here we find some essential principles of the church's inward functioning.

A second matter of concern must be to uncover the supreme outward function of the church in our age in order to accomplish the purpose and plan of God. It is my contention that the Holy Spirit demonstrates such functions in Acts 8–12. It is evident that the New Testament presupposes the possibility of such discovery and achievement.

To the definition of the inward and outward function of the church we must devote our next two chapters—to define some guiding principles in building a quality community, a church as I have portrayed it in chapters 9 and 10. Upon this we must define the supreme function of the church according to the plan and purpose of God in our age and present a series of principles to guide us in accomplishing His divine design.

Mission of the Church

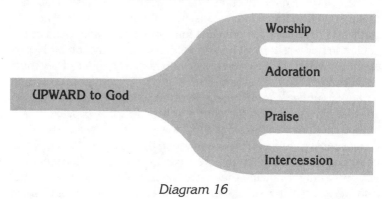

Diagram 16

Mission of the Church

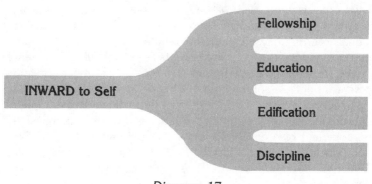

Diagram 17

Mission of the Church

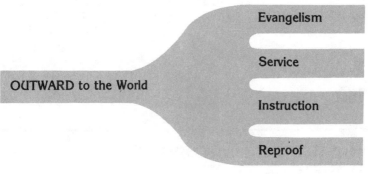

Diagram 18

12

The Inward Function of the Church

Fundamental Building Principles

In order to minister to others the church must learn to minister to itself and built itself into a quality community. For this we glean some guiding principles from Acts.

BASIC BUILDING PRINCIPLES

1. **The Principle of Balanced Ministry—Teaching, Witnessing, Evangelism**
2. **The Principle of Quality—Quantity Balance**
3. **The Principle of Addition—Multiplication Balance**
4. **The Principle of Concentration—Multiplication Balance**
5. **The Principle of Balanced Evangelism—Breadth, Depth**
6. **The Principle of Balanced Relationships—Autonomy, Association**

Diagram 19

The key word in all principles is the word "balance," a word easily pronounced but difficult to achieve and consistently practice.

"I will build my church," Christ assures us (Matt. 16:18). Immediately following this majestic and assuring statement, our Lord turned to Peter and informed him that He would entrust the keys to the building process to human hands (Matt. 16:19). Thus the church building program became a divine-human cooperative enterprise.

Like human culture, so the church as a fit vessel and qualitative community is being built according to specific and defineable principles, patterns, and procedures. I define six such building principles.

1. *The principle of balance in the ministry of evangelism, teaching, and witnessing.* All three of these ministries are mentioned in the first five chapters of Acts. The word "evangelism" is found only once in the verb form (5:42). The word "witness" is ascribed only to the apostles in the first part of Acts. No doubt, the words of the Master had registered deeply in their minds. His farewell charge had been "You shall be my *witnesses*" (Acts 1:8). Thrice Peter boldly declares "we are witnesses" (2:32; 3:15; 5:32). Once Luke tells us that with great power the apostles gave witness (4:33). The emphasis, however, seems to be on *teaching.* Therefore we read of the early church that "they continued steadfastly in the apostles' doctrine" or as the New English Bible has it "they came daily to hear the apostles' teaching." There seems to have been daily public instruction of believers (2:42). In 5:42 we read that much teaching was performed from house to house. Teaching refers to method as well as to content and again reflects the impact of the Master on the disciples' lives. Was He not known as the Teacher? Forty-eight times He is so designated. Also, teaching is most effective in discipleship making.

The content of the instruction material is not spelled out. From Hebrews 2:3–4 and Luke 1:1–2, we may confidently conclude that the teaching consisted largely in the recounting of the life, words, and works of Jesus Christ. The disciples related the coming of Christ to the Old Testament, as the phrase *that it might be fulfilled* indicates. They expounded the meaning and significance of the Christ event, His words, miracles, life, death, and resurrection for the Jews, the world, and the believers. The record of the teaching material is found in the Gospels.

Judging by the epistles that the apostles left behind, it is evident that they were quite detailed and deeply ethical in their instructions, in addition to being expository. Christianity was more than a doctrine or a religious philosophy. It was the life-transforming power of God for all who believed. Therefore, their ideals are high and their expectations taxing. They knew the source of strength, the Holy Spirit, who is able and willing to enable the believer to live up to the expected standards and ideals.

The total program of indoctrination was designed to *make disciples* as they had been instructed by their Master to do. For the apostles this meant to equip the believer for the ministry of their calling (Eph. 4:11–16), and to qualify them to give intelligent and reasonable answers for the hope that was in them (1 Peter 3:15).

The manner of their teaching can be deduced only in general terms from their messages and writings. Here it is evident that indoctrination was purposive (Eph. 4:11–16), highly ethical, and life related. An outline of the Pauline epistles bears this out. Although some of the epistles open with an elaboration on the greatest doctrines, they end in high ethics. This is particularly so in Romans, Ephesians, and Colossians. The lists of ethical precepts both positive and negative are numerous and extensive as we find it illustrated in such passages as Galatians 5:19–24; Ephesians 5:3–5; Philippians 4:8; Colossians 3:5–17; 2 Timothy 3:1–7; Titus 3:4; 1 Peter 4:3. The concreteness of apostolic instruction is remarkable. It was designed by the Holy Spirit to build, sharpen, and prick the Christian conscience. The great revival that had been released on the day of Pentecost must not only be preserved but also relayed. This can be accomplished only if a balanced ministry of evangelism, witnessing, and teaching is initiated and maintained. It is not a question of either/or, one or the other, but a healthy balance in the emphasis is needed if a qualitative community is to result.

2. *The principle of quality-quantity balance.* Both aspects are important. Our Lord wants many believers and followers and He desires strong believers and obedient followers. It is biblically not

permissible to make it an either/or in the matter of quality-quantity growth. Because of this I hyphenate these two concepts. They are not two separable poles. They are two sides of a genuine coin. Quality is to be produced that quantity might result, and quantity is garnered in that quality might be produced. God is a God of holiness and also a God of greatness. It is neither divine nor scriptural to separate these two aspects, though we must distinguish between them. It is possible to seriously suffer because one or the other aspect is neglected. A balance is needed if a healthy and prospering church is to result. The first section of Acts evidences the fact that the apostles were concerned to *make disciples* as they had been made and as they had been instructed to do. Therefore, we find the emphasis on instruction in doctrine, fellowship, and prayer. These are essential elements to create quality disciples.

To achieve balance in quality-quantity is not always easy; in fact, it is difficult. All of us are inclined in one direction or the other. In the Western world where quantity is difficult to achieve, churches are quick in excusing themselves by saying that they prefer a membership of quality. The reasoning is that if quality is accomplished quantity will naturally result. Ideologically this sounds logical and appealing; practically this does not match reality. It may be more rationalization than honest admission of some basic weakness and/or failure. However, it need not be if quality is of the true kind even if quantitative growth may seem to lack. It could be that a church finds itself in a non-missionary situation and the populace is well cared for spiritually and regular in church attendance. The church's only possibility to grow quantitatively is by transplanting, or sending some of its members into a missionary situation. As the home church shares in such a ministry by prayer and generous care for the dispatched *delegation,* it extends itself qualitatively and also quantitatively by the principle of multiplication rather than addition. This principle will be considered later.

This described experience should not be advanced as an excuse for a stalemated home base. It is not a substitute for growth at home but it may be a strong supplement to the home congregation under specific circumstances and should not be completely discounted.

A Theology of Church Growth

The quantitative growth of the church in a missionary situation may be a direct result of the qualitative growth of the church in a non-missionary situation because of a healthy relationship and spiritual cooperation between the two bodies. This is the experience of some Western churches who find themselves in well-churched places with little room to grow. Therefore they extend themselves into missionary situations to plant daughter churches.

Let it be said with all emphasis, and I believe on solid scriptural deductions, that no church will experience the blessings of God and grow qualitatively unless it is balanced in quantitative growth on the home base or on a base operated and supported by the church. God does not bless His church in order to fatten it. He builds muscle-quality and not fat baggage. A stalemated, non-evangelizing, non-missionary church definitely comes under the "woe is me if I do not preach the gospel" as Paul expresses it in 1 Corinthians 9:16. Sooner or later the sap will dry up in the tree, branches will wilt, wither, and dry up and death will seep down to the roots. History is our evidence that the Holy Spirit will bow to no rationalization or accept excuses not to keep a healthy balance of quality-quantity in the church. Such balance must be achieved if the churches desire to experience the full measure of the blessings of God and prosper for His glory.

A different situation prevails in much of the non-Western or Third World areas. In much of it quantitative growth abounds. Churches are increasing in some places from 10 to 35 percent annually.[1] Here quality becomes the pressing issue. When quantitative growth rate exceeds 10 to 15 percent, the quality of the average church will soon be endangered. Few churches have a program to absorb and incorporate such growth rate. No thought must be entertained to seek to slacken the numerical increase. Ways and means must be created to intensify and enhance the efficiency of the teaching and training ministry in the church. A creative and well-staffed church should be able to integrate and socialize an annual increase of 20 to 25 percent without endangering its quality. It will take energy and work, wisdom and creativity, and courage to restructure the program of training and organization for efficient operation in addition to dependence on the Holy Spirit. But it can be done!

The principle of qualitative-quantitative balance must be energetically and persistently pursued if we would build prospering churches.

3. *The principle of addition-multiplication balance.* Here we face another delicate and complicated issue. It is in the mind of ambitious (in a positive sense) church builders to have large and also many churches. This is not abnormal or unhealthy. It is biblically ideal. However, it is difficult to achieve both ideals simultaneously. In such cases where must the emphasis lie? The Book of Acts presents both emphases and practices, not necessarily as alternatives but as ideals. Twice the word *added* appears immediately following Pentecost in Acts 2:41, and 47. Luke mentions it again in 5:14 and 11:24. This concept seems to indicate an enlargement of the local group and increasing it in size and number. However, the word *multiplied* soon follows and is used in Acts 6:1, 7; 9:31; 12:24. It is recorded that disciples multiplied, churches multiplied, and that the word of God grew and multiplied. The concept of multiplication seems to point in the direction of an increasing number of groups and churches rather than an expansion of the existing ones. Thus both practices prevailed in apostolic times. The emphasis was upon both aspects— churches were enlarged and they increased in numbers.

Nevertheless, there seems to be a biblical order indicated by the fact and record that addition preceded multiplication. This may be pointing to an important practice. *In most ordinary circumstances our first concern should be given to adding to existing groups or churches to build them into bodies sufficiently large enough to function responsibly as churches.* It seems unwise in the light of apostolic practices and history to overextend ourselves in multiplication and leave behind numerous ill-functioning small groups or detachments. *The apostolic practice of Christian fellowship, the biblical assignment delegated to the church, the responsible functioning of a body of believers,* and *the expectations of the world seemingly dictate a body of some numerical size and social and economic strength.* In the light of this the principle of addition demands attention. It is also true that history seems to substantiate the fact that larger churches make a greater contribution to in-depth evangelism or the Christianization of culture and structures of society than numerous smaller groups do.

Such seem to be some advantages of the emphasis of the addition principle. To remain here, however, is to fall short of the New Testament ideal. *Multiplication is absolutely essential to achieving the biblical ideal of New Testament church growth.* The church must be planted in all lands, among all peoples and communities, and made visible and audible everywhere until every person has the privilege to become acquainted with the gospel. This demands a continuous process of multiplication of churches. It is not a question of the necessity of multiplication; it is more a question of the time and place of such multiplication. When it is recorded that in Europe alone there are some 250,000 towns and villages without an evangelical witness or an evangelizing center and/or church, then the way is clear. Here multiplication of churches and living witnessing groups is absolutely essential. Most certainly America has its needs here. What about the hundreds of thousands of communities around the world for whom nothing has been prepared thus far? Can we honestly question the absolute imperative for the most rapid process of multiplication of churches throughout the world? Is it Christian fairness that an American community of 6,000 people has twenty churches to attend and a community in India of 250,000 people has no church? And this is no exceptional case.[2] Only blindness of mind and hardness of heart could here reply in the negative or remain indifferent. Thus the principle of addition and multiplication of churches must be kept in balance if the church of Jesus Christ is to achieve its true dimensions as envisaged in the New Testament.

It is also true that a mother church that plants a number of daughter churches not only demonstrates concern and wisdom but usually experiences great blessings and joy because of such multiplications. It lives in obedience and in the ideal of the Lord who wants His church to grow and multiply. Spiritual health and riches increase as it multiplies. A non-multiplying church is a barren church and a fig tree without fruit.

4. *The principle of concentration-expansion balance.* Jeru-

salem became the first center of Christian activities. Here our Lord suffered, died, rose again, commissioned His disciples, and ascended on high. Here Pentecost became a historic reality and here the church of Jesus Christ was born. Jerusalem was also the city that was first saturated with the gospel of Jesus Christ (5:28), experienced great blessings, and witnessed a great revival of spiritual life and vitality. The record of Luke states that literally thousands of Palestinian Jews, Hellenists, and proselytes became followers of Jesus Christ (2:41; 4:4; 5:14; 6:1, 7). All of this over a period of a few short years, perhaps two or three.

a. *Some justified questions.* A serious question arises, Was it the will of God and the plan of the Master that Christianity in its beginning years should remain confined to Jerusalem? Is such a prolonged and complete concentration in one city justifiable, wise, and for the good of the church? Could the Christians not have lessened the opposition of the Jewish hierarchy, prevented the wrath of the religious leadership, and also avoided the persecution had they instead of such heavy concentration in Jerusalem expanded over all Palestine and beyond its borders before the wrath of the Jews was unleashed? We cannot avoid asking some such questions and many more. It almost seems contrary to our Lord's expressed command to go into all the world and to preach the gospel to every creature. Yet, we will see much wisdom and great advantages of such concentration *in the initial stages* of the church of Jesus Christ.

b. *The need of concentration.* On the day of Pentecost something new was born. The church of Jesus Christ came into existence, and as the body of Christ and as a living organism it was unique. As a divine-human institution it had no definite pattern to follow. Its basic ecclesiastical doctrines, its practices, and its relationship to Judaism had not been specifically defined. The living and risen Lord had made the demands and responsibilities of Christian discipleship and the mission of the apostles in world evangelization very emphatic. But He had not left a general framework for the structure of the church behind Him.

In the divine counsel the realization, ministration, and the historical and cultural institutionalization of the church of Jesus Christ had been delegated to the divine Paraclete, the Holy Spirit. He was performing initially His task through the apostles whom Christ had nurtured and trained (1 Cor. 3:11; Eph. 2:20; 3:5). They incarnated the principles of the Master, and later spelled them out for the churches in the New Testament.

It was therefore of utmost importance that the church be concentrated in a specific locale in order to remain under the immediate instructions, example, and tutorship of the apostles. Only thus could the total body of believers be molded according to the principles of the Master, melted and knit together into an exemplary community, instructed in the right doctrines, receive a relative institutional stability, and serve as model for the future churches. We can hardly imagine what would have happened had the Christian believers immediately or soon after Pentecost dispersed into all the world. It is not impossible that there would be no Christian church. Doctrines and practices would have diversified endlessly and confusion would have resulted. In wisdom and grace the Holy Spirit kept the saints concentrated in Jerusalem to create a holy, wholesome, and lasting community. The believers became a church, a quality community, a brotherhood in Christ Jesus. Thus concentration proved its worth.

c. *Expansion is an essential necessity.* Concentration is purposive and temporary. It does not belong to the essential nature of the gospel and Christianity and must not be permitted to become a habit. *Expansion does belong to the essential nature of the gospel and Christianity.* Therefore the living church breathes expansion. It is a living organism, and growth and multiplication belong to its very being. It must expand if it would live. It must expand geographically and numerically if it is to be healthy and vigorous, true and obedient to its Lord.

The expansion of the Christian church is not left to the judgment and sentiments of man. It is not to be made dependent on invitation and conveniences or pleasant circumstances. No human power has a right to legislate in this matter. Here only He to whom all authority is given in heaven and on earth speaks the decisive word. His command is law, His desire is motivation, His will is the direction, His presence in the Holy Spirit is the power and comfort, and the need of the world is an impelling call to action.

d. *Expansion is imperative.* The Lord wants His church to expand around the globe and offer blessings to all people that are procured in Christ Jesus. Expansion is not optional; it is imperative. It is imperative because of the nature and design of the church (Matt. 5:13–16; Eph. 2:11–22; 3:6); it is imperative because of the need of the world (Eph. 2:1–3; 1 John 5:19); it is imperative because of the redemptive design of our Lord (Matt. 28:18–20; Luke 24:45–48); it is imperative because of the Pentecostal design of the ministry of the Holy Spirit (John 16:8–11; Acts 2:39); it is imperative because expansion is written in the boldest manner across the pages of the New Testament. Who can honestly and sincerely doubt it when he listens attentively to the command of the Lord, reads the New Testament with an open mind and ready will, and when he sees the lands of the world without the wholesome influence of the gospel?

Therefore, while initial concentration may be wise and advantageous, expansion is necessary and demanded by the very nature of the church and the purpose of God. The release of the expansion and multiplication power come before us in Acts 8–12. Suffice it here to say that these two seeming polarities must be kept in healthy balance if the church is to grow into a qualitative community of God and prosper in its way.

5. *The principle of evangelism-in-depth and in-depth-evangelism.* We have noted that somehow Christianity at its beginning was able to cut through vertically and draw people from all strata of society into the church. This was so in Jerusalem and it was so in Antioch in Syria, the first mission and missionary church. It manifested the power to reach up as well as to reach down and out. In addition, it drastically changed the total life orientation of the people. Believers gladly shared their substance (instead of hoarding it or putting it into security) with the needy and lived in fraternal relationships as a great family of God. These two aspects of the manifestation of the power of the gospel of Jesus Christ may well be likened to two ambitions of more recent philosophies of evangelism that have been strongly advocated. At least one of them has shown

considerable success. I am thinking of evangelism-in-depth and in-depth-evangelism. These may well be formulated into a principle of church operation. All care must be taken to keep the two aspects in balance if the church is to perform its responsibility and mission in this world, remain healthy, and grow according to the design of God.

I have dealt with the first part of the principle—evangelism-in-depth—in a separate book (Zondervan). Here I give a brief definitive statement.

a. *Meaning of evangelism-in-depth.*[3] By evangelism-in-depth I refer to the scope of and depth in evangelism. It includes geography, society, and culture. Every individual needs the gospel of Jesus Christ. It is well to assume that every person can be won if we can only find the right key to his affections and heart's door. And every person can be saved by faith in the Lord Jesus Christ as Savior from sin and condemnation. In evangelism-in-depth no geographical area, no social strata, no ethnic grouping of people, no religious community, or any other distinction of peoples is to be omitted. All must be reached with the gospel of Jesus Christ and given an opportunity to say yes to Christ as Savior and Lord. Here it must come true literally that we are reaching the reached and the unreached—the hidden people.

In our days of specialized evangelism—child evangelism, teen and youth evangelism, student evangelism, etc.—it is essential to emphasize the fact that in all our specialization we must be careful that our program is extensive and comprehensive enough to omit no one. This is God's plan and purpose. This is His missionary design. God will have "all men to be saved and to come to the knowledge of the truth. For there is one God, and one mediator between God and men, the man Christ Jesus, who gave Himself a ransom for all, the testimony borne at the proper time (1 Tim. 2:4–6). Such a program will call for various special efforts and methods, materials, and different types of training. But such must be the scope of evangelism.

Scope alone does not exhaust the meaning of evangelism-in-depth. It is evident that at the beginning, when the designation evangelism-in-depth was coined by Kenneth R. Strachan in Costa

Rica and Waylon B. Moore in Tampa, Florida, that the term included not only the scope of evangelism but also the downreach of its transforming power in the individual personality, in society, and also in the structures of culture. It was anticipated that the power of the gospel would bring about social, moral, and cultural transformations that would result in more effective and efficient church members and churches to serve in this world, be greater lights and more salt in a decaying society, and thus positively affect society as a whole and bring about a better society with a deeper sense of justice, peace, and love. Human realism sensed the need of a depth restructuring of the total social and cultural society on the continent of South America in a special way. Although the latter emphasis was mild and cautious in practice for various reasons, it was not absent in theory and purpose in the minds of the originators.

b. *Meaning of in-depth-evangelism.*[4] Eventually the seeming dichotomy between scope and depth gave rise to a separate structure in Latin America known as in-depth-evangelism. Although the latter never became a movement, its philosophy is important.

From the New Testament we must conclude that the gospel of Jesus Christ seeks depth as well as breadth. It reaches into life and transforms it in all its personal and social relationships and also into the cultural structures as well as saving man from guilt, peril, and personal depravity. It was on the basis of this personal, social, and cultural transformation that Paul expected Philemon to accept and to treat the runaway slave Onesimus as a brother, which was contrary to prevailing social practices and legal rights. It is also on this basis that Paul exhorts masters and slaves in words of instructions of mutual relationships and behavior, which instructions are not culturally oriented. The gospel in many ways is a counterculture movement. It does transform relationships and attitudes, although not necessarily does it change status and position.

Jesus Christ came to save man from sin in all its forms, powers, strongholds, and structures, whether they are personal, individual, social, or cultural and bring liberation to humanity. He came to destroy the works of the devil and to set humans free. The gospel is a liberating and transforming power. The method in such liberation, of course, is love and a love all the way to the cross and not armed force. As Paul expresses it: "For though we walk in the flesh, we do not war according to the flesh, for the weapons of our warfare are not of the flesh, but divinely powerful for the destruction of fortresses. We are destroying speculations and every lofty thing raised up against the knowledge of God, and we are taking every thought captive to the obedience of Christ" (2 Cor. 10:3–5). It was because of this that the Christian messengers in the New Testament were decried as those who turned the world upside down (Acts 17:6) and those who "are throwing our city into confusion, being Jews, and are proclaiming customs which it is not lawful for us to accept or to observe, being Romans" (Acts 16:20–21). The gospel of Jesus Christ literally went contrary to many Jewish, Roman, and Greek customs and practices, religious as well as social.

c. *Biblical theology of liberation.*[5] There is a biblical theology of liberation. The redemption of humankind is not only from guilt and sin and eternal condemnation but also from oppression and power of sin in its varied forms. Whenever Christ appears, when He is permitted to enter in as Lord and Savior and exercise His lordship, a transformation takes place, the ramifications of which no one can foretell. Christ leaves no personality, society, and culture as it is. He is the great Liberator and Transformer. He did come to preach the gospel to the poor; He did heal the brokenhearted; He did preach deliverance to the captives (captives in what sense?); He did recover the sight of the blind; He did set at liberty those who are bruised, or as the last is translated, He did release the oppressed or crushed (again, oppressed or crushed in what sense?) (Luke 4:18). Indeed, this was a novel approach to society and exegetes differ greatly in the exposition of this portion of Scripture. How literal, how figurative are some of these expressions? This is today's debate. Has the West distorted this passage? Have we finally come to realize that we have truncated the message and ministry of Jesus? These are weighty questions and must not be pushed aside lightly. It seems to me, however, that not our present situation and aspirations must give to us the final key to the interpretation of these statements. The gospel records themselves are the safest guide and best commentary on the above declarations and the summation of the earthly life and ministry of our Lord and Savior Jesus Christ.

d. *Two serious perils.* The *first peril* arises out of evangelism-in-depth. Eagerness to advance as rapidly as possible and cover much scope, easily glides into superficiality in evangelism. Numbers of professions and coverage of areas pose a real threat to depth in the work. Superficiality is a real enemy of evangelism and a disease that paralyzes much work. Overextensiveness in coverage and territory often breeds shallowness, which results in indefinite decisions, half-heartedness in Christian commitment, laxness in fellowship, indifference in Christian responsibilities and imperiling entanglements in pagan practices and relationships. To argue that culture as such is neutral is vain talk. Hendrik Kraemer has disestablished such views. Culture is the embodiment of a soul that has created it, dwells within it, unites with it, and expresses itself through an appropriate frame of structure (Luzbetak). Culture takes on the form, structure, design, and purpose of that which lives within the person and which the person idealizes, seeks to preserve, to utilize, and hopes to benefit from. It is the expression of one's total value system, with all its hopes, yearnings, cravings, anticipations, and aspirations. Basically it is a unit, an organismic whole, held together by a cement that is one's religion (Lowie). Because of this, culture holds the person in its grips (Marney).

To hope that the convert will eventually grow out of his semi-paganism into a pure form of Christianity is not realistic. History gives little support to such hope. The opposite is far more likely. The New Testament clearly calls on the Christians to "come out from among them and be separate" (2 Cor. 6:17) and not to walk as the Gentiles do (Eph. 4:17).

The gospel of God does not come to reinforce us in our self-chosen way of life, philosophy, and religion, but to confront us with Jesus Christ. Every conversion to Christ, therefore, is a power confrontation and a power encounter with the totality of humankind in its total life milieu. This is true not only in animism. It is true also in the living historic religions of the world including Christendom.

Our Lord met personal attraction, personality cult, and superficiality in evangelism with His most stringent demands for Christian discipleship (Luke 14:25–35).

The *second peril* arises out of in-depth-evangelism. There is the constant danger that in in-depth-evangelism the concept of the church is relegated to a secondary emphasis and the concept of the kingdom is set forth as dominant. This becomes determining in sensitive issues in the relationships of Christianity, or better, the gospel of Jesus Christ to social movements, power structures, and culture as a whole.

It is not possible here to enter into a debate of this complex issue. The principal question is whether the New Testament sets forth a personal and church ethic or whether we have here a comprehensive kingdom ethic that governs all institutions and relationships of humankind, including political, economic, social, cultural, etc. Too frequently the latter emphasis overshadows the basic spiritual realities. In other words, is the New Testament principally concerned with evangelization of the world and the calling out and building of the church of Jesus Christ, or is its main emphasis on humanization and the restructuring of society and culture? That the church is in the world to exercise a positive and moderating influence is not questioned. However, what is *the chief thrust* and the dominant emphasis of the New Testament? Here lies the danger of in-depth-evangelism. It easily tilts over into social activism and humanization and the end result is Kultur-Christentum (culture-Christendom or a Corpus Christianum).

In-depth-evangelism has a place as well as evangelism-in-depth, but both movements must submit themselves to the directives and criteria of the Scriptures, keep themselves within biblical scope and realm, and operate within that framework. A healthy balance must be retained.

Several facts are sure from Scripture and history. Christ is the Light of the world (John 1:4; 8:12; 9:5; 12:46). We are assured that eventually the Light will brighten the whole globe and all humanity will see the Light. We are also informed that the Christian community is light and salt in this world (Matt. 5:13–16) and is called upon to shine as light in the midst of a crooked and perverse generation, holding high the word of life ("gospel"—Phil. 2:15–16). The full meaning of these words is difficult to determine. The fact remains, however, that the salutary impact of the gospel of Jesus Christ must not be measured only by the growth of membership in the outer fold of Christendom, but also by the pervasive wholesome influence on the whole world. This, of course, cannot be measured by degrees and statistics. It is something that escapes the scientist with his measuring rod. Yet it is a reality of life difficult to deny. Christianity in the life of an individual and a nation does make a difference. And therefore evangelism must remain the central thrust of the church of Jesus Christ, and evangelism-in-depth and in-depth-evangelism must be kept in healthy balance if a community of quality is to result.

6. *The principle of associational relationships.* The gospel and the church spread rapidly throughout Jerusalem. We read of 3,000 converts (Acts 2:41), of 5,000 men (family heads) who believed (Acts 4:4), of multitudes that were added (Acts 5:14), and that the number of the disciples multiplied in Jerusalem greatly; and a great company of the priests were obedient to the faith (Acts 6:7). The apostles were accused of having filled the city with their doctrines (Acts 5:28).

Somewhat later the gospel spilled over and Judea, Samaria, and Galilee were evangelized and multitudes became followers of the new faith. Thus groups of believers sprang up in many places even in far-off Damascus (Acts 9:2, 10, 11, 25), Cyprus, Cyrene, and in Antioch, Syria (Acts 11:20–26).

In Jerusalem the people gathered in numerous houses for fellowship, instruction, and evangelism (Acts 2:46; 5:42). We may well surmise that similar plans were in vogue in all other places. House churches were the order of the day for all of the first and most of the second century. History bears this out. And yet, despite these numerous places of gatherings, *the church is spoken of in the singular.* Thus we read of the church of Jerusalem (Acts 2:47; 8:1–3; 11:22; 12:5; 15:4, 22). Similarly the church of Judea, Samaria, Galilee, and the church of Antioch are spoken of in the singular (Acts 9:31 [in the Greek]; 11:26; 13:1; 14:27).

It would seem irresponsible to build a doctrinal, ecclesiastical framework on the usage of the singular in the above references. It would be equally irreverent to pass it over as insignificant. It seems to bespeak the closeness of association of the believers of apostolic times. They could speak of the church in a local situation in the singular. Most certainly this is not related to our present usage of the word when used of a denominational designation or as we speak of the Roman Catholic Church, or Anglican Church, etc. It was not a super church with all local congregations belonging to its fold. It was not a united church in the modern sense of the word. But neither do we find in Acts separated and autonomous churches in the modern sense of the word. The house churches in Jerusalem united in a common worship and for common instruction and prayer in the temple (Acts 2:42, 46; 3:3; 4:1-2; 4:23-31; 5:42). They seemingly were unified first under the leadership of the apostles and then by a common eldership (Acts 11:1; 15:2, 4, 6, 22, 23; 21:18). Seemingly the same pattern prevailed in Antioch and in Ephesus where multitudes had come to believe in Jesus Christ (Acts 13:1; 19:8-20; 19:26; 20:17-28). We observe that the words flock and church are used in the singular.

It is evident from the New Testament that the autonomy and independence of the local congregation are carefully balanced by interrelatedness and interdependence.

We do well to note this important principle. It cannot be lightly discounted. History favorably endorses such interrelatedness and association. As no man lives to himself, so no local congregation lives to itself. This is particularly so in fields where churches are surrounded by a sea of paganism and an atmosphere that is destructive to the church. Here they need each other more than ever.

History seems to bear out the fact that churches in association, in chain relationships and close proximity, grow more rapidly and healthier than churches in isolation. Fellowship and association make for health, strength, quality, and growth. It is wise, therefore, to seek to plant clusters of churches in limited geographical areas rather than scatter the church planting force over wide stretches or several cities, especially in the beginning of a work in a city or country. No one has proven this more true than the Southern Baptists of the USA in a number of cities around the globe. In this wisdom, church leaders must moderate their enthusiasm and ambition to occupy territory. Interchurch relationship may prove as important as interpersonal relationship in the health of the local church and the eventual spread of the gospel.

13

The Outward Function
of the Church

"It is not desirable for us to neglect the word of God in order to serve tables . . . we will devote ourselves to prayers and to the ministry of the word" (Acts 6:2b, 4). Such was the insight, the decisions, and the direction of the apostles. Their priority had been set by their Master. They had been sent forth to proclaim the gospel. Tables on social service were not to be neglected, but they must not endanger the priority of gospel preaching. Priorities are important. The ability to discern and the courage to select and pursue energetically that which is "best" (Phil. 1:10) are gifts of God and must be sought in prayer.

NEW TESTAMENT PRIORITY

In the threefold function, a certain priority must become focal. Our upward reach must become motivating as we are being related to God. Our inward ministry, while it is supremely edifying, must also equip the saints for a ministry. Eventually all must eventuate in service to the world. In this service *evangelism* becomes central and focal. This is in perfect keeping with God's general thrust in the Bible and particularly in the New Testament. It is beautifully expressed in John 3:16 when we read: "For God so loved the world that he gave his only begotten Son." If God so loved the world that He gave Himself for it, is it not natural to expect that He would also give the church and through the ministry of the Holy Spirit motivate the church to give itself for the world? It is essential to grasp this movement of the Trinity. God's movement is a world-ward movement. This was so in the Old Testament through Israel. This was so in and through Christ Jesus. This must be so in and through the church. Election is purposive and must lead to service. A church that has itself as central is a vanishing church. Not the church but the world is the focus in the New Testament as the theater of God's activities. The church is basically instrumental, purposive, mediating. It is and must be a Servant-church. As the gospel (evangel) is central in the New Testament message, so must evangelism be central in the function of the church. According to the New Testament the church lives by evangelism and for evangelism.

This fact is clearly set forth in the portion of Acts we are considering (Acts 8–12). Seven times we are told that the church evangelized (8:4, 12, 25, 35, 40; 10:36; 11:20; most translations read "preached the gospel" instead of "evangelized" as the Greek has it). We find the church membership, Philip the deacon, and Peter and John evangelizing. All served as agents of the Holy Spirit in making known the good news of God. It is evident that at the very heart of church growth in the New Testament is an energetic endeavor of evangelism, the persuasive telling forth of the good news of God in Christ Jesus. *From the perspective of human involvement, evangelism becomes the central principle of church growth.*

This should lead the student of church growth into a full inquiry into the place and practice of evangelism in the New Testament church.

Paul writes: "Christ sent me not to baptize but to preach the gospel (evangelize)" (1 Cor. 1:17). The only woe that seemingly threatens him is a divine woe if he should fail or neglect evangelism (1 Cor.

9:16–18). In consequence he describes his ministry twenty-three times as evangelizing and Luke in Acts adds another five passages with the same term. In this Paul followed His Master of whom we read that He went about in all the cities and villages and evangelized. He knew Himself sent from above to evangelize (Luke 8:1; 4:43; 4:18; Matt. 11:5). The total movement of the New Testament is a movement of the gospel. The gospel is the power (dynamic) of God. It is never static as power is never static.

In the practice of evangelism for church expansion, we must be mindful that a tremendous gulf exists between God and the world. This gulf has not narrowed through the centuries. In fact it is constantly widening. Sin incarnates itself not only in the sins of the individual, but also in the mood and sentiments, pleasure hunting, amusement and aspirations of the time, the institutions and establishments of culture, the power structures of society and in the philosophies of the generation, be they religious or secular. At the present time religious relativism, religious privatism, situation ethics, humanism, secularism, materialism, agnosticism, scientism, atheism, etc. are creating havoc in human society and are keeping multitudes away not only from the church but also from God of salvation.

As Israel was to be a bridge builder (priesthood) in Old Testament times, so the church of Jesus Christ is to fulfill this ministry in this age. It must become God's priesthood, the earthly mediator between God and the world. This is the fundamental calling of the church. It is God's earthly people to mediate the gospel of our Lord Jesus Christ to the world (2 Cor. 5:18–21; Eph. 3:1–11; Phil. 2:14–16; Col. 1:21–29).

The church therefore must sincerely face the question how this can be done most effectively. How can the church be made to expand most soundly and most rapidly? Again we turn to the Book of Acts.

Fundamental Expansion Principles

New Testament words as planting, watering, building, growing, increasing, adding, multiplying (Matt. 16:18; Acts 2:41–42; 6:1, 7; 1 Cor. 3:3, 6–7; Eph. 2:21–22) speak of diligent work. At the same time they imply orderly procedure mainly in quantitative, numerical, and geographical expansion.

Church growth takes place according to definite principles, many of which can be observed or uncovered and defined. From Acts 8 through 12 we are able to deduce a series of fundamental principles underlying the strategy and methodology that enabled the early church to operate most efficiently and effectively and to succeed in its primary function of world evangelization and global expansion. These principles can be stated with amplifications in thirteen propositions. For emphasis and clarity's sake, I enumerate them first before I present them more fully in detail.

1. A church grows to the degree that it is able to move from a state of introversion to a state of extroversion.

2. A church grows to the degree that it is able to overcome barriers that would naturally inhibit the expansion of the gospel.

3. A church grows best when it functions energetically in extensive and intensive evangelism.

4. A church grows best when the total body of believers is mobilized and trained in continued ministries of praying, sharing, witnessing, evangelizing;

5. A church grows best where the soil has been carefully and prayerfully prepared for the gospel;

6. A church grows best when evangelism is undergirded by a Spirit-directed strategy and relevant structure that rests on biblical principles to guide the onward movement;

7. A church grows best when the work is properly people related;

8. A church grows best by homogeneous units of society;

9. A church grows best by corporate-personality decisions and conversions in cultures of family, tribe, community, and people groupings;

10. A church grows best when the church releases the ablest, most experienced, and most qualified men of God for evangelism and church expansion;

11. A church grows best by team ministries under the guidance of strong and wise leadership;

12. A church grows best where the gospel is clearly, relevantly, and persuasively preached, Jesus Christ is most honored as Savior and Lord, and the Holy Spirit is believed and obeyed;

13. A church grows best where men of divine calling and qualification, faith, and prayer are able to guide the church body to live in the experience of the reality of God in the midst of His people and meet their needs.

With this outline before us we proceed to study them more in detail in the light of the early church.

1. *A church grows to the degree that it is able to move from a state of introversion to a state of extroversion.* Stated in another way, a church will grow to the degree that it is able to transform centripetalism into centrifugalism. A church will grow to the degree, therefore, that its membership becomes mobile in witnessing (Acts 8:1, 4; 11:19–21).

Principally this transformation is from Old Testament procedure to New Testament procedure. In the Old Testament the people of the world were both privileged and obligated to *come* to Jerusalem in order to hear and learn the law of God. Indeed, the Old Testament envisions a time when *nations* will come to Jerusalem to worship the Lord. There is no specific missionary command in the Old Testament such as that which the church received from its risen Lord and which is encoded in the Great Commission. The New Testament does not promote a central place for divine worship. The church is commissioned to "go into all the world," to "preach the gospel to every creature," to make the gospel message available "among all nations." The New Testament does not invite the people to the church but commissions the church to go to the people. It is this difference that leads Johannes Blauw to show that while the message and intent of the Old Testament were universalistic, the people of Israel were not commanded to be a missionary people.[1] The New Testament fuses the two aspects and makes the gospel a universalistic missionary message and the church a universalistic missionary people. Diagrams 20 and 21 illustrate this distinction.

The New Testament therefore demands the "conversion" of the church. Such conversion is not an easy matter, yet, a mental and

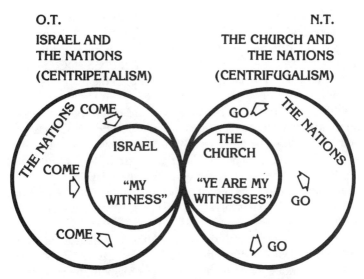

O.T.
ISRAEL AND
THE NATIONS
(CENTRIPETALISM)

N.T.
THE CHURCH AND
THE NATIONS
(CENTRIFUGALISM)

THE NATIONS — COME

ISRAEL

COME

"MY WITNESS"

COME

GO — THE NATIONS

THE CHURCH

"YE ARE MY WITNESSES"

GO

GO

BIBLICAL UNIVERSALITY AND REVERSED METHODOLOGY

Diagram 20

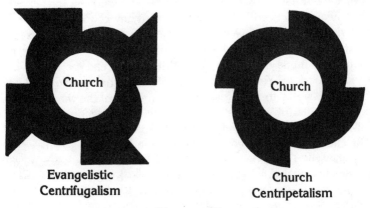

Church

Evangelistic Centrifugalism

Church

Church Centripetalism

Diagram 21

211

practical conversion from being introverted to becoming extroverted must take place if the church is to grow. The church must be turned inside out if it is to turn the world upside down. Outreach must characterize the church that would fulfill the Great Commission whether that is in Jerusalem and in Judea or in the uttermost part of the earth.

In the case of the church in Acts the Lord had to permit persecution to arise in order to disperse His witnesses. For some years they had been nurtured by the apostles and had enjoyed the fellowship of the saints (Acts 2–5). This had been a necessary time of consolidation. Now the time had come to *practice* discipleship in public and private witnessing. A Pentecost revival that is divinely released must be relayed. Unless a revival results in evangelism and missions, it will lose its fire and soon die out.

2. *A church grows to the degree that it is able to overcome barriers that would naturally inhibit the expansion of the gospel.* There are various kinds of barriers, five of which are overcome in Acts 8.

a. *Geographical barrier.* Geographical roadblocks can confine the spread of the gospel to a particular place and soil.

According to the record in the beginning chapters of Acts, all the gospel ministries were limited to the city of Jerusalem, although people from the surrounding area came in, heard the gospel, and were healed (Acts 5:12–16). Of course, many of the visiting Jews who had become believers on the day of Pentecost returned to the home countries where they had settled in the Diaspora. However, no mention is made of any plan of activities to spread the gospel beyond Jerusalem. Yet our Lord had informed the apostles that the field is the world, that His followers are the light of the world and the salt of the earth. Was the church in danger of becoming another Palestinian religious "Dead Sea" with too much salt in one place? The church had to overcome the geographical barrier and move out into the world. The vast masses of the people were elsewhere and not in Jerusalem. He had instructed them to be His witnesses in Jerusalem *and* in all Judea *and* Samaria, and even to the remotest part of the earth (1:8). This must be accomplished.

b. *Community barrier.* By nature humans are gregarious beings; life in society is their natural habitat. In the spiritual realm this natural tendency is reinforced by the spiritual instinct of fellowship. Thus when the church was born and individual believers were baptized into one body, a bond of unity was established.

The church is divinely designed to be the spiritual home of the believers. In it they find spiritual nurture, instruction, fellowship, and discipline—all that they need to grow in grace and in the knowledge of the Lord Jesus Christ. The believers must be brought to spiritual, doctrinal, ethical, and social maturity. This is scriptural (Acts 2:42; Eph. 4:11–16), and this is essential (1 Peter 2:1–9; 2 Peter 1:3–9). But this is not an end in itself. Believers are called to bear fruit, to be witnesses, to proclaim the excellencies of Him who has called them out of darkness into His marvelous light. To fulfill this wonderful purpose the believers must move out of the warm nest of the church into the cold world. It is *pleasant* to abide in the community of the saints, but it is *profitable* to be in the world and to share Christ with the world.

Community-centeredness was expressed on the Mount of Transfiguration when Peter exclaimed: "Rabbi, it is good *for us* to be here; let us make three tabernacles, one for You, and one for Moses, and one for Elijah" (Mark 9:5). However, this mentality, while noble in itself, does not perceive God's highest. There was a people in desperate need at the foot of the mountain. They needed the Master and His healing and liberating ministry. This fact was momentarily forgotten by Peter. The sentiments of Peter have continued to characterize and to paralyze the church in its proper functions in the community. Too easily the saints have enjoyed the coziness of blessed fellowship and have forgotten the world in its needs and desperation. Nationalism, peoplehood, tribalism, community relatedness, as well as the coziness of the fellowship become blinding and binding forces in evangelism. Evangelism and mission interest and fervor often wane when the people of the group, tribe, or community have been reached. It is not easy to climb across community and ethnic barriers.

c. *Ecclesiastical barrier.* In Acts 2 through 5 all activities are ascribed to the apostles. The church membership was listening, learning, observing; they participated only in a limited sense in sharing and praying. But the apostles were the main actors (Acts 2:42–47; 4:23–37). A limited division of labor was initiated in Acts 6:1–6 and continued to develop through the rest of Acts. Soon there were elders in the church (Acts 15:2, 4, 6, 22, 23; 20:17, 28–35). In Acts 8 all the people became active in the service of the Lord as evangelizing agents and scatterers of the gospel. Thus the ecclesiastical barrier of apostles vs. congregation was overcome and a new epoch in the movement of Christianity was initiated. Lay mobilization of the church will be discussed in a later section.

   d. *Religio-cultural barrier.* No doubt, this is one of the most formidable obstacles to overcome. Religion both unites and separates. The sentiments are expressed in such words as: "'How is it that You, being a Jew, ask me for a drink since I am a Samaritan woman?' (For Jews have no dealings with Samaritans)" (John 4:9). The Jews spoke of the Gentiles as dogs. And the Gentiles reciprocated in no milder manner. The Jews were hated among the nations and the Gentiles turned on the Jews in a most despicable and at times most brutal manner. The Jews were not appreciated in most cities of the Roman world.

   It was Philip, in all probability a Hellenist, who crossed the line, broke the religio-cultural barrier, and labored in Samaria. The Lord was with him and confirmed the work with sign and miracles. Many came to believe in the Lord Jesus Christ and both men and women were baptized. News of these happenings reached Jerusalem, and Peter and John were dispatched to see what was taking place. The gospel had leaped the line and the Samaritans had become Christians without first becoming Jewish proselytes.

   Somewhat later Peter entered the home of Cornelius of Caesarea, a Roman centurion and a man who feared God (Acts 10:1–2). Luke makes it clear that this was a difficult experience for Peter and only a divine summons could persuade him to break through the religio-cultural barrier (Acts 10:28–29, 45; 11:12). His daring step was not permitted to go unchallenged (Acts 11:1–3). But even Jerusalem had to acknowledge the grace of God bestowed on the Gentiles (Acts 11:18). With this experience the religio-cultural wall was breached. Then the barriers were theologically liquidated at the council of apostles and elders according to Acts 15. This, of course, did not mean that the struggle between Jewish legalism and Christian unity and equality ended. The Epistle to the Galatians reflects the continued battle.

e. *Racial barrier.* It was Philip who became the instrument of the Lord to cross the racial line as well. The story is found in Acts 8:26–40. The Ethiopian had made a long journey. He was yearning for divine light. He was searching for it at the right place (Jerusalem) and in the right book (Old Testament). Nevertheless, he needed human help. Philip had been divinely summoned to go to the place of the Ethiopian's journey. Here representatives of two races and cultures met in one carriage, around one book, and around one concern to discover one Savior. Thus the Lord broke down the wall of racial separation and united them in a common faith. Here is the power to break down the racial barriers that separate many people in the church of Jesus Christ and much of humanity. The church at Antioch of Syria was a healthy and fast-growing multi-racial church as its leadership indicates (Acts 11:19–26; 13:1–4). Racial and cultural heterogeneity gave way to unity and equality in Christ Jesus.

Acts 8 is evidence that the Lord does enable His church to break through the many barriers that could have become serious roadblocks in world evangelism and hindered the growth of the church.

3. *A church grows best when it functions energetically in extensive and intensive evangelism* (Acts 8:4, 12, 25, 40; 11:20; 13:32; 14:7, 15, 21; 15:35, 16:10, 17:18).

Our Lord's command is that the gospel must be preached (Mark 13:10). This is a divinely promulgated and Spirit-motivated imperative. Somehow this divine *must* did lay hold of the early church and a gospel explosion followed. The church expanded rapidly throughout the area of Palestine and beyond its borders, multitudes were added, churches grew and multiplied, to the consternation first of the Jews and soon of the Roman government.

In a New Testament church evangelism must be *central;* it must involve the energies of the total church in witnessing and praying; it must be *extensive,* reaching out to all classes and peoples of the community and all nations of the globe. In addition, evangelism must be *intensive,* touching all phases of human experience and bringing all of life under the lordship of Christ. Only thus it becomes saturation evangelism, or as discussed in the previous chapter, evangelism-in-depth and in-depth-evangelism. Finally, evangelism must be *perennial* rather than sporadic. It must become the life throb and life style of the total church. Thus the New Testament makes one of its last appeals an evangelistic and salvation appeal when John writes: "And the Spirit and the bride [the church] say, 'Come.' And let the one who hears [every believer] say, 'Come.' And let the one who is thirsty come; let the one who wishes take the water of life without cost" (Rev. 22:17). Here is evangelism by the Spirit, the church, every believer; it is all-involving, all-encompassing, perennial. Evangelism must go on to the ends of the earth until the end of the age. (See diagram.)

Diagram 22

Patterns of Evangelism
Identified from Acts

1. Public Proclamation evangelism
2. Small Group evangelism
3. Household evangelism
4. Community evangelism
5. Regional evangelism
6. Personal evangelism
7. Informal evangelism

Diagram 23

4. *A church grows best when the total body of believers is mobilized and trained in continued ministry of praying, sharing, witnessing, evangelizing.* Body life in the church is not a modern invention. The priesthood of all believers was not a fabrication of sixteenth-century reformation. Both emphases are New Testament doctrines that have been sadly neglected for many centuries. The apostles of Jesus Christ were disciple-makers. New disciples in turn were to be instruments of the Holy Spirit in world evangelism and in making disciples.

Distribution of responsibilities is a divine order. God uses men and women in various capacities; there are none He does not need or does not desire to use. The fact that all members do not have the same assignment or the same gifts and that all are not equally efficient and effective does not mean that some are excused and others must be overloaded.

All this is beautifully demonstrated in Acts 8–12. Luke records that all believers except the apostles were scattered throughout the regions of Judea and Samaria. They evangelized everywhere they went (Acts 8:4). Later Luke refers to those who went beyond Palestine (Acts 11:19–20) who also made known the gospel in their areas. Thus all believers went forth with the gospel.

Acts seems to indicate that layworkers evangelized and planted churches in Judea, Samaria, Galilee (Acts 8:14; 9:31), Cyprus,

Cyrene, Antioch (Acts 11:19–21), Pontus, Bithynia, Cappadocia, and Rome (cf. Acts 2:9–10; Rom. 1:7; 1 Peter 1:1). And who planted the churches mentioned in Rev. 1:11? Paul was in Ephesus for a lengthy period, but who planted the other churches? Again, did not Paul commend the churches in Rome and Thessalonica for their evangelistic zeal (Rom. 1:8; 1 Thess. 1:7–8)? And who evangelized the region round about Antioch in Pisidia (Acts 13:49) and the vast territory between Jerusalem and Illyricum (present-day Yugoslavia) (Rom. 15:19)? No doubt, much of the work was done under the personal direction of Paul by his coworkers. But certainly this alone cannot account for the tremendous expansion.

Many historians have discussed the reasons why Christianity spread so rapidly in the first three centuries, including among those reasons the fact that every member was mobilized and actively involved.[2] Professionalism had not yet drowned out the concept of the general priesthood of all believers. All functioned as responsible members in the body life of the church.

This principle is so significant that I am adding a special section on lay mobilization. Its importance was beautifully stated by the late R. Kenneth Strachan when he wrote: *"The expansion of any movement is in direct proportion to its success in mobilizing its total membership in continuous, constant propagation of its beliefs."*[3] This became known as the "Strachan theorem" and was the cornerstone of evangelism-in-depth (see diagram 24). W. Dayton Roberts writes: "Mobilization is the key word in Evangelism-in-Depth. In its simplest terms, it is an effort to mobilize every Christian believer—man, woman, child, illiterate, intellectual, new Christian and mature disciple—in an all-out witness to Jesus Christ."[4]

It is neither scriptural nor practical to expect that the complex ministry of the church and the ever-expanding task of world evangelization can be realized by a small group and special class of formally trained ministers. Neither can it be expected that all local congregations will be supplied with a fulltime theologically trained leadership. This holds true particularly for the churches of the Third World. In fact, trained leadership in the local congregation should be considered the exception rather than the norm in most cultures and

"The expansion of any movement is in
direct proportion to its success
in mobilizing its total
membership in continuous, constant
propagation of its beliefs."

STRACHAN THEOREM

Diagram 24

communities and at most times. This is especially so in periods of accelerated church growth such as our times. The mobilization and development of capable lay leadership for the local congregation and the training of all church members in evangelism and supportive ministries is an urgent necessity in the ongoing program of the Christian church.

However, active participation of all members in the life and ministry of the church is desirable not only for practical reasons. The very nature and constitution of the church demand it.

The church locally as well as collectively is the body of Christ. Membership in the body of Christ involves responsible functioning. The church is spoken of as the temple of God in whom the Holy Spirit dwells (Eph. 2:22). As such every member of the church is endowed by the Holy Spirit to render a meaningful service (1 Cor. 12:1–31). Every priest has a duty, responsibility, and sacred function to fulfill (Heb. 10:19–25; 1 Peter 2:9; Rev. 1:6). The New Testament privilege of the priesthood of all believers is a most gracious and glorious bestowal. At the same time it is a most serious responsibility.

The representative priesthood of Old Testament days came to an end at the death of Christ, when the veil in the temple was rent. On the day of Pentecost all believers received the anointing in the gift of the Holy Spirit. Therefore, the Aaronic priesthood was ended in the church of Jesus Christ.

The New Testament priests are exhorted to offer their bodies (Rom. 12:1), their praise (Heb. 13:15), their substance (Rom. 12:13), and their service (Heb. 13:16) to God as a reasonable response to the mercy of God. The New Testament priests are encouraged to enter boldly into the holiest by the blood of Christ (Heb. 10:19–22) and to exercise the office of an intercessor (Rom. 15:30–31; Eph. 3:14–21; 6:18–20; Phil. 1:3–11; Col. 1:9–12; 4:2–4; 1 Tim. 2:1; Heb. 10:19–22). The New Testament priests have a vital role to play in the ongoing work of the Lord. They must learn to walk circumspectly, accept their prerogatives boldly, and discharge their duties faithfully. There are no non-priests in the church of God.

Somehow history has modified this biblical concept. Unawares, a new type of representative priesthood has crept into the church and beclouded, if not crowded out, the New Testament order as ushered in on the day of Pentecost. The ordinary priests (church members) have been relegated to the place of bystanders and spectators. They have been deprived of their highest prerogative, noblest calling, and holiest functions. It was tragedy of all tragedies when the *Spirit-endowed, sacrificial* priesthood and ministry of all believers was transformed into the *sacramental* priesthood and ministry of some ecclesiastical specialists. The Reformation restored the biblical doctrine of the priesthood of all believers but re-established the practice in a very limited sense, except in the Anabaptist movement.

To remain and/or leave the membership of the church passive is not only to fail in the ministry but to sin against the specific calling and design of God for the church. It sets aside the intent of God and frustrates the grace of God in the individual believer. Church membership mobilization is impelled first and foremost by the nature of the church and reinforced by the design, intent, and calling of the church. It is therefore absolutely essential to enlist every member in the cause of the Lord if the church is to be awakened, revived, renewed, if the life and ministry in the church is to remain balanced and if the church is to flourish.

It must also be emphasized that the church will become meaningful to the individual only to the degree that a member becomes an active participant in the life and service of the church. Involvement is of utmost significance. Inactivity breeds disinterest, indifference, and eventually apathy. Therefore the vitality and welfare of the individual member demands it. In simple words, the health of the church and each member in particular demands mobilization, training, and involvement.

It is unfortunate that history has developed such concepts as laity and clergy, for it has brought classification and stratification into the membership of the church. The Bible does teach that God gave, or appointed, some to be apostles, prophets, evangelists, teachers, pastors. He also ordained that there should be elders and deacons. Such designations, however, are descriptive of sacred functions and should be recognized and respected as such. *Functional distinctions* are clearly scriptural. The church leadership—the elders and presbyters—are to be held in honor and respect, are to be obeyed and followed. The leaders are exhorted to watch over the church; to feed the flock; to teach, admonish, and encourage the membership. But to constitute such leadership into a separate and peculiar category within the church is an extrabiblical idea. *Positional distinctions* in the body of Christ are foreign to the New Testament. Such distinctions are historical and cultural.

Personally I do not find such classification scriptural. Neither do I believe that there is biblical support to circumscribe ordination by academic standards and examinations. Rather than academic and theological achievements, the Bible requires spiritual, moral, and social qualities, soundness in doctrine for the gospel ministry, and the ability to communicate the message (2 Tim. 2:2). Nor are serving in the congregation and the administering of sacraments bound up with ordination. Such limitations and demands are designed by men and are not necessarily divine and binding. Frequently they limit the growth of the congregation and the expansion of the gospel of Jesus Christ.

Lay gospel witness is a biblical norm that is buried under centuries of clerical, ecclesiastical tradition; it is badly in need of being resurrected and practiced. Wherever it is permitted to break through, progress is soon reported. It is one of the dynamics of the rapid expansion of Jehovah's Witnesses, Latter-day Saints and some other quasi-Christian movements and cults. It is one of the secrets also behind the rapid growth of the Assemblies of God and world-wide

Pentecostalism in general. It is the secret of the steady and rapid spread of the gospel in Korea, among the mountain tribes in Taiwan, in the tribal areas of Ethiopia, among the Tiv people in Nigeria, in Papua—New Guinea, and in countless other areas.

Lay mobilization and training should take place on several levels. Some lay workers will be found who will make excellent contributions in leadership, administration, and communication ministries. Others will be suited for different aspects of evangelism, such as friendship evangelism and personal or small group Bible ministries. The rest must be harnessed for prayer and supportive services. All, however, must be mobilized and trained to become useful and fruitful members in the congregation.

For study purposes, I add an outline on total membership mobilization as gleaned from the Scriptures.

1. *Mobilization is practiced in the churches.* It is led by the apostles as recorded in Acts 2:41–12:24. In Acts 2:41–5:42 the believers are in discipleship training—being made witnesses. In Acts 8:1–12:24 the believers are out in actual discipleship practice—witnessing.

2. *Mobilization is divinely ordained.* Ephesians 4:11–16 says that for this purpose the Lord gave the church apostles, prophets, evangelists, and pastor-teachers.

3. *Mobilization is implied in the descriptive terms of the church:*

—in the body function of all believers (Rom. 12:3–8; 1 Cor. 12:1–31).

—in the priesthood of all believers (Heb. 10:19–22; 1 Peter 2:9; Rev. 1:6).

—in the fact that the local church is the *people of God* (1 Peter 2:9–10).

4. *Mobilization is implied in the commands to the believers:*

—in the fact that the Holy Spirit indwells and endows every member of Christ with a *special enablement* (Rom. 12:3–8; 1 Cor. 12:1–31).

—in the fact that believers are created unto *good works* (Eph. 2:10; Titus 2:14; 3:8; James 2:17; 1 Peter 2:12).

5. *Mobilization is illustrated in the Old Testament:*
—in the building of the tabernacle (Exod. 35:4–29).
—in the conquest of Palestine (Josh. 1:10–15).
—in the building of the temple (1 Kings 5:13–18; 1 Chron. 29:1–9).
—in the building of the second temple (Ezra 1:5–6; 3:8–13; Hag. 1:2–15).
—in the building of the walls of Jerusalem (Neh. 2:17–6:15).

Thus the total church must be mobilized to remain healthy and strong and serve its divinely ordained purpose.

5. *The church grows best when the soil has been carefully and prayerfully prepared for the gospel.* This truth has been emphasized in chapter 4 and needs no further discussion here.

6. *A church grows best when evangelism is undergirded by a Spirit-directed, biblical strategy.* The Holy Spirit is the great *Strategist* in Acts. He is undisputably the Superintendent in the great missionary endeavor. He empowers and initiates (Acts 1:8; 13:1–4), guides and directs (Acts 8:29; 16:6–10). Although the strategy is not explicitly spelled out in Acts, or anywhere in the New Testament for that matter, yet it is implicit and traceable.

The beginning point in any strategy is setting the goal. The goal of the Christian church was clearly set forth by the Lord Himself as recorded in Acts 1:8 when He commissioned His disciples: "You shall receive power when the Holy Spirit has come upon you; and you shall be My witnesses both in Jerusalem, and in all Judea and Samaria, and even to the remotest part of the earth." Even though the goal only gradually unfolded in Acts, the Holy Spirit, as Superintendent, surely motivated the church in its onward movement. The remotest part of the earth remains the goal of all Spirit-directed evangelism.

The following observations show us the strategy that had resulted in evangelism and church multiplication.

1. *Originating place.* The divine breakthrough came about in

Jerusalem, the center of Old Testament worship and the Judaism of that day. That this happened in Jerusalem was most significant. Something new had been born on the day of Pentecost, yet it was related to the Old Testament. A new people of God had been born; a new institution—the church—had been created. This did not happen somewhere on the periphery. God invaded the very center of Judaism to dwell in His new temple and to manifest Himself from Jerusalem. Thus Jerusalem became once more the center of the manifestation of God.

2. *Appropriate timing.* The breakthrough came at a most strategic time. Thousands of Jews, proselytes, and God-fearers were filling Jerusalem for religious celebrations. Acts 2 mentions some of the representatives from the Diaspora. It was at this time that God sent the great outpouring, multitudes were converted and became members of the Christian church. The significance of this is seen in the fact that a wide variety of men such as Barnabas, Stephen, Philip, and others (Acts 6:5) became prominent advocates of the gospel. Also, when the persecution forced the believers to leave Jerusalem, they carried the gospel with them to their home countries (Acts 8:4; 11:19–22). We may well imagine that these reports are representative and that they were duplicated many times over.

3. *Preparation time.* The Lord provided time for the new believers to develop new spiritual, social, and economic relationships, and to be made into disciples of Jesus Christ. They were indoctrinated as witnesses in order to preserve the unity and soundness of the faith and were trained to function as responsible members in witnessing, praying, and communal living (Acts 2:42–46; 4:23–31; 5:42; 6:1–7; 8:4; 11:19–21; 12:5).

4. *Prepared areas.* The witnesses went to prepared people when they scattered abroad because of persecution. Samaria, Judea, Galilee had been the communities in which Christ had served, so the Lord Himself had prepared these people for the message. It is not surprising that the churches here prospered and multiplied (Acts 9:31). The situation seems to have been similar in other Jewish communities (Acts 9:32–43; 11:19–21; 13:43–45, 49).

Paul, for example, labored mainly in cities where there was a concentration of Jews, where the soil had been prepared by the presence of the synagogue and possibly by believers returning after Pentecost to their adopted homelands. Most of these cities were strategic cultural and commercial centers of Roman administration so that order and safety were assured. Also, they lay on national and international communication and trade routes from which the gospel could radiate into the communities round about (Acts 13:49; 19:10, 26; 1 Thess. 1:8) and be carried to distant places (Rom. 15:19–23).

5. *Coordinated ministries. Cooperation, coordination,* and *subordination* in the movement gave unity, strength, and direction to it. There was a unifying superintendence of the work at the very beginning in order to prevent the work from over-diversifying and thus creating small units of isolated groups. Philip did not mind that Peter and John were dispatched from the mother church to check into the work in Samaria and add to and enrich his ministry (8:4–25). The Christians of Antioch in Syria did not object to Barnabas being sent from Jerusalem to investigate and regulate the work and take charge of the teaching ministry (11:22–26).

Coordination was seen in the division of the fields of labor (Gal. 2:7–10). Peter directed his strength toward the evangelization of the large non-Palestinian Jewish colonies, and Paul went more to the Roman centers.

Cooperation was seen in the teamwork concept. Paul surrounded himself with a team of laborers who worked together in mutual confidence and respect. Such team ministries were psychologically wholesome. The team provided support as they confronted paganism. Teamwork also facilitated gospel saturation of total communities (Acts 13:49; 19:7–10) by the impact that comes from the presence of a group rather than a lone worker.

Writing of the Pauline team ministry Dr. Arthur Glasser observes:

> This team occupies most of the later chapters of the Book of Acts. It was a supranational team. Paul as a member of the team forgot he was a Jew; in certain situations it was necessary for him to repudiate his racial origin. The team interacted with local congregations yet was separate from them. Authority for

the team came from within itself—not from the local church. Guidance was received directly from the Lord, yet they sought later approval of churches from which they had come. The team recruited its own workers and manifested a leadership principle even while respecting individual guidance. The team was mobile, moving to the outer fringes, evangelizing men, training converts, and planting churches.[5]

6. *Global vision.* Paul had a definite world strategy. After he had been driven from Jerusalem, he turned his attention to Asia Minor laboring first in Tarsus and Antioch (Acts 11:25–30; 13:1–3), then West Asia-Minor with Ephesus as his center (Acts 19:1–20:38). From there he looked west with Rome as the center and Spain as the remotest part (Acts 19:21; 23:11; 28:14–31; Rom. 1:9–15; 15:24, 28). Here was a man with the world in view.

The effectiveness of this strategy may be deduced from the following summary expressions in Acts:

- "You have filled Jerusalem with your teaching" (5:28).
- "And the word of God kept on spreading; and the number of the disciples continued to increase greatly . . . and a great many of the priests were becoming obedient to the faith" (6:7).
- "There was much rejoicing in that city" (8:8).
- "And all who lived at Lydda and Sharon saw him, and they turned to the Lord" (9:35).
- "The word of the Lord continued to grow and to be multiplied" (12:24).
- "And the word of the Lord was being spread through the whole region" (13:49).
- "The churches were being strengthened in the faith, and were increasing in number daily" (16:5).
- "All who lived in Asia heard the word of the Lord, both Jews and Greeks (19:10).
- "The word of the Lord was growing mightily and prevailing" (19:20).
- "From Jerusalem and round about as far as Illyricum I have fully preached the gospel of Christ" (Rom. 15:19).

Here was a movement with a global vision and strategy. It was superintended by the Holy Spirit and obediently, persistently, and sacrificially pursued by a band of valiant men and women.

Let no one think lightly of strategy. Strategy is not scheming. It is wise, purposeful planning and orderly procedure to accomplish a set goal. It is essential to church growth.

7. *A church grows best when the church and the work are people-related.* The gospel is for the people because Jesus Christ is for the people, and our Lord constantly related Himself to people. To be people-related is much more difficult than to be subject-related. A person can acquire subject matter in his study, but not so people-relatedness. It must also be emphasized that a church can become a holy huddle of self-interested members.

The key to people-relatedness is genuine love for people, interest in people, sharing with people, understanding people, becoming involved with people in their experiences and needs, their anxieties and anticipations, praying with and for people, humbly depending on the Holy Spirit and expecting that He can and will create that needed relatedness.

Jesus was people-related. In His childhood, youth, and early adulthood He shared all their experiences, growing up in Nazareth and toiling as a carpenter. Later He labored in their midst from early morning till late into the night in such dedication that He was accused of being out of His mind (Mark 3:21). No one is more exemplary in his love for people than our Lord who visited with, healed and served, and spoke the message of love and the kingdom of God in such a way that throngs followed Him and great crowds enjoyed listening to Him (Mark 12:37). His parables are unparalleled in the history of communication and vividly and concretely present the message of God with emphasis and persuasion. They grip the imagination, capture the interest, illumine the mind, warm the heart, and motivate the will. In His service He was sought out by people in need and His presence and help was solicited at numerous occasions. Jesus was a man of the people.

How people-related was the early church in the ministry it sought to render in the world? A study of the Book of Acts will show that it drew large numbers into its fold. It had favor with all the people and the people held them in high esteem (Acts 2:47; 5:13). Without such relatedness it would have been impossible for the church to expand as it did.

The church must be people-related in message and service if it wishes to capture the attention of the people and draw them into the fold of Jesus Christ. It needs to ask itself such questions as: Do we actually meet the deepest and most pressing needs of the people? Do we grip and guide their conscience? Do we scratch where they itch? Do we bring warning where they are negligent or indifferent? Do we bring correction where they are wrong? Do we rebuke where they are failing? Do we bring healing where they are hurting? Do we bring hope where they are depressed? Do we bring encouragement where they are downcast? Do we bring strength where they are weak? Do we bring light where they are ignorant? Do we bring comfort where they are brokenhearted? Do we bring redemption where they are in bondage? Do we bring forgiveness where they are guilty? Do we bring reconciliation where there is enmity? Do we bring peace where there is strife? Do we share liberally of our substance with the needy in the world? Is our presence, message, and service related to the people? Would it be missed if it were to disappear? To be people-related may be a costly game of life, however it is a Christlike life and will be a great force in building the church.

To be people-related is not a simple matter in a diversified world. It is apparent that people differ in their languages, psychological mood, feelings and sentiments, in their mentality or ways of thinking, in their societies or interpersonal roles and relationships and their cultural values, systems of beliefs, behavior, patterning, and structuring. This calls for differences in communication, in methodology of operation and organizational ordering to be relevant to the individuals and to be people-related. Diagram 25 presents this vividly.

Several principles evolve from such differences. The mentality of the people determines the principles of communication. This we have studied before. The roles and relationships within society determine the methods of operation. Therefore one method or program that operates most effectively in one type of society may not be

CULTURE IMPACT

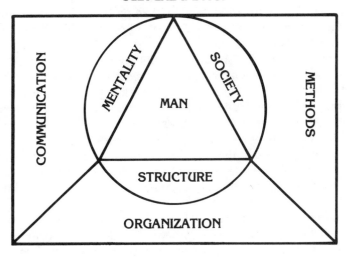

Diagram 25

relevant in another society. The form and structure of culture determines organizational patterns in which people will feel at home and operate efficiently and effectively. Basic religious philosophy shapes the world and life view of people and also their value system, hopes, and aspirations. It becomes determining in the approaches that will appeal to the individuals. These are differences that cannot be overlooked and must be bridged if the church is to relate itself to the people.

Christianity is new and renewing but it should not be strange and estranging. The people should know that the church is created to serve the people and not that the people are there for the aggrandizement and expansion of the church.

8. *A church grows best by people units of society.*[6] The emphasis is on *people units,* often spoken of as homogeneous units. We do not find scriptural support that there were churches formed along

homogeneous lines in apostolic times. This may have happened. However, this seems more unlikely than probable. It would be difficult to establish such a fact and practice from biblical and historical sources. *Biblical idealism* and *apostolic practices* do not support it. In fact, biblical idealism seems to cut across this social and cultural practice and rule it out, at least consider it sub-ideal (1 Cor. 3:4; Col. 3:10–11). The unity and equality of all believers in Christ were dogmatically defended in the letters to the Ephesians and Colossians. Divisions, divisiveness, partyism, and social distinctions were practically condemned (1 Cor. 11:1–22; James 2:1–13). Such was not to be practiced in the churches. It may, however, be that small group fellowships in the homes and household churches *naturally* fell into this pattern without having been consciously designed that way.

However the churches and fellowships may have been structured, and whatever role homogeneity may have played in them, *in evangelism and in movements toward Christ and the gospel peoplehood did play a significant role.* Whether we speak of such movements as mass movements, community movements, tribal movements, people movements, or whatever other designation we may choose, it cannot be denied that people in a bond of belongingness and a sense of togetherness have moved quite frequently in larger units or totality into the fold of Christ or at least into Christendom. Whether this is biblically ideal and practically advisable may be debated, but *the fact* of such movements is biblically and historically established.

Consider the following biblical records: Abraham moved with his extended family—servants and slaves—into the covenant of God (Gen. 17:1–14, 23). All major revivals in Israel and reported in the Old Testament were national in scope. Extensive community movements were experienced under the preaching of John the Baptist (Matt. 3:1–6; Luke 3:1–14). It should be noted that the tax-gatherers and soldiers came in groups to John as did the sinners and publicans later to Jesus (Luke 15:1), seemingly later the priests in groups came into the church (Acts 6:7). There were large community and village movements in Galilee, Samaria, and Decapolis during the ministry of Christ (Matt. 3:23–25; John 4:39–41). Certainly Pentecost was a breakthrough of no small proportion (Acts 3:19–45), and soon the masses followed (Acts 4:4; 5:14–16; 6:1, 7). Peter experienced a community movement in Lydda, Sharon, and Joppa (Acts 9:32–43) and Philip saw it in Samaria (Acts 8:5–25). Other evangelists must have witnessed similar things in Galilee, Samaria, and Judea (Acts 9:31), or how else could the churches have multiplied? We are informed that great numbers believed in Antioch of Syria (Acts 11:10–26). Paul seemingly saw churches multiply daily (Acts 16:5), and Antioch, Pisidia, and Ephesus experienced great ingatherings (Acts 13:42–45; 13:49; 19:10, 20, 26).

Of special significance are the household conversions mentioned in the New Testament.[7] In Luke 19 we hear our Lord say to Zaccheus: "Today salvation is come to this household" as the father had been converted. John reports the household conversion of a royal official of Capernaum whose son was healed by the Lord—"So the father . . . himself believed, and his whole household" (John 4:53). The story of the conversion of Cornelius is told in great detail in Acts 10. Cornelius had called together his relatives and close friends (Acts 10:24). To this congregation Peter spoke and "while Peter was still speaking . . . the Holy Spirit fell upon all those who were listening to the message" (Acts 10:44). In consequence Peter ordered the extended family and friends to be baptized in the name of Jesus Christ (Acts 10:48). The conversion of two households in Philippi are reported (Acts 16:15; 16:27–34). Crispus, the leader of the synagogue in Corinth believed in the Lord with all his household (Acts 18:8) and so did Stephanos and his household (1 Cor. 1:16). The households of Aristobulus, Narcissus (Rom. 16:10–11), Onesiphorus (2 Tim. 1:16), and Philemon (Philem.) are mentioned. However, the details are not specific whether these remarks refer to the conversion of the total household. We must point to Acts 2:37–41 and 4:4. It is probable that the 3,000 converts on the day of Pentecost were *men* who had gathered in the precincts of the temple and thus represented that many households. These were increased soon to 5,000 men (Acts 4:4; "as distinct from women and children"—F. F. Bruce). It is in the light of this that the early believers were able to meet in the homes for fellowship, prayer, evangelism, and teaching (Acts 2:46; 5:42). Similar was the experience of Paul in Ephesus (Acts 20:20).

The New Testament knows of household conversions, household baptisms (Acts 16:15; 16:30–34; 1 Cor. 1:14–15), and of household churches (Rom. 16:3–5; 1 Cor. 16:19; Col. 4:15; Philem. 2).

We find household conversions among Jews, Greeks, Romans, and Samaritans. Seemingly household evangelism is one pattern that fits all cultures. Household conversions in the New Testament are not exceptional cases. *They are a divine ideal and apostolic norm.* They are biblically sound, socially wholesome, and beneficial to church growth and church strength. Well does Boer say: "The church was not built up of so many individual Christians but of *basic social units,* of *organic wholes,* and these units, these wholes, were the fundamental cells of society, namely *families."* It is too bad that household evangelism figures very little in present-day evangelistic programs.

We are not lacking biblical data that people move in groups, in families, blood relationships, in communities or social relationships, and in professional groups in religious matters. Peoplehood is a divine-human factor that cannot be ignored in evangelism and church planting. It is a fact of life and of the total structure within humanity.

The significant fact is that *the New Testament does not reflect negatively on people movements.* They have continued throughout the history of Christianity and added countless multitudes to the church of Jesus Christ or at least to professing Christendom.

In the light of history, it must be stated that such larger movements are not without serious dangers to the church. These must be guarded against. They need not become reality. Let me sketch some dangers.

First, there is little carry-over of evangelism concern and effort from one group of people to another. There is a tendency to slacken in the work of evangelism and missions when the *home-group* has been reached with the gospel. This tendency must not be permitted to become practical. Therefore, missions to people outside of the home circle must be emphasized from the very beginning. People must become involved in missions at an early stage.

Second, there is a tendency toward exclusiveness and unwholesome separateness. It becomes easy to remain aloof from the larger fellowship of the church of Christ. Provincialism and parochialism bring with them a practical denial of the unity and equality of all believers in Christ Jesus. This danger is real not only in tribal areas of Africa or elsewhere. It is uniquely serious in India because of the deep-rooted caste system. Only a healthy spiritual life and a strong teaching program of New Testament principles can build a conscience that will not tolerate such separateness and exclusiveness.

Third, larger group accessions can constitute a real danger to change the New Testament believer's church of personal voluntarism into a *folk church* that belongs to the people. This is a most serious peril. From a practical standpoint it converts the church into a religious club of the community that everyone ought to and is expected to join. It is also a fact that in large group and community movements many individuals either drift along with others or because of social pressure are pushed along without having personally experienced salvation and regeneration. Nominalism, therefore, becomes a real threat to the church of Jesus Christ. This becomes most evident in the second or third generation when the first glow of the religious change has cooled down and Christianity has been *domesticated.* All belong to it as natural descendants of its founders.

Fourth, the line between indigenization and socialization, syncretism and nativism is not always easily drawn. While indigenization and socialization are enhanced by large movements, the dangers of syncretism and nativism are deepened. This is evident to every observer who visits mass movement areas in South India and Indonesia. In many areas of the former country Christo-paganism is rife. In the latter place syncretism saps the finances and strength of the church. Here ancestor and spirit worship and even occultism are most threatening realities. It is well to read a book like *Post-Christianity in Africa—A Theological and Anthropological Study* by G. C. Oosthuizen. It is a sobering study.

Such dangers, while alerting us, must not frighten us to the degree that we hold back from working toward and expecting great movements to come about, bringing multitudes into the kingdom of God.

While we are conscious of such perils we must work so much harder to assure as much true spiritual experience and Christian growth as possible.

9. *A church grows best by corporate-personality decisions in cultures of family, tribe, community, and people relationships.* This point is closely related to the previous two propositions and leads us into the process of decision making in societies other than Western.

Western individualism is not necessarily the highest norm and absolute ideal. The Bible has much to say about households. It is my impression that household evangelism, conversion, baptism, and churches are a higher norm according to the New Testament than Western individualism. Certainly it is not the only type and form as we have seen above, but the family as the pre-Fall divine institution remains the highest and noblest institution in the Bible. Its salvation and edification must always be before us. Though the emphasis on community and people is not as pronounced, it is significant in the Bible.

We ought to distinguish more carefully between two concepts that are often wrongly used as synonyms. *Individual* is a *social concept* and when used as a noun *individualist* most often connotes negative qualities. *Personal,* on the other hand, is a *psychological term* and most often expresses positive characteristics. Thus we speak of a strong, a pleasant *personality.* Something may become very personal even if experienced in and with a group. This distinction must be kept in mind.

A corporate-personality society is not necessarily a lower level or a lesser type of people than an individual-personality or autonomous-personality people. In fact, it may be stronger and more balanced in many ways because of the bond of relationships and sense of interdependence that it experiences and that is its milieu of functioning.

Corporate-personality decisions are decisions made by deliberations and by common consent rather than by one person or a few persons making the decision for all the others. Corporate-personality decisions and consequently conversions are experienced in large numbers in Asia and Africa. They are just as natural out there now as they were when experienced by the early church. The problem is not corporate-personality decisions and conversions but our mode and method of communication, operation, and dealing with such decisions. The problems of miscarriage may rest more with us than with them. Our bondage to individualism easily blinds us to broader realms of operations and psychological and social relationships.

Operations in corporate-personality societies require their own method and time. Here evangelism does not aim at sudden and immediate decisions. The Western-style altar call has no place in such ministries and may do more harm than good in the long run. It may be a show with little lasting reality behind it. Rather, here the practice of gospel presentation-penetration-permeation-confrontation must be carried through with diligence, patience, and persistence with continued follow-up to answer questions and come with additional information and motivation. Dialogue and discussions are more suitable than Western-style monologue preaching. The result of patient, persistent ministries as societies or total communities deliberate and make decisions to move in unity into the kingdom of God may be testing and taxing, but it is wholesome and wise. *It is not a people-movement but rather a people-in-relationship is being moved by gradual depth persuasion and on deliberative decisions to turn to the living God from their idols and to Jesus Christ as the only sufficient Savior of humanity* (1 Thess. 1:9–10). It is not a bulk being pushed along. This may be so if the evangelist is not wise and patient. Rather, it is a *people and personalities in relationships deliberating, deciding, and moving along in unity without disrupting the inter-relationships.* This most certainly is not a lower level of functioning than Western individuals operating independently and without consideration of relationships.

In corporate-personality societies evangelism aims first of all at people *responsible for guiding* the community, tribe, or family in decision making. To lay hold initially of some key people may prove more effective in the long run than to reach a considerable number of peripheral individuals. Because of this the Bible emphasizes the role of the father in evangelism and conversion. In Israel the emphasis was on the king, the princes, the priests, and prophets. Here were the keys to the people and the whole nation.

Evangelism must note the organizational and functional power structures and seek to channel the gospel along the natural and socially acceptable lines of communication. This is not manipulation but submission to and adaptation of the ways of the people the evangelist seeks to reach with the gospel of Jesus Christ. This is the adaptation Paul advocates when he writes: "I have made myself a slave to all, that I might win the more . . . I have become all things to all men, that I might by all means save come. And I do all things for the sake of the gospel, that I may become a fellow-partaker of it" (1 Cor. 9:19–23). There was reason for Paul striving to enter some of the main centers of civilization of his time and for his ambition to preach the gospel in Rome also. (See diagram.)

Patterns of Conversion

1. **Mass responses**
2. **People in relationship**
   corporate personality
   professional
   occupational
   filial
3. **Cities**
4. **Communities**
5. **Individual**

Diagram 26

10. *A church grows best when the church releases the ablest, most qualified, and experienced servants of God for evangelism and church expansion.* So it was in the Book of Acts. This point needs no argument. It will be readily agreed that the apostles, who had been trained by the Lord Himself, were the most qualified men

of their time. To the apostles prominent teachers were added such as Barnabas, Saul (Paul), Apollos, Silas, Timothy, Titus, Epaphras, Luke, and many others. With the exception of James, the brother of the Lord, who remained in Jerusalem, all men were released by and from the churches for itinerant ministries of evangelism, church planting, and church confirmation.

This set the example for and pattern in the early church. It was a church on the go, a church in evangelism. It is not surprising, therefore, that the church expanded rapidly. The band of able evangelists and missionaries, supported by large numbers of volunteers, lay people, and professionals, fanned over large territories to spread the good news. Only so it was possible that all Jerusalem was filled with the new doctrine (Acts 5:28); only so could churches multiply and increase in numbers daily (9:31; 16:5); only so could the word of the Lord be published throughout all the regions of Pisidia and Asia and Galatia (13:49; 19:10); only thus could the words of Paul, in Romans 15:19, sound reasonable when he wrote that the gospel message had been preached from Jerusalem to Illyricum; and only so could the gospel reach Rome (Rom. 1:7), Pontus, Cappadocia, Bithynia (1 Peter 1:1), and Babylon (1 Peter 5:13).

Should we add extra-biblical material, the noble band would lead us into Arabia, Iran, India, Egypt, Spain, and around the Black Sea. This spread of the church and the gospel under the most adverse circumstances, without any modem facilities of communication, and by an originally small and insignificant group is absolutely fantastic. Only the impact of a risen Lord and the supernatural endowment of the Pentecost power in the Person of the Holy Spirit can account for it. On the human side it was the readiness of the churches to release the ablest, most qualified, and experienced men to lead and inspire such a ministry. The sacrifices of the churches in missions must not be measured foremost in the amounts of money they collect but in the number and quality of people they are offering and releasing for world evangelism. Here is the real measure of sacrifice.

It is estimated that at the end of the Apostolic Age (A.D. 100) some 500,000 believers (Martin) had been won and most of the larger centers in the Roman Empire had a church as a witness to the gospel of our Lord Jesus Christ.

11. *A church grows best by team ministries under the guidance of strong, devoted, and wise leadership.* In this our Lord Himself is the prime example. The band of twelve were not merely disciples and learners. This they were, but they were chosen to be *with Him,* and that He might send them forth to preach (Mark 3:13–14). Luke significantly adds "Whom also he named apostles" (Luke 6:13). It was these to whom He gave authority, power, a commission, and detailed instructions (Matt. 10:1–15). Thus the disciples became members of a team led by our Lord, and at least to some degree, His colaborers.

The second outstanding example in team ministries is Paul, whom we have already met with his band of colaborers.

In neither of the teams was there ever a question who the leader of the team was. He had not been elected by a majority vote, nor was he dependent on their favor. He knew his appointment from above. Neither was the team a team of joiners. Our Lord carefully chose His disciples and so did Paul. Neither team was completely successful in holding the trained. Christ had a Judas in His company and Paul had those who forsook him. Such experiences, however, did not discourage either leader. Wherever human beings are involved, failures may occur.

12. *A church grows best where persons of divine calling and qualification, faith and prayer are able to guide the church body to live in the experience of the reality of God and have their spiritual needs met by the study of the Word of God.* Leadership is important. It may well be the main key to church growth and health. Not academics but the knowledge of divine spiritual reality and the Word of God are its highest prerequisites. Nothing is more tragic than a pulpit and a church out of touch with reality. No one senses the state of the church more quickly than the world does. It cannot be expected that the world will be attracted by a realitiless church or leadership. On the other hand, there will always be people who will be attracted to a church that lives in the reality of the divine and the spiritual. This is evident in the Book of Acts. No opposition and

persecution was able to stop the growth of the church because here divine reality was experienced.

13. *A church grows best where the gospel is clearly, relevantly, and persuasively preached; Jesus Christ is honored as Savior and Lord; and the Holy Spirit is believed and obeyed.* This point has been studied previously under the topic, "The Message of God." It is stated here in propositional form in order to remind the student of church growth that it is *not only* a vital point but that it is the beginning and the end, the foundation and the culmination, and that it binds the factors into a dynamic whole and perfect circle. It is the message of God that matters above and in all.

CONCLUSION

The thirteen points we have listed are not merely suggestions for church growth. We believe these are *biblical principles* that determine strategy, methodology, and communication. They cannot be disregarded or lightly set aside as practices that belong to the ancient world or early church. They are *principles* according to which the Holy Spirit operates in and through the church. Therefore, only to the degree that a church conforms to such biblical principles does the Holy Spirit function freely and can the church perform dynamically. Its growth and prosperity are related to them. While the incarnation and configuration may differ with time and cultures, the principles themselves are abiding. The church needs to rediscover and practice them in obedience to and dependence on the Holy Spirit. The church may yet experience the abiding effects of Pentecost in revival, relaying the revival and church growth and multiplication.

14

Pillar Four—
The Focus of the Church

To be in focus demands at least two things—an object to be focused on and clarity of perception. We all know that looking at a slide or movie that is out of focus makes us dizzy. The picture must be clearly focused so that we can see the object clearly.

The church is much like a movie that may be in or out of focus. Its objective is to accomplish the purpose of God. Its concern must be to clearly perceive this purpose and then carefully, wisely, and energetically pursue that goal. Cost, convenience, and time are not considerations. Rather, the choice is between knowing the will and design of God or remaining ignorant of it; between obeying the will of God and fitting into His purpose or disobeying His will. What is the church to focus on? What is its object? What is the purpose of God?

First, the total world view of the Bible is theocentric. God is central to all that exists and everything is dependent on Him. However, though the Bible is theocentric, it is not deistic. God remains in intimate relationship to the world and to mankind. God is the gracious sustainer and benevolent ruler and just judge of all that exists. He is and remains in just and loving relations with all that is and particularly so with human beings whom He created in His own image and to His own likeness. Never has God totally abandoned His creatures. We have never become totally autonomous or total forsaken. Only in the second death will people be forsaken. God's concern for us is clearly evident from the pages of the Old Testament and demonstrated in the *Heilsgeschichte* of the old economy. It broke through in full radiance and glory in the miracle of Incarnation, the sending forth of His only begotten Son, our Lord Jesus Christ, to be the Savior of the *world.* God exists in a love relationship to the world. Jesus Christ, the Lamb of God, took on Himself the sin of the *world.* He is the propitiation for . . . the sins of the world. He *reconciled* the world to God (John 1:29; 1 John 2:2; 2 Cor. 5:18–21). The Holy Spirit is *convicting* the *world* and *drawing* all individuals to Christ (John 12:32; 16:8). *The Trinity, thus, is focused on the world.*

Second, the Lord expressed His will and purpose in the Great Commission. God wills that the *gospel* be proclaimed by His messengers. Whatever a witness may take with him and whatever he may do, if he does not take the gospel with him, he does not operate in the framework of the Great Commission. The gospel is to be *preached.* It must be orally communicated in such a manner that it will win a hearing and elicit a response. It must appeal to the conscience, heart, mind, will, and emotions. It must penetrate the listener's whole personality to evoke response. Again, the gospel must be preached among *all nations.* The word *all* is too emphatic to be ignored or slighted. To make it specific, it is restated in Acts 1:8 in geographic terms—Jerusalem, Judea, Samaria, and the extremity of the earth. Well does Blauw interpret the phrase in terms of intensity and extensity of universal gospel proclamation.[1] *The Great Commission focuses on the world.*

Third, the missionary outreach of the early church was under the direction of the Holy Spirit. Study the record of the Book of Acts. It is common to mark a basic division of the book between chapters 12 and 13. Luke devotes twelve chapters to the emergence of the church, its structure and function, and sixteen chapters to the missionary outreach of the church. The missionary focus was under the direction of the same Holy Spirit who gave birth to the church on the day of Pentecost. The world focus began at a specific place, at a specific time—a time of ministering and fasting—to a specific congregation. Specific men—Barnabas and Saul—were called out for a specific work—the work to which the Holy Spirit had called them (Acts 13:1–4). The Holy Spirit accepted the superintendency of the work—He sent them forth. *The Holy Spirit focuses the church on His work that must be done in the world.*

Fourth, the plan of God is that the church be made up of people of all nations. We turn to a crucial passage in Paul's writings. No other epistle expounds more fully the plan and purpose of God than the letter to the Ephesians. Here the purpose of God comes to a clear focus: first, in the greatness and glory of the salvation of God (1:3–23); next, in the greatness and glory of the church of God as it is being gathered in our age (2:1–22). In chapter 3 Paul mentions the whole mystery of salvation and the church (v. 6) and says that all this is according to the eternal purpose of God (v. 11). Verse 6 summarizes the several essential emphases of God's plan:

a. The church of Jesus Christ is to be composed of people from all nations. The definite article before *Gentiles* (non-Jewish people of the world) is significant. It omits no people.

b. In the church of Jesus Christ there is total equality positionally in Christ. All are fellow-heirs, fellow-members of the body, fellow-partakers of the promise.

c. All of this is *in Christ Jesus.* He is the only source and cause of such a qualitative body, such a church, such a community.

d. All of these benefits can be experienced *only by means of the gospel* of Jesus Christ. Therefore the apostle continues: "of which I was made a minister . . . to preach to the Gentiles the unfathomable riches of Christ" (vv. 7–8). Here the purpose of God becomes clearly evident. *God's purpose is focused on the nations of the world* because the church is to be composed of members from every nation.

To sum up, the Trinity, the Great Commission, the work of the

Holy Spirit, and the purpose of God focus on the world. The church, too, must focus on it.

God focuses on the world in a great and glorious missionary purpose and plan. Initially this purpose was perceived only dimly by the apostles and early church. This is both natural and understandable. Pentecost did not necessarily snap the apostles out of their traditional concepts, moods, and mentality; nor did it mold them in a miraculous manner and refocus them so completely that they found themselves spontaneously moving in the stream of God's missionary purpose. Their spiritual horizon, thinking, experiences, and also missionary ministries, were a matter of growth and progress. That they finally did perceive God's focus is evident in Acts and the Epistles. The world missionary purpose shone forth most brilliantly and was incarnated most fully in the apostle Paul. This chapter will look at, first, the church moving into focus, and then Paul moving into focus.

THE CHURCH MOVES INTO FOCUS

The first foreign missionary endeavor (cross-national and cross-religious) is recorded in Acts 11:19–21. It is true that we have already read of Philip going to Samaria and then being divinely led to meet the Ethiopian on the Gaza road. Peter and John had evangelized in many villages of the Samaritans, and Peter had proclaimed the Good News in the house of Cornelius. Philip's evangelism in Samaria and Peter's ministry to Cornelius did not, however, result in a sustained ministry to non-Jewish people. They were preaching projects into which divinely ordered circumstances had led them. In addition, these incidents did not necessarily occur prior to the events recorded in Acts 11:19–21. Acts 11:19 seems to be directly related to Acts 8:4 as the wording in it suggests.

In Acts 8:1 we read that at the time of the stoning of Stephen a great persecution broke out in Jerusalem. Christians dispersed in every direction. However, they did not go into hiding. They went about evangelizing. As would be natural, they fled back to their home countries. Therefore, some scattered into Judea, Galilee, and Samaria (8:2; 9:31). Others went back to the large Jewish settlements in Phoenicia, Cyprus, and Antioch (11:19–21). The result of the ministries of those who went into the Palestinian provinces is summarized in Acts 9:31—the churches there were built up and increased. The disciples of Phoenicia—Tyre and Ptolemais—are mentioned in Acts 15:3 and 21:3–7. But, for specific reasons Antioch is singled out for a report.

No doubt, a goodly number of people from Antioch had responded to the gospel of Jesus Christ already in Jerusalem. One of their representatives, Nicolas, a proselyte, had been made a deacon in Jerusalem (Acts 6:5). We can also deduce that the response to the new message in the large Jewish community in Antioch was good (Acts 11:26; 13:1; 14:26–15:2; Gal. 2:11–14). Therefore, a substantial church must have grown up around the synagogue consisting of believing Jews and proselytes. Then, however, something new happened. Some of the evangelizing men took heart and preached to the Greeks *also*. The Greek words for *Greeks* and *also* seem to indicate that here was *a new endeavor resulting in a breakthrough with continuing effects.* Seven specifics are mentioned about this mission in Antioch:

1. The men who are singled out in this mission were unauthorized laymen from Cyprus and Cyrene. They were not natives of Antioch; they had been guided here for a specific mission.

2. These men proclaimed the gospel *also* to the Greeks (that is, to the Hellenes, Greeks by origin, not the Hellenists, Greek-speaking Jews). In this they departed from previous practice. So far the gospel had gone only to the Jews and proselytes (Acts 11:19). Here was a change not only in strategy but in basic principle. That this did not go without challenge is evident from Acts 11:22–24; 15:1–2; Galatians 2:11–14.

3. The evangelizing men experienced the blessings of the Lord in a remarkable way: "the hand of the Lord was with them." This may mean that manifest signs and miracles accompanied their ministry, indicating divine approval of this new departure (cf. Acts 4:30).

4. Genuine conversions were registered among the Greeks. The words are convincingly descriptive: they became believers, they turned to the Lord, and Barnabas saw the grace of God at work.

5. This new departure demanded a great deal of teaching to mold this believing multitude from non-Jewish background into a church, a qualitative community of God. It is not improbable that serious tensions arose between the believing Jews and proselytes of the synagogue and the Greeks converted from paganism to Christianity, tensions that continued for many years and eventually led to the Jerusalem council and a visit by Peter to Antioch, perhaps on the invitation of the synagogue Christians (Acts 15:1–3; Gal. 2:11–14).

6. In Antioch the believers were first called Christians, a designation whose origin is difficult to define. It seems to indicate an active, aggressive witness in the community.

7. Somewhat after these first days of Acts 11, Antioch had the honor of sending forth the first world missionaries and thus become the missionary center of early Christianity.

That such a breakthrough should come in Antioch in Syria is in one way natural and in another way strategically significant. It is natural because of the mood and population of the city, and it is strategically significant because of the geographical location of the city and its importance in the eastern regions of the Roman Empire.

Antioch was a microcosm of racial, national, social, and religious pluralism. At the same time wealth, pleasure, debauchery, tolerance, openness, and freedom were its characteristics. It was the gateway that linked East and West. Here God providentially planted the first church with a substantial non-Jewish element.

Three substantial groupings are identifiable—the Jews, proselytes, and Greeks. These people were united in Christ and molded into a unified church (the church is always spoken of in the singular, 13:1; 14:27; 15:3). They became one in learning situations (Acts 11:26); in a common leadership (Acts 13:1); in their identification with Barnabas and Paul in their missionary endeavor (Acts 13:3); in receiving reports from the returning missionaries (Acts 14:27); in dispatching a delegation to Jerusalem for the council meeting (Acts 15:3); in receiving the report from the Jerusalem council (Acts 15:30).

Thus the Lord established *the Christian ideal* toward which His church must always strive and which His people are to emulate. Only thus can the church become a model community and a counterculture in this world. Only thus can His people be focused effectively on the whole world with its broken humanity and stratified and classified people. *All* are to be reached with the gospel; *all* are to be wooed to Christ; *all* are to be brought into the family of God and into the church; *all* are welcome in the kingdom of God. Only thus can a new humanity (Eph. 2:15) be created in the church and the divine ideal demonstrated before the world. This ideal must remain the focus of all mission endeavor. If such ideals are neglected at the beginning of the work, it will be most difficult to achieve them in the course of the movement.

It is significant that this ideal church was established *before* the Lord sent forth His missionaries into the vast Roman world. It is also noteworthy that it is out of this model church that the Lord of the harvest called His servants for the great missionary enterprise. This happened some fourteen or fifteen years after Pentecost, and it happened by the sovereign instruction of the Holy Spirit while the church was gathered in the presence of the Lord in prayer.

With this momentous event foreign missions was inaugurated and the church of Antioch was focused on the world. Thus God demonstrated His power and grace in order to project the gospel of Jesus Christ into the Roman Empire according to His plan and purpose. Soon Antioch displaced Jerusalem as the center of vital Christianity. It remained so for several centuries. Only gradually did Constantinople (Istanbul) overshadow Antioch in the eastern part of the Christian church. Not only did Paul launch his great missionary journeys from Antioch, but from here also came such famous men as Ignatius, bishop and martyr (A.D. 110), Chrysostom (c. 390), and Theodore of Mopsuestia (c. 390). Here also ten significant councils convened, A.D. 252–300. Here a school was conducted with emphasis on the literal interpretation of the Bible to counter the school of Alexandria with its allegorizing tendencies. Thus the strategic significance of Antioch is well established, for from there the church focused on the world.

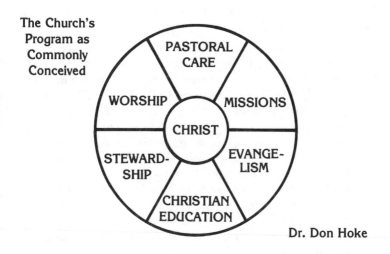

Diagram 27

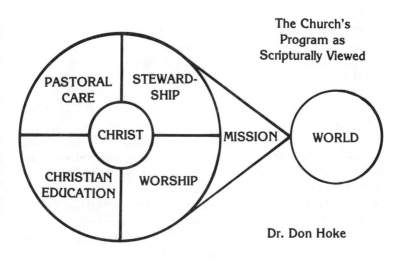

Diagram 28

Paul Moves Into Focus[2]

No one demonstrates the focus of the church more clearly than Paul does. More than half of the Book of Acts constitutes a report on the life and labors, sufferings and accomplishments of this apostle: Paul's personal antagonism and public opposition to Christianity (Acts 7:58; 8:1; 9:1–2); his conversion (9:1–22; 22:1–21; 26:4–23); his call as an apostle to the Gentiles (9:15; 13:1–3; 26:16–18); and his three missionary journeys (13:4–14:26; 15:40–18:22; 18:23–21:17) are fully recorded. Cities, churches, and coworkers are mentioned, and his ministries and sufferings are detailed. His capture, subsequent hardships, and difficult journey to Rome as well as his reception there are reported with much care. His thirteen letters fill in much-needed information, so that we know more about Paul than about any of the Twelve after Pentecost. The mark of Paul is stamped on the New Testament, on the history of the church, and on world history.

1. *Paul's certainties.* The life of Paul was marked by unshakable certainties. His faith was rooted in the absolute truths of revelation, his conscience was bound by authoritative ethical standards, and his ministry was guided by the unchanging will and purpose of God.

a. Paul knew who had met him on the way to Damascus, and he never tired of ascribing names and titles to this person. Paul referred to Him as Jesus Christ of Nazareth, the Son of God, the man Christ Jesus, the Messiah of Israel, the Savior of the world, the only Mediator between God and man, the image of the invisible God, God incarnate, the crucified man, the risen Lord, the coming judge and consummator of the plan and purpose of God, the Lord Jesus Christ in whom all the fullness of deity dwells in bodily form, in whom are hidden the treasures of wisdom and knowledge, in whom the fullness of the Godhead was pleased to dwell, who became wisdom to us from God and righteousness and sanctification and redemption, the name above every name and before whom every knee shall bow. Repeatedly he couples His name with that of God and speaks of "God our/the Father *and* the Lord Jesus Christ." He also writes of Him as "our great God and Savior, Christ Jesus." The Damascus road experience—the Person, the vision, the commission—never grew dim or stale in Paul. He knew *who* had met him, though he could never fully comprehend or describe Him. Therefore, in full devotion and total commitment he served Him and in doxologies extolled Him.

b. Paul knew with an unshakable certainty that he had been called to be an apostle of Jesus Christ by the will of God. This he reiterates frequently, defending his apostleship with vigor and persuasion. For this calling he suffered the loss of all things; to this he was fully devoted as a bond-servant of God. He did not consider himself a volunteer in this mission and position. Nor did he look on himself as a draftee in the service who was merely fulfilling certain duties. The choice and the calling of God had so attracted and persuaded his conscience, mind, and will that he became a bond-slave in deepest love and unreserved commitment to his Master. Repeatedly he calls himself a bondslave of Jesus Christ.

c. Paul had a clear perception of the eternal and cosmic purpose of God throughout the ages and God's special design for this age. To that purpose he devoted himself in an unreserved and joyous manner. In full certainty that God had reconciled the world to Himself in and through Christ Jesus and that He purposed to gather His church from among *all* nations, Paul focused his life and service on the world. His Jewish particularism and ethnicism vanished; the universality of God and equality of all people filled his heart, guided his mind, dominated his will, and shaped his life purpose and mission.

d. Paul accepted his assignment as an apostle and ambassador to the Gentile world in gratitude and as a special grace bestowed on him; he spoke of it on numerous occasions (Acts 9:15–16; 22:15, 21; 26:6–10; Rom. 1:5; 11:13; 15:15–16; Gal. 1:15–16; 2:7–9; Eph. 3:1–12; 1 Tim. 2:7; 2 Tim. 1:11). Based on Paul's initial experiences in Damascus and Jerusalem (Acts 9:20–30; 22:17–21) and on our knowledge of his history, academic preparation, burning zeal and intense love for his people (Acts 22:17–21; Rom. 9:1–5; 10:1–4; 11:13–14; 11:25–28), we may well gather that Paul would have loved to spend his life in the evangelization of his own people. His unusual knowledge of the Old Testament and intimate acquaintance with the psychology, hopes, and aspirations of his "waiting" people would have qualified him as no other apostle to remain in Jerusalem and evangelize the strategically religious people of his time. This seems to have been his original intention and desire. But the call and commission of the Lord made him a world missionary.

e. Paul accepted his apostleship to the nations as a lifetime assignment, as a course he must follow to the end of the way and to the end of his life (Acts 20:18–25; 21:11–14; 2 Tim. 4:6–8). Nothing could be allowed to stand in the way of his pursuit of the goal.

f. Paul served in the certainty that the church was a unique treasure to his Lord and Master—that He had purchased it with His own precious blood, that He had given Himself for it in deepest love, that He was guarding it as a shepherd watches his flock, that He was building it as a most sacred sanctuary, that He had promised to preserve it in the midst of the fiercest trials, that He would not permit it to be tempted and tested beyond its ability to endure, that He would be with it to the very end of the age, and that He would eventually gather it to Himself to be with Him forevermore and share His glory. Such certainty and devotion to His Lord inspired the apostle to undaunted labors for the church of Jesus Christ.

g. Paul endured untold hardships, privations, physical and mental sacrifices, and sufferings of every kind. His ministry ended in martyrdom. The catalog of his sufferings staggers our imagination (2 Cor. 6:4–10; 11:21–33; Gal. 6:17; Phil. 3:7–8; 4:10–12; 2 Tim. 1:8–12; 4:6–8). But none of these things could move him from his course, blur the focus of his calling, or cause him to swerve in his path of duty.

> In the grip of the eternal purpose of God, in devotion to his Lord and Master, in commitment to his call and assignment, in love and concern for the church, and in anguish for a world in peril of eternal separation from God and the kingdom of God, he strove persistently and heroically, with or against the stream, understood or misjudged, laboring, praying, suffering, sacrificing, dying in and for the purpose of God and the glory of His Master.

With Christ he was building the church of God (Col. 1:24). From the historical perspective Paul became its masterbuilder, laying a firm and enduring foundation that is Jesus Christ Himself (1 Cor. 3:9–11; Eph. 2:20).

h. Paul attributed all his greatness and success to the grace of God (1 Cor. 15:10). God had chosen him before he was born (Gal. 1:15). God had revealed His Son in him (Gal. 1:16). God had made him an apostle and focused his ministry on the nations (Rom. 15:15–16; Eph. 3:1–12). And God had prepared him for his ministry.

2. *Paul's preparation.* Paul's first ministry was in Damascus in the synagogue. His second attempt was in Jerusalem among his own people and peers. However, in both places his enemies plotted his destruction. Finally he found himself in Tarsus for several "quiet, hidden" years. The Lord was molding His servant. Four stages seem to be evident: on the Damascus road, in Arabia, in Tarsus, and in Antioch.

On the Damascus road Paul was *born as a Christian.* He became a new creature in Christ Jesus. The man of law became a man of grace and faith. Judaism gave way to Christianity. His life was transformed, his heart was changed, and his loyalties were transferred. "Jesus of Nazareth—the Son of God" became his initial message (Acts 9:20). More than this. In his great experience Paul received his *divine call* to become an apostle of Jesus Christ to the non-Jewish nations of the world. No suffering later could dim his conviction. The greatness, decisiveness, and glory of‚ the Damascus experience never vanished.

However, more than that had happened on the Damascus road. His system of theology was challenged and it crumbled. The experience of reality in Jesus of Nazareth and the truth revealed in Him collided head-on with his Old Testament exposition and his system of belief. The impact left his theological system and his messianic hope in ruins. He was left with a theological wreckage. In consequence, his theological system had to be rebuilt. The rebuilding seems to have taken place in the searching years of Arabia (Gal. 1:17). Returning from there, he confounded the Jews who lived in Damascus with the truth that this Jesus is the Christ (Acts 9:22). Somewhat later he spoke boldly in Jerusalem "in the name of the Lord," indicative of his identifying Jesus of Nazareth with Jehovah of the Old Testament and the Messiah of Israel. This was a tremendous step forward and upward in building a New Testament christology. Evidently a theological reconstruction had taken place. The Old Testament became a contemporary book with a message of salvation already at hand.

Paul needed further broadening to become the chosen instrument of the Lord to bear His name "before the Gentiles and kings and the sons of Israel" (Acts 9:15). Paul's horizon needed to be enlarged to see *the purpose of God for the whole human race.* His narrow Judaistic views and approaches had to give way to a vision of the love and purpose of God for all of humanity. This enlarged vision and theology seem to have come to him during the several hidden years in Tarsus. From them Paul emerged as a true internationalist and evangelical universalist. He saw that the love and purpose of God embraces everyone and reaches as far as creation stretches. He perceived that the salvation work of Christ is potentially as comprehensive and intensive as the sin of Adam had made necessary. He discerned that the regenerative ministry of the Holy Spirit reaches down as deep as the disobedience of Adam and the cumulative sin of humanity had plunged the human race. So we could be made free from guilt before God and renewed in our innermost beings and restored to the image of God. He received a universalistic perspective of the Old Testament hidden from most people. Paul understood that God is the God not of the Jews only but of the Gentiles also (Rom. 3:29), and that Jesus Christ is the Savior of all people (Rom. 5:12–21).

Paul also realized that the preaching of the gospel of God is the only way to inform people of the Good News of God in Christ Jesus and that by means of the gospel the Holy Spirit convicts and illumines the human mind and motivates the person to respond to the free gift of God in Christ Jesus. Thus it became imperative to preach the gospel to all people everywhere. Such theological persuasion substantiated his subjective call and command which Ananias had clearly put before him (Acts 22:12–15). Thus Paul proclaimed Christ, "admonishing every man and teaching every man with all wisdom, that we may present every man complete in Christ"

(Col. 1:28). Emphatically he added: "And for this purpose also I labor, striving according to His power, which mightily works within me" (Col. 1:29).

Paul needed one further aspect of preparation. This came to him in Antioch. Here he was privileged to fellowship and minister in a *model church,* a church in which a heterogeneous people from a pluralistic society had become a homogeneous fellowship and people of God in Christ Jesus as we described it on privious pages. Here, too, he was conditioned to work in an *international team* and with brethren of greatly varied background. As their name and location indicate they represented a broad scope of religious and cultural experiences and background. Only their common loyalty to the same Lord and purpose could hold them together.

That is, in part, the story of the making of the man of the Lord's sovereign choosing. The potter's wheel made a vessel useful to the Master, prepared for every good work (2 Tim. 2:21), a vessel for honor, a chosen instrument. Gradually but surely Paul's life was moved by the hand of God into the clear focus of God—the world.

Paul's journeys, ministries, and accomplishments are recorded in part in the last sixteen chapters of Acts and in part in his own epistles. Only eternity will show what the impact of this remarkable man has been and what it has meant in the history of the Christian church and the world as a whole. Reverberations from his life and work will continue to affect the Christian movement until the return of the Lord writes the last chapter of its activities. Because of Paul's ministry, the church will always be aware that true Christianity must focus on the world, live in the world, and serve in the world.

It may not be easy but it is absolutely essential that a church that desires to be acceptable to the Lord, and experience the fullness of His blessings, that church must become a community of quality and quantity and be focused on the world. Only thus does its focus merge with the focus of God, and assures spiritual prosperity and progress in the world. The world focus of the church is important— all important—for God so loved the world. . . .

15

Toward a Theology
of Church Growth

Concern for church growth has been a part of modern Christian missions from the very beginning. Many pioneer missionaries were not only energetic evangelists but also great churchmen. They loved the church, understood its purpose, and sought ways and means to build and expand the church. They set up ideals, formulated theories, devised methods, developed institutions, and, in dependence on the Holy Spirit, they moved forward to build the church.

There have been, however, serious theological as well as practical questions hovering over missions and church growth: Is missions principally building the kingdom of God with all its social and cultural implications, or is missions principally a church-building ministry? What is the basic meaning of the biblical concept *ethnos* (*ta ethne* of Matt. 28:19)? Comprehension and careful exegesis seems to verify that its basic scriptural reference is to the non-Jewish nations. Does this justify the expectation of great national movements from the nations of the world? Can missions expect "Volkskirchentum," churches constituted of total peoples? This has been a debated question for more than a century. Is conversion by individual decision or by corporate-personality decisions made by common consent after meaningful deliberations? It is natural that the answers to such basic questions have determined the methods of operation on the fields of labor to a considerable degree.

These weighty questions and many more, such as the relationship of the gospel to the non-Christian religions, the relation of the gospel to culture and the the structures of society, etc., must be most carefully considered, and the principal and decisive answers must come from the Bible through diligent exegesis and sound theological studies. The behavioral sciences can render great help in the development of relevant methods and procedures, and can point ways to more effective communication and more efficient structures. However, *they cannot give scriptural principles.* Serious dialogue on missions has begun between biblical exegetes, theologians, and missiologists. There are positive signs of progress to bring church growth more fully under the searchlight of the Scriptures. I can only hope that missions and church growth will come more under the dominance of the Bible and theology to receive their direction from this perspective and authority.

I am convinced that as the Scriptures are searched, fuller and clearer answers will be found. These, in turn, will lead to a more steadfast and sure walk and conduct of missions. I am also convinced that the *message,* the *servant,* and the *quality of the church* operating in missions and church growth will become more central than methods and techniques. While methods are important, they are only tools and not directly agents and instruments of the Holy Spirit. The Holy Spirit is in the message; He anoints the messengers, and He operates in and through the church. Therefore, church growth must be seen in biblical and theological perspective and must continue to be subjected to scriptural scrutiny. God wills His church to grow. And His promise is: "I will build My church!"

NOTES

Preface

[1]Compare the writings of such men as Karl Graul of the Leipzig Missionary Society (1814–1964), Henry Venn of the Church Missionary Society (1796–1873); Rufus Anderson of the American Board of Commissioners (1796–1880); Gustav Warneck, Mission Inspector at Barmen (1834–1910); Bruno Gutmann of the Leipzig Mission (1876–1966); Julius Richter of the Berlin Missionary Society (1862–1940); John Livingston Nevius, Presbyterian missionary to China (1829–1893); Roland Allen and the World Dominion Movement (1868–1947); John Merle Davis, Director of the Department of Economic and Social Research, and Counsel of the IMC (1875–1960); J. Waskom Pickett, Methodist missionary and bishop of India (n.d.).

Consult especially these writings: Roland Allen, *Missionary Methods: St. Paul's or Ours?* (London: World Dominion, 1930), and *Spontaneous Expansion of the Church and the Causes Which Hinder It* (Grand Rapids: Eerdmans, 1962); John M. Davis, *The Economic and Social Environment of the Younger Churches* (London: Edinburgh House,n.d.), and *New Buildings on Old Foundations* (New York: International Missionary Council, n.d.); John Nevius, *Planting and Development of Missionary Churches* (Nutley, N.J.: Presbyterian and Reformed, 1974); J. Waskom Pickett, *Christian Mass Movements in India* (Nashville: Abingdon, n.d.).

[2]The original title of the series was *Studies in the Life and Growth of the Younger Churches;* this was later changed to *Churches in the Missionary Situation—Studies in Growth and Response.* The general editor of these volumes was Victor E. W. Hayward. The books are published by Lutterworth and SCM, London, and distributed in the United States by Friendship Press, New York. Regrettably, most of these volumes are out of print.

[3]Arno W. Enns, *Man, Milieu and Mission in Argentina* (Grand Rapids: Eerdmans, n.d.); K. E. Hamilton, *Church Growth in the High Andes* (India: Lucknow, n.d.); Donald McGavran, *Bridges of God* (New York: Friendship, 1955), *How Churches Grow* (New York: Friendship, 1965), and *Understanding Church Growth* (Grand Rapids: Eerdmans, 1970); William Read, *New Patterns of Church Growth in Brazil* (Grand Rapids: Eerdmans, 1965).

[4]Wilbert R. Shenk, ed., *The Challenge of Church Growth* (Scottdale, Pa.: Herald, 1973), p. 21.

[5]Annually a study group convenes in Oxford, England, to study factors contributing to revival and awakenings and the effect of such experiences on the church and its expansion.

[6]Author's personal research.

[7]Compare statistics of their annual reports.

[8]Latourette's volume *A History of Christianity* (New York: Harper, 1953) builds on this principle. This was confirmed to me in personal conversation.

[9]Emilio Willems, *Followers of the New Faith* (Nashville: Vanderbilt U., 1967).

[10]F. P. Cotterell, *Born at Midnight* (Chicago: Moody, 1973).

[11]Harold R. Cook, *Historic Patterns of Church Growth* (Chicago: Moody, 1971).

[12]Donald C. Palmer, *Explosion of People Evangelism* (Chicago: Moody, 1974).

[13]Dean M. Kelley, *Why Conservative Churches Are Growing*, rev. ed. (New York: Harper & Row, 1977).

[14]Consider such books as: C. E. Autrey, *Evangelism in Acts* (Grand Rapids: Zondervan, 1964); F. F. Bruce, *The Book of the Acts* (Grand Rapids: Eerdmans, 1955); F. V. Filson, *Three Crucial Decades* (Richmond, Va.: John Knox, 1963); E. F. Harrison, *Acts, the Expanding Church* (Chicago: Moody, 1976); D. V. Hurst, *The Church Begins* (Springfield, Mo.: 1959); H. A. Kent, Jr., *Jerusalem to Rome* (Grand Rapids, Baker, 1972); W. S. LaSor, *Church Alive* (Glendale, Calif.: Gospel Light, 1972); August Van Ryn, *Acts of the Apostles: The Unfinished Work of Christ* (New York: Loizeaux, 1961).

Chapter 1

[1]Thus far I have been unable to discover the origin of these concepts but I find them used freely in Dutch and German missiological literature.

[2]Compare Erich Beyreuther, *Kirche in Bewegung* (Berlin: Christlicher Zeitschriftenverlag, 1968).

[3]Author's personal research.

Chapter 2

[1]I am greatly indebted to my professor, the late principal of St. Andrew's College, Saskatoon, Saskatchewan, Canada, Dr. David Strathy Dix for an expanded understanding of the kingdom of God concept and its glory. Also helpful have been: John Bright, *The Kingdom of God* (New York: Abingdon-Cokesbury, 1953); A. B. Bruce, *The Kingdom of God*, 3rd ed. (Edinburgh: T. & T. Clark, 1890); Fritz Hubner, *Weltreich und Gottesreich* (Bad Liebenzell/Wuertt.: Liebenzeller Mission, n.d.); George Ladd, *The Kingdom of God* (Grand Rapids: Eerdmans, n.d.), and *The Gospel of the Kingdom* (Grand Rapids: Eerdmans, 1959); Alva McClain, *The Greatness of the Kingdom* (Grand Rapids: Zondervan, 1959).

[2]Gerald Anderson and Thomas F. Stransky, *Mission Trends* Nos. 1, 2, 3, 4. These articles are only a mild reflection of the dialogue, debate, and crisis that is developing. The documents of Uppsala and Nairobi of the WCC are indicative of the direction of the course of theology. For summarization of the issues and debate I suggest: Wolfgang Guenther, *Von Edenburg nach Mexico City;* Klaus Bockmuehl, *Was heisst heute Mission?*; and Walter Kuenneth and Peter Beyerhaus, *Reich Gottes oder Weltgemeinschaft.*

[3]O. Michel as quoted by Johannes Blauw in *The Missionary Nature of the Church* (Grand Rapids: Eerdmans, 1962), p. 104.

[4]Ibid., p. 79.

[5]J. C. Hoekendijk, "The Church in Missionary Thinking," *International Review of Mission,* 41 (1952), p. 325.

[6]Ibid., pp. 324–336.

Chapter 3

[1]As an example of this approach see article by Choan-Seng Song, "From Israel to Asia—A Theological Leap," in G. Anderson and T. F. Stransky, *Mission Trends No. 3: Third World Theologies* (Grand Rapids: Eerdmans, 1976), pp. 211–222.

[2]For an expanded study of this see G. W. Peters, *A Biblical Theology of Missions* (Chicago: Moody, 1972), chapter 3.

[3]The outline is based in part on E. H. Bancroft, *Christian Theology* (Johnson City, N.Y.: Johnson City Pub. Co., 1946), pp. 100–103.

[4]Peters, *Biblical Theology of Missions,* pp. 202–203.

[5]Elton Trueblood, *The Company of the Committed* (New York: Harper & Row, 1961).

[6]Lesslie Newbigin, *The Household of God* (New York: Friendship, 1954).

Chapter 4

[1]W. H. Griffith Thomas, *The Holy Spirit of God* (Grand Rapids: Eerdmans, 1955), pp. 138–139.

[2]Ibid., p. 185.

[3]Ibid., p. 197.

[4]Ibid., p. 184.

[5]A. A. van Ruler, *Theologie van het Apostolaat,* p. 46, as quoted by Blauw, *Missionary Nature of the Church,* p. 113.

[6]Peters, *Biblical Theology of Missions,* p. 149.

[7]McGavran, *Bridges of God.*

[8]Georg Vicedom, *The Mission of God* (St. Louis: Concordia, 1965), pp. 17–19.

Chapter 6

[1] I am acquainted with the past debate on whether the Bible *is* the Word of God, whether it *contains* the Word of God, or whether it *becomes* the Word of God, and with the present dispute over the inerrancy question. Literature abounds in these realms and can be found in any standard theological library.

[2] Hoekendijk, "The Church in Missionary Thinking," p.

[3] Hendrik Kraemer, *The Communication of the Christian Faith* (Philadelphia: Westminster, n.d.).

[4] Ibid., p. 13.

[5] The reader will recognize my indebtedness to Louis Luzbetak, *The Church and Cultures* (Techny, Ill.: Divine Word Publications, 1963), pp. 229–238.

[6] R. E. O. White, *Apostle Extraordinary* (Grand Rapids: Eerdmans, 1962), p. 18.

[7] For further reading on cross-cultural communication, especially note these: J. F. Engel and H. W. Norton, *What's Gone Wrong With the Harvest* (Grand Rapids: Zondervan, 1975); Jacob Loewen, *Culture and Human Values: Christian Intervention in Anthropological Perspective* (South Pasadena, Calif.: William Carey Library, 1975); Eugene Nida, *Message and Mission* (New York: Harper, 1960); and the many articles in *Practical Anthropology* by Dr. William A. Smalley.

[8] E. Stanley Jones, *The Christ of the Indian Road* (New York: Grosset & Dunlap, 1925), p. 182.

[9] Huston Smith, *The Religions of Man* (New York: Harper & Row, 1958), p. 110.

[10] Ibid., pp. 111–112.

Chapter 7

[1] I owe a great debt for this section to the following writings: A. B. Bruce, *The Training of the Twelve* (1894. Reprint. Grand Rapids: Kregel, 1971); R. E. Coleman, *The Master Plan of Evangelism* (Old Tappan, N.J.: Revell, 1977); H. H. Horne, *Jesus the Master Teacher* (1920. Reprint *Teaching Techniques of Jesus*, Grand Rapids: Kregel, 1971); R. P. Meye, *Jesus and the Twelve* (New York: Harper, n.d.); F. B. Meyer, *Peter, Fisherman, Disciple, Apostle* (London: Marshall, Morgan & Scott, n.d.); A. Smith, *The Twelve Christ Chose* (New York: Harper, n.d.).

Chapter 9

[1] S. M. Zwemer, *Into All the World* (Harrisburg, Pa.: Christian Publications, 1942), pp. 164–165.

[2] Personal conference with a group of theologians in Korea.

Chapter 10

¹Willems, *Followers,* p. 250. I also urge that the student read Howard A. Snyder's book, *The Problem of Wineskins: Church Structures in a Technological Age* (Inter-Varsity Press, 1976).

²Robert Lee, *Stranger in the Land* (London: Lutterworth, n.d.).

³The relationship of the gospel, Christianity, the church, and culture has been debated since the beginning of the Christian movement. From the pages of the New Testament it is evident that the Jews had fused religion and culture and found it practically impossible to distinguish between the two aspects of life. This is natural to non-Western people, cultures, and religions.

In modern times the West has almost completely divorced the two aspects and finds it practically impossible to interrelate them. A threefold woe has befallen the West: humanism has no real need for God, naturalism has no real place for God, secularism sees no real value in God. Therefore, a godless culture is developing. While the existence of God is not necessarily denied, He is not given the proper place in life and culture. This basically godless philosophy and life style, more than other Western cultural patterns that the early missionaries exported, is the "hidden fear" and the real problem between East and West. Dr. Bong Ro states that the Orientals dread nothing more than Western secularism and Japanese economic imperialism.

Any student of this issue would do well to read such books as: Emile Cailliet, *The Christian Approach to Culture* (New York: Abingdon-Cokesbury, n.d.); E. A. Judge, *The Social Pattern of Christian Groups in the First Century* (London: Tyndale, 1960); H. Kraemer, *The Christian Message in a Non-Christian World* (New York: Harper, n.d.), *Religion and the Christian Faith* (Philadelphia: Westminster, n.d.), and *World Cultures and World Religion* (Philadelphia: Westminster, 1960); B. E. Meland, *The Realities of Faith* (New York: Oxford U., n.d.); G. C. Oosthuizen, *Theological Battleground in Asia and Africa* (New York: Humanities, 1972), and *Post-Christianity in Africa* (Grand Rapids: Eerdmans, 1968); Lothar Schreiner, *Adat und Evangelium* (Guetersloh: Guetersloher Verlagshaus, 1976); W. A. Visser't Hooft, *No Other Name* (Philadelphia: Westminster, n.d.).

Chapter 12

¹This happens to churches in Korea, certain parts of Indonesia, the Philippines, Guatemala, Brazil, Nigeria, Zaire, and other countries in Africa. In the churches related to the Sudan United Mission in Africa, namely Nigeria, only ten percent of the church attenders are church members. Ninety percent are

insufficiently discipled to be baptized to become church members.

²This does not necessarily mean that the American community is over-churched. However, it points up the inequality of opportunity to hear the gospel that exists in this world and that must be remedied.

³For a detailed evaluative study of evangelism-in-depth the reader should consult my book *Saturation Evangelism* (Grand Rapids: Zondervan, 1970).

⁴For studies of in-depth-evangelism see some of the writings of Orlando Costar.

⁵More than 200 volumes have been released in Latin America on Liberation Theology, and the end is not yet here.

Chapter 13

¹Blauw, *Missionary Nature of the Church,* ch. 2.

²Michael Green, Evangelism in the Early Church (Grand Rapids: Eerdmans, 1970); Kenneth S. Latourette, *The History of the Expansion of Christianity,* Vol. 1 (Grand Rapids: Zondervan, 1970); Adolf Harnack, *The Expansion of Christianity in the First Three Centuries* (Magnolia, MA: Peter Smith); Haus-Werner Gesichen, *Glaube fuer die Welt* (Guetesloher Verlagshaus Gerd Mohn, 1971), pp. 165–172.
Gesichen, *Glaube fuer die Welt* (Guetesloher Verlagshaus Gerd Mohn, 1971), pp. 165–172.

³Latin American Mission (Staff), *Evangelism-in-Depth* (Chicago: Moody Press), p. 25.

⁴W. Dayton Roberts, *Revolution in Evangelism* (Chicago: Moody Press, 1967), p. 100.

⁵Arthur Glasser, in an unpublished paper.

⁶Waskom Pickett, *Christian Mass Movements in India* (Nashville: Abingdon Press), and numerous writings of Dr. Donald McGavran.

⁷G. W. Peters, *Saturation Evangelism,* Part III (Grand Rapids: Zondervan, 1970).

Chapter 14

¹Blauw, *Missionary Nature,* pp. 111, 117.

²Books on the life, ministry, and theology of Paul abound. Of special value for this study have been: F. B. Meyer, *Paul, Servant of Jesus Christ* (New York: Revell, 1897); Olaf Moe, *The Apostle Paul,* 2 vols. (Minneapolis: Augsburg, n.d.); W. Ramsay, *The Cities of Paul* (1907. Reprint. Grand Rapids: Baker Book House, 1960), and *St. Paul the Traveller, and the Roman Citizen* (1897. Reprint. Grand Rapids: Baker, 1960); J. E. Rattenburg, *The Religious Experience of Paul* (Nashville: Cokesbury, n.d.); J. E. Stewart, *A Man in Christ* (New York: Harper, n.d.); R. E. O. White, *Apostle Extraordinary* (Grand Rapids: Eerdmans, 1962); X. P. Wilfley, *St. Paul, the Herald of Christianity* (Nashville: Cokesbury, n.d.).

BIBLIOGRAPHY

There is no special need to add an extended bibliography. I have referred to five major publishers of this type of literature—Lutterworth Press, London; William B. Eerdmans Publishing Company, Grand Rapids; Zondervan Publishing House, Grand Rapids; Moody Press, Chicago; William Carey Library, South Pasadena. The Church Growth Book Club, 1705 N. Sierra Bonita Avenue, Pasadena, CA 91104 publishes bimonthly lists of books on church growth and related subjects in the *Church Growth Bulletin,* P.O. Box 66, Santa Clara, CA 95052. Here the reader will find up-to-date lists of books as well as brief annotations on the content of the books. An extensive bibliography is listed in *Acts, the Expanding Church* by Everett F. Harrison, (Chicago: Moody, n.d.).

INDEXES

Scripture

Scripture Index

12:5	126, 203, 224	15:13–18, 28	124
12:24	22, 46, 125, 193, 226	15:14	19
13:1	146, 203, 204, 244, 245	15:25	145
13:1–3	226, 248	15:35	145
13:1–4	55, 141, 157, 215, 223, 242	15:40–18:22	248
13:1–28:31	134	16:4	165
13:3	245	16:5	22, 226, 231, 237
13:4–14:26	248	16:6, 7	141
13:9	124	16:6–10	223
13:16	101	16:10	215
13:17	98	16:14	104
13:17–23	98	16:14, 15	146
13:23	99, 100	16:15	231, 232
13:23, 32	98	16:18	99
13:23, 33–39	35	16:20, 21	200
13:32	215	16:22–28	156
13:38, 39	99, 100, 101	16:25–34	157
13:38–41	100	16:27–34	146, 231
13:39	100	16:30–34	232
13:41	101	16:31	96, 100, 101
13:42–45, 59	224	17:4	146
13:44–50	73	17:5, 13	99
13:48, 49	22	17:6	200
13:49	22, 218, 225, 226, 231, 237	17:18	214
14:4, 5	73	17:18, 31	99
14:7, 15, 21	215	17:22–31	81, 101
14:14–18	101	17:22–34	80, 109
14:15	96, 98	17:24	98
14:16	98	17:26	98
14:17	78, 79	17:27	79
14:22	37, 40	17:30	96, 98
14:23	165	17:31	98
14:26–15:2	244	17:34	146
14:27	204, 245	18:2	146
15:1ff.	177, 215	18:8	146
15:1–3	245	18:21, 25, 28, 42	151
15:1–29	148, 149	18:23–21:7	248
15:2, 4, 6, 22, 23	165, 204, 213	18:24–28	146
15:3	244, 245	19:1–7	148
15:4, 22	203	19:1–20:38	226
15:9, 11	100	19:8	37
15:13, 14	81	19:8–20	204
15:13–18	39	19:10, 20, 26	231

Scripture Index

3:5	158	3:4	190
3:6–15	58	3:5	40, 67, 90, 141
		3:8	223
1 Timothy			
1:17	78	*Philemon*	
1:18, 19	34	1, 2	146, 231, 232
2:1	220		
2:1–4	79	*Hebrews*	
2:1–5	76	1:1–3	34
2:3–6	61, 71	1:2, 3	62
2:4–6	198	1:6	219
2:5	34, 78	2:2, 4	152, 154, 159, 189
2:5, 6	34	4:9	54
2:17, 19	165	4:12	91
3:1–13	165	4:14–16	34
3:5, 15	54	5:5–10	34
3:14, 15	58	8:13	154
3:15	139	9:24	34
3:16	34, 35	10:19, 25	219
3:16, 17	94	10:29	62
4:5	90	11:1–12:3	141
5:1	165	11:6	141
5:19, 20	58	12:14	42
		12:23	54
2 Timothy		12:28	43
1:7	121	13:15	219
1:8–12	250	13:16	220
1:10	100	13:17	165
1:16	231	13:20, 21	44
2:2	154, 221		
2:7	249	*James*	
2:15	94	1:5, 6	157
3:1–7	190	1:18	65, 67, 90, 93
3:16	95	1:25	121
4:6–8	250	2:1–13	230
4:18	37	2:5	37
		2:8	121
Titus		2:17	223
1:5	165		
1:5–9	165	*1 Peter*	
1:7	165	1:1	176, 218, 237
1:11	249	1:2	90
2:14	223	1:3–9	49

Subject Index

Subject